To Mike

Happy Christmas 2007

Eddie, T.

Bernie Smith and Maureen Hunt

GEORGE BEST

A CELEBRATION

Untold true stories of our most
legendary footballer

JOHN BLAKE

Published by John Blake Publishing Ltd,
3 Bramber Court, 2 Bramber Road,
London W14 9PB, England

www.blake.co.uk

First published in hardback in 2007

ISBN: 978 1 84454 455 4

British Library Cataloguing-in-Publication Data:

A catalogue record for this book is available from the British Library.

Design by www.envydesign.co.uk

Printed in Great Britain by William Clowes Ltd, Beccles, Suffolk

1 3 5 7 9 10 8 6 4 2

Papers used by John Blake Publishing are natural, recyclable products made
from wood grown in sustainable forests. The manufacturing processes conform
to the environmental regulations of the country of origin.

George Mott

Dedication
To all those who need a chance in life, and those
who are willing to take it

ACKNOWLEDGEMENTS

To Bernie's wife Angie and Maureen's husband Ron, our families and friends who have supported and encouraged us through the whole process of writing this book; to the many people who have been so willing to share their stories, memories and tributes to George without whom the book wouldn't have come so alive.

Many thanks also to: Malcolm Wagner, George's long-time friend and business partner; Jim Weaver, official photographer of Aston Villa FC for those long hours photographing so much; Graham, Tom and Ellie Smith for their valued contributions; Bernie's mum-in-law, Margaret Booth, and Ian Trevethick for reading the stories and making constructive comments; Jay Thethi for his invaluable technical support; The University of Central England TIC for help in designing and developing the website.

Of course, our thanks to Michelle Signore at John Blake Publishing for guiding and supporting us through the process and to John Blake for believing in the project.

And finally to George Best for living such a colourful and fascinating life and our thanks for being given the opportunity through this book to celebrate and pay tribute to his memory.

FOREWORD

BY MALCOLM WAGNER

I'm so pleased that Maureen Hunt and Bernie Smith have given me the opportunity to write a few words about my friend and business partner George Best. George and I shared a friendship that spanned over 40 years, and lasted until the day he died. He was a true friend in every sense of the word.

I still find it hard to believe that George is no longer with us, no longer phoning me at all hours of the night and day just to chat. I spent some of the best times of my life in his exciting and charismatic company and miss him like mad. I think everyone who ever met George was enthralled by him.

I remember him being invited to No. 10 Downing Street in the 1960s, when Harold Wilson was Prime Minister. George was in the company of lots of other invited stars from sport, stage, screen and television, but everyone seemed intent on talking to him… and he couldn't quite understand why. 'I couldn't believe it, Waggy,' he told me later, in that quiet unassuming way of his, 'everybody wanted to talk to me. They didn't know how star struck I was of all of them.'

But that was Bestie for you. He had no edge, no flash; he was just an ordinary guy with a talent that was so special. He was a wonderful person, and as a footballer he had no equal. George had a confidence on the football field that defied description. He could do anything with a football, and play in any position. Alex Stepney, Manchester United's goalkeeper, once enthused, 'You want to see him during training, Waggy, when he plays in goal. He's a better keeper than I am.'

Over the years when I've watched him play, I've never failed to marvel at his balance, his pace and his never-ending ability to beat an opponent in a new and exciting way. George had everything: he had two good feet, was as brave as a lion, was as strong as an ox and was a fantastic header of the ball. He had everything required to be the best footballer in the world… and, for me, he was. George Best was the best. I'm so proud of him and what he achieved in his short football career. I'm also proud of George Best the man, with his quiet genuine manner and casual attitude towards fame and life in general. That's something he never lost throughout his life. George was one hell of a good human being.

That said, George was Britain's first superstar footballer and he received neither advice nor help of any kind on how to deal with the pressure superstardom heaped on him. I only wish I could have done more to save him, especially in the latter years, but, as anyone who knew him will tell you, George was his own man and did things his own way. I used to have a go at him whenever I thought he was out of order, but it was all to no avail. So much so that he'd complain, 'You're like my conscience, Waggy, always sitting on my shoulder telling me how things should be done… you're a proper nuisance.'

Sir Bobby Charlton said at the time of George's death, 'We at Manchester United have learned from our experience with Eric Cantona, we had to treat him differently, make allowances. If, instead of being hostile to George – which I was – we had leaned a bit his way and tried to help him, who knows?' For my part, despite his consistent disregard for the advice I used to offer him, I did my utmost never to judge him… at the root, George and I were true friends and I loved him as a friend should… and, in return, I know he loved me. That was always the basis of our friendship.

George and I met in 1965, when he was beginning to make the headlines on the back pages of Manchester's sports papers. It was at the end of the 1964/65 season after Manchester United, with a rampant George Best, had claimed the league title. He was 19 years old and I was 20. That was the beginning of a relationship that would see me travelling around the world with him. During the intervening 40-odd years, we've shared some amazing journeys to places such as Spain, South Africa, Mexico, Canada and the United States – to name but a few. During that time, life was so eventful and so exciting. We had a fabulous time together.

In May 2003, George, in the company of our mutual friend Michael Parkinson, gave an after-dinner speech at my hotel in Ramsbottom, Lancashire, in aid of 'The Foundation for Liver Research'. After the dinner, my wife Jane was taking George and his wife Alex back to Manchester Airport for their return flight home, when I suddenly remembered I'd forgotten to ask him for some autographs for friends. I rang George in the car and explained I'd promised the autographs to some people. 'Sorry to be a nuisance, George,' I ended. 'But, Waggy,' George playfully replied, 'you've been a nuisance for 40 years, why would you want to change now?' I could hear them laughing in the car. That was the George I knew and loved.

As far as I'm concerned, nobody can say a bad word about George Best. I feel so privileged to have known him and to have been a part of his life. George did so many good things that went unheard of – visits to hospitals to brighten the lives of sick kids, helping charities whenever he could; all unreported because he wanted it that way.

I'm delighted to have been asked to write this foreword and tell you a little bit about him. I only wish that George Best was still around, so I could continue being a nuisance to him.

INTRODUCTION

How many more words can be written about George Best? There must be thousands upon thousands of column inches describing, commenting on and evaluating his performances on and off the pitch, all settled and collecting dust in the archives of every newspaper right through the land, and indeed throughout the world. Hardback and paperback books either written in partnership with or by the man himself, some translated into other languages, still grace the bookshelves of fans, libraries, book fairs and bookshops. All this along with collections and portfolios of photographs depicting every stage of George Best's life, most of his action shots, goal-scoring poise and celebration poses he has become so famous for, together with the more compromising pictures that the paparazzi has earned large sums of money in selling. So why the need for more?

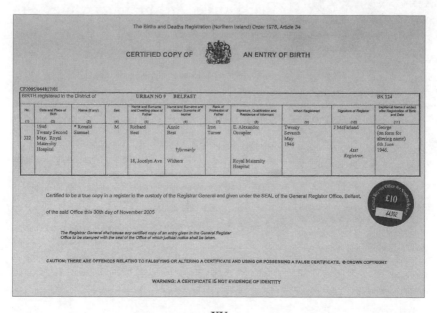

Growing up, George made a football part of his anatomy. That incredible body swerve which terrorised top-class fullbacks was there even as a kid. As were the deceptive changes of pace, the lightning shooting and the determination never to be on the losing side. As Christmases and birthdays came and went George was easy to buy presents for. Football was a near religion for him so he invariably got books on football, football boots or footballs.

George became possibly the most controversial of all post-war football stars, not only in the way he played but also in the way he was built and the way he looked. George was so different to footballers of the past. Remember those grim faces, short-back-and-sides haircuts, massive shinpads, burly bodies and barn-door shoulders, with perhaps a few busted noses and cauliflower ears thrown in, evident in photographs of pre-1950 football teams? Then look at George. Small

framed with not an ounce of fat on his body, hairstyles that changed regularly, a rather shy but face-splitting smile that revealed his brilliant white teeth and an added extra sparkle to those already twinkling blues eyes.

George Best the football star, the photographic pin-up of thousands who never even watched him kick a ball. George Best the boutique owner, the nightclub owner who could spot a business idea as well as he could spot a chance to avoid a tackle on the pitch, weave his way through mesmerised defenders to score a goal and rejoice with his trademark one-arm-raised jubilation.

Some may say that George's fame and fortune unfortunately coincided with the social explosion of the

1960s. The total opposition of ideas, ideals and freedom of decades prior to the 1960s and the 1960s themselves has become the subject of social historians and the 1960s written about profusely as being a decade of complete change and social revolution. George Best became part of the 'in' scene in the 1960s and his engagement in every facet of this change has been documented to death. George Best became a commodity that everyone wanted a part of. Companies and businesses craved for and wanted him to promote everything from aftershave to sausages, from overalls to oranges.  He was part of the first generation of footballers who enjoyed the demolished capped wages in the footballing world and so began to earn money he could never in his wildest Irish dreams have ever thought of earning.

The life of George Best has been documented, deliberated, debated and in some cases argued over. There are differences of opinions on his decision to leave Manchester United, the reports on his off-pitch antics, the number of beautiful women who became a part of his life – some for a very short time, others over a period of time. The most controversial aspect of George's life is of course his life-changing addiction to alcohol, an illness that eventually beat him and resulted in a claim on his life.

One thing is for sure, there was absolutely no doubt that George Best was special. A young man from a Belfast council estate blessed with the most astonishing talent the world of football was fortunate to witness, who spent 11 years with Manchester United displaying his almost superhuman skills in the Theatre of Dreams as well as the world stage of football. George was central to Manchester United's post-Munich disaster successes and, towards the end of his time at United, he was relied upon by an ageing team to pull them through difficult matches at certain times. He became a legend before he was 30 years of age and some would say that he spent the rest of his life trying to deny any legendary attributes.

George Best was part of the first English club to win the European Cup Final, he was voted English and European Footballer of the Year during the same year United raised that trophy. He was young, gifted, beautiful, talented, skilful – but he lived a totally unprotected superstar lifestyle, something that nowadays would never happen.

George Best combined mercurial talent with pop-star looks, his attributes attracted men and women alike, a combination that vaulted him to the pinnacle of celebrity in London's Swinging Sixties. But there is no way of avoiding the fact that his love of champagne and playboy lifestyle slid George into alcoholism, and that George was unable to shake the disease.

At George's funeral at Stormont, the home of Northern Ireland politics, on 5 December 2005, Eamonn Holmes said, 'Today we celebrate his life. In a country that often cannot rise above religion and politics, George Best did more than most to bring us together as people to make us recognise that maybe there is more that unites us than divides us.'

Consider this just for a moment: tributes and wreaths laid at the foot of Parliament Buildings included ones from former Prime Minister Tony Blair and the UK government, Bertie Ahern, his former clubs Manchester United and Edinburgh side Hibernian. The Duke of York sent white roses with this tribute: 'An inspirational footballer from Northern Ireland whose skills captured the imagination of fans from around the world.' Hollywood actor Mickey Rourke sent a wreath and there was a floral tribute from one of east Belfast's other famous sons, the singer/songwriter Van Morrison. The turnout and the tributes that flooded in after the death of George Best, a Protestant, show his immense popularity, one that crossed Northern Ireland's sectarian divide. This public outpouring was recognised as the biggest nationally since the death of Princess Diana.

All this and more in recognition to a footballer? Yes, because most people know that George Best was actually more than that, and *George Best – A Celebration* seeks to unveil some of what the man was really all about. It looks behind the tabloid headlines and diverts away from his flaws and questionable chosen way of life to see the man himself and tries to uncover why George Best was loved so much by so many.

The different phases of George's life always included within them his capacity to entertain. Throughout George's post-United years he was still able to display his God-given talents on the football pitch. At times it was only for 15 or 20 minutes of the game but that didn't matter, he was also able to use his natural way that he had of making people feel that they mattered. He may not have been showing his skills on a weekly basis in the Theatre of Dreams but in Dunstable Town, for example, he was still able to increase the usual gate of 53 to a capacity gate of 10,000. This was the game that officially 'switched on' the new floodlights when Dunstable played Manchester United Reserves. When George Best graced a football pitch whether it was for the Jewish Guild in South Africa, Hibernian F.C. in Scotland or Bournemouth F.C. in the south of England people still poured into the ground to see him play.

The famous and record-breaking six goals scored by George for Manchester United against Northampton Town in 1970 are much talked about, deliberated over and are part of many people's memories. In fact, the video clip of this event was used when George was introduced on a chat show in 1991 for the now infamous interview, when Terry Wogan said, 'What happened to the man Pelé himself called the world's greatest footballer?' But equally so is the goal talked about by those who were fortunate enough to see George in action when he scored for the San Jose Earthquakes in the United

GEORGE BEST

Date of Birth - 22nd May 1946
Place of Birth - Belfast
Height 1.75m
Position Winger/Forward

Manchester United Record 1963–1974

Total Appearances 466
Total Goals 178

International Record 1964–1973

37 Caps for Northern Ireland - 9 Goals

Honours with Manchester United

1st Div League Championship 1965
1st Div League Championship 1967
European Cup 1968
European Footballer of the Year 1968

States in 1981, when he wove his way through six players to score an outstanding and near impossible goal.

George Best couldn't help being idolised, he couldn't help being popular and he couldn't help being top of the list of interesting stories for the press to get hold of. True, some of his antics off the pitch were a journalist's dream to 'hold the front page' for – and who knows whether perhaps he may have done some of the headlining behaviour just for the hell of it? We just don't know, but what we do know is that many, many people were pleased to have George as their friend, even though at times he let them down. People were oh so glad when they saw George Best and were able to go up and chat with him like old mates and to maybe share a drink with him.

George himself knew that he wasn't perfect and perhaps coming to terms with how many thought he was a genius, an extraordinarily gifted person that the game of football had never seen before was a part of his decline. When Sir Alex Ferguson (who could have been speaking for the masses) said that George Best was 'unquestionably the greatest', to George it was just normality.

Similarly, someone who lived not far from George in Northern Ireland, who would often see him around, said that 'George was special to everyone and his faults were overlooked'.

In his book *Blessed* George is open and honest about himself and about his mistakes. He looks back at his regrets, of which he had a few, and admits, 'It all went wrong with football, the thing I loved most of all and from there my life slowly fell apart.' But clearly he also didn't forget the good times, of which there were many, and the successes and achievements.

George Best was for many a player who never reached his full potential on the field, so why then did so many wannabes want to emulate him? Michael Parkinson said of George: 'The only tragedy George Best had to confront is that he will never know how good he could have been.' He helped Manchester United win the First Division title in 1965 and 1967 and the European Cup in 1968, but he never played in a World Cup tournament. Quite sad to think that such dynamism never graced the world football stage at that level. George even suggested at times that perhaps things may have been different had he been born an Englishman or even a Brazilian, or born ugly.

George was renowned not only for remarkable footballing genius, skills and talents but also for his Sixties playboy lifestyle and eventual alcoholism. He was the first footballing 'celebrity' on and off the pitch who became involved in more than just the beautiful game, but he tried to combine football with glamour and some would say practised overindulgence in most things.

George Best – A Celebration is just what the title suggests. It is a selection of stories, tributes and memories that celebrate George Best the man, the son, the father, the brother, the friend, the genius, the footballing icon, the business man, the once-in-a-lifetime talent that many have had the pleasure of either seeing, meeting, watching, playing with or against, knowing or simply have heard about. The authors of the book have also used objects and memorabilia linked to George Best and have uncovered the story behind the real people who either own or have previously owned such items.

George Best – A Celebration weaves in between his colourful life and seeks to piece together some of the stories left on his way from those who will always remember their close encounter with the Best.

It reveals some of the more everyday activities and the less well-known and commentated aspects of a genuine, loving and caring person. Some of the stories make known the more unusual events and happenings in the lives of people, the famous and the not so famous, who have encountered George Best and have held their memories of him very close to them for a number of years. Some of these memories are simple but poignant, some are very personal while others are told from a different perspective. Some tributes are from those known to many of us, others are made from people you would pass by on the street.

George Best – A Celebration is an opportunity and a way of joining together all of these experiences, tributes and memories and a way of sharing as well as maybe bringing your own memories back to the surface. It enlightens the celebration of a life worth celebrating – the life of the kid off the streets of Belfast who became a superstar, the genius and the man, George Best. A man who in 1981 was described by a long-serving octogenarian tour guide at Old Trafford as 'the best man and footballer ever to have played the field or walked the corridors. A man who had as much time to give to the tea lady as he would to the main board director. A man dearly loved by all true Manchester United fans.'

FIRST HALF

Manchester United
May 1963 – January 1974

Event	Appearances	Goals
League	361	137
FA Cup	45	23
League Cup	25	9
Europe	34	11
Total	465	180

GEORGE'S FIRST TASTE OF SILVERWARE

In 1961, George made the journey of his lifetime, all the way from the Emerald Isle and the love and security of his family and friends to Manchester, the centre of the 19th-century industrial revolution, and the inspiration behind Charles Dickens's novel *Hard Times*. Little did George Best know what his journey to Manchester would lead to: undeniably to his own personal revolution. He did without doubt have many good times and provided the many thousands of his fans with such memories of a talented and gifted footballer in action on the pitch. But also, sadly, through circumstances and inappropriate choices, his life would also lead to some personal hard times and, on occasion, financial hard times.

After joining United as an amateur in 1961, George made his professional debut for the club as a 17-year-old against West Bromwich Albion in September 1963. He was a vital member of the Manchester United side that won the league championship in 1965 and 1967, and the European Cup in 1968, when he was voted both English and European

The young George turns out for Manchester United.

The FA Cup Youth Team.

Footballer of the Year. He also famously scored six goals in an FA Cup fifth-round tie against Northampton. But what happened of note in 1964?

The 1964 FA Youth Cup semi-final between the Manchester rivals – City and United – on Wednesday, 8 April at Old Trafford had great significance. Any match between City and United has always been, and always will be, a big match, with probabilities being discussed, and scorelines and performances forecast by the fans and pundits on both sides. The previous season Manchester United had won the FA Cup and Manchester City had been relegated – by none other than United. The result of this was that for the first time since 1949 there would be no Manchester derby – so the FA Youth Cup was the only way the blue half of the city could gain some honours and indeed for some kind of derby to take place.

The Busby Babes had won the FA Youth Cup for the first

five years of its existence – 1953–1957 – but since then United had failed to even reach the final. In 1964 the silverware was now in sight once more for United youths and the 17-year-old George Best received his call-up back into the youth side to give City some welly!

One of the players for City, John Clay, remembered, 'The only memory I have got of those two games was of Bestie. We got him in a corner, two of us, and he just turned and left us both for dead. He was incredible.'

What was also incredible was the gate for the match – 30,000 at a youth match – who watched an entertaining and uncompromising game with an abundance of enthusiasm and plenty of skill, and with an end result of Manchester United 4, Manchester City 1, leaving City a considerable task to achieve at the second leg played 12 days later at Moss Side. George Best was on top form for the second leg and City lost 3–1 on the night making the score 7–2 on aggregate, taking United comfortably through to a final against Swindon Town.

The town's community website www.swindonweb.com looked back on the match thus: 'You could say George Best's career officially started the night Manchester United beat Swindon Town. As an 18-year-old apprentice [sic; he would have been 17], he came of age when the next bunch of Busby Babes defeated Swindon 5–2 on aggregate to lift the FA Youth Cup on Thursday 30 April, 1964. It was his first real trophy. And he always described the moment he received his medal as being "extra special".

'"It was my first taste of silverware, and I liked it," he said.

"I wanted to play my best for Manchester United even more after that."

'Best even scored at the County Ground during the first leg on the previous Monday, 27 April. He shot low to beat Swindon Town keeper Tony Hicks on 70 minutes. It ended 1–1. Swindon's scorer that night was their answer to Best, Don Rogers. He remembers the match quite vividly: "I fired home past Jimmy Rimmer on about the half-hour," he said, "We were just thrilled to be in the final. But for a while we thought we could win it. Then Best turned on the skill. He had everything: ball control, courage and intelligence. He was the complete player even at 18."

'Swindon Town then succumbed 4–1 in the second leg at Old Trafford, with Best flying in from Northern Ireland to play after appearing for his country the previous night – his fourth match in six days (one Division One game for the first team, a two-legged final for the youths and an international).

'It was the start of something special for Manchester United. Seven of the 1964 youth team went on to win the League in 1965 and '67, and lift the European Cup in 1968. Equally inspired, Swindon Town also went onto enjoy a golden period – if slightly less glamorous; the 1969 League Cup win with Don Rogers scoring the winner.'

David Sadler recalls, 'I remember in the final I scored three [for United], and none of them was from outside the six-yard box, but Bestie won it. He was unstoppable!' Sounds familiar, doesn't it?

HERE'S TO YOU, MRS FULLAWAY!

How can four random photographs and a dry-cleaning ticket tell a story? Easy when they're all linked to George Best!

Living life in a goldfish bowl was becoming a way of life for George Best during the 1960s. So when, in the late 1960s, he moved into his Frazer Crane-designed and built house in Blossoms Lane, near Bramwell, Cheshire, to name

The dry-cleaning ticket for George's trousers.

7

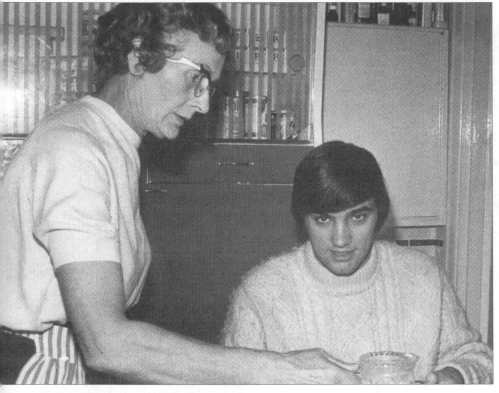

George with Mrs Fullaway, the landlady at his digs.

it the Goldfish Bowl was maybe more than a description of the modernist, split-level house encased in glass with a flat roof. It was perhaps metaphoric of George's life.

The luxurious 'Goldfish Bowl' lifestyle and having a great time of drinking, partying and girls only lasted for three years before George was found to have broken some of the Manchester United club rules. As a result of

8

9 Aycliffe Ave.,
off Merseybank Ave
Chorlton
<u>TUESDAY</u>'

Dear Bob,

Thanks a million for your most welcome letter. Sorry I didn't write sooner but I have been too busy training. At present the weather isn't too good but lets hope it will improve. We have training tomorrow morning and then a march in the afternoon There are a lot of lads from Dublin here and 3 new boys arrived today Better get off to bed now. an early rise tomorrow See you soon.

Geordie

George outside Mrs Fullaway's front door.

this George found himself deported back to his early days with Manchester landlady Mrs Fullaway in Chorlton-cum-Hardy, for her to keep a motherly eye on him and to try to curb his unruly ways. Quite a change in lifestyle and surroundings – but still the same George Best.

Just prior to Frazer Crane designing the infamous Goldfish Bowl, he also designed George's city-centre boutique that sold up-to-the-minute fashion for the man of the 1960s. Included in this fashion were checked hipster trousers, something George (and many other fashionable men) would often be seen wearing with his amazing style and flair.

Life still went on while George was back residing with Mrs Fullaway. One such everyday occurrence was when George needed to have a pair of his infamous checked pants dry-cleaned, and so took them along to the local dry cleaners. When he returned to collect them he discovered that he had lost the dry-cleaning ticket. The Saturday girl working in the shop asked George to complete a ticket agreeing not to try to claim anything from the Granada Pressing & Cleaning Co. Ltd should he find the original ticket – and complete it George did.

Were these the trousers?

10

And so it was that ticket number 00443 for 'Check Pts' was signed for by George Best living at the now famous 9, Aycliffe Avenue, Chorlton, and that same ticket kept safely so that we can now be aware of a very small but significant episode in George's life.

It's in such a life that four random photographs can be linked together to give a taste of what things were like for George Best during the sixties, and how something as insignificant as a dry-cleaning ticket has a greater story to tell about Chorlton life for George. And so to you, Mrs Fullaway, thank you.

THREE PROS AND THE BEST

3 pm, 17 September 1963, Old Trafford, Manchester. Ian Moir injured, a late replacement puts on the number 7 shirt for Manchester United to play against the blue and white stripes of West Bromwich Albion. Who is this young strip of a lad from Northern Ireland in the number 7 shirt, in his debut match, who has been put out on the wing and not getting a look at the ball? After some 15 minutes having never kicked the ball, let alone made any impact on the game, this young unknown got bored and decided he had had enough, changed places and went to play in central midfield. Unusually Bobby Charlton moved over from midfield and took up a post on the wing – something unheard of.

Following this youngster's bold decision, Graham Williams, captain of West Brom, had his first encounter with George Best, who ran the defender inside out on many occasions during the match. George didn't score, but played his part in the 1–0 win for Manchester United.

The match report in the *Daily Telegraph* read like this:

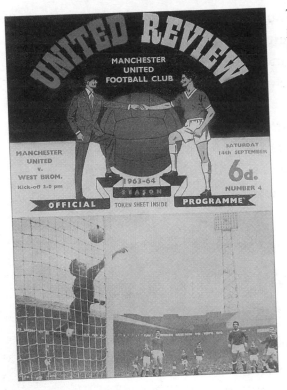

The programme from George's first professional match – played at home to West Bromwich Albion.

'There was the prospect of young George Best to brighten a dullish match. Despite the ordeal of a league debut after only three reserve matches, a gruelling duel with full-back Graham Williams and a painful ankle injury, he played pluckily and finished the game in style. None of the handicaps could disguise a natural talent. I know manager Matt Busby is looking forward to seeing this Belfast boy in a team with Law to help him. I agree, and it is an exciting prospect that will brighten up even the dullest of games.' A star was born that day, and an era had begun.

The debut appearance on that Manchester day of an unknown but extremely talented footballing boy from Belfast – just a year before regular television highlights began – was the beginning of many memories held by three of the West Brom greats from the 1960s and '70s, Graham Williams, Tony Brown and Bobby Hope. Their memories of playing against George, meeting him off the pitch and their comments about him as a person are as fresh as ever, with not a negative comment or thought about this 'once in a lifetime' talent they had the absolute pleasure to know.

Graham Williams fondly remembers George on holiday in Majorca at the same time as he and his family were. George, never being a swimmer, was delighted to baby-sit Graham's children on the beach while he and his wife enjoyed swimming in the sea. The children loved George, and he enjoyed being with the kids. Graham recalls that to him George was 'a person you would like to be your son, such a nice guy'. What an accolade for this shy, good-looking football genius.

Tony Brown, a lifelong Manchester United fan, made his debut for West Brom just a few weeks after Best's debut for Man U. He recalls the Busby Babes playing in a Youth Cup with a crowd of well over 20,000 – such was the increasing popularity of Manchester United.

Tony also recollects that George never had tricks on the pitch but he came at his opponents with such pace and balance that, although physically small, he had a way of turning players inside out. Graham agreed and suggested that 'Jesus is known for walking on water, but George Best could walk on mud, as he seemed to fly over the uneven and deep muddied pitches.'

Tony Brown, Bobby Hope and George Best all exported their footballing talents to the United States. Tony brought to mind the time when he was playing for the New America team against San Jose Earthquakes – the team George Best had bestowed his flair and genius on.

Graham Williams, former captain of West Brom, had fond memories of George.

13

Before the game Tony was invited to explain to his teammates George's capacity on the football pitch and told them that they 'were playing against one of the best'. He remembers how the team appeared to take his 'warning' lightly, and some even questioned what he was suggesting. His words soon rang true when George displayed a spark of brilliance and 'murdered them on the day' and those who had questioned his genius had to agree that George Best had everything – including scoring a goal on the day. Nonetheless, there was a general consensus from the squad after the match on how they were 'amazed how nice he was'.

Bobby Hope, playing for Dallas in the 1970s, remembered with almost sadness how George didn't seem to understand everything that was happening to him and recalls seeing him sitting with children as if he were an outsider.

It seemed such a sad reflection as Tony Brown considered George in his heyday, how a short time ago, when Manchester United played West Brom at home, Halfords Lane would be crammed with people, mainly girls and women, all wanting to see George Best. An hour or more before the game it was impossible to move because of the crowds waiting for him to arrive on the club coach, and George would never disappoint the fans, smiling and giving his shy wave.

'So generous' is also how Graham Williams remembers George Best, and questions some of the people who became 'hangers on' around him, only wanting his friendship for what they could get. Graham remembers that when on holiday George would always have a flight bag full of money ready to hand out to those around him to join him for a drink, and unfortunately this led him to be part of bad company.

All three ex-West Brom players remembered how in any team talks prior to playing against George they knew that because he could play anywhere it was difficult to be advised on how to deal with him. In fact there were never tactics discussed, just thoughts on how to combat him. George was such a brave player, and, as Bobby Hope recalls, they were never told to deal with George one-to-one but would always have to have a potential support route planned.

The debut performance of George Best was reported thus: 'He turned professional in 1963 and made his debut that autumn at home against West Bromwich Albion, who were then second in the League. Best had a fine game, giving West Brom's experienced fullback Graham Williams a roasting. One of his first moves was to show Williams the ball – and then he "nutmegged" him.'

Yet there is a lovely story that, years later, Williams, the seasoned pro he had embarrassed, met Best and said to him, 'Will you stand still for a minute so I can look at your face?' 'Why?' asked Best. 'Because all I've seen of you,' explained Williams, 'is your arse disappearing down the touchline.' This is one occasion where the story gets better with the telling!

Graham Williams, the West Brom fullback, is happy to let the media inflate such a story, or for Wilf McGuinness to use it in his after-dinner speeches. Truth is that George Best did give Graham the runaround on that September day in 1963 and, yes, he can remember wondering what this young slip of a boy was about. It was when Graham and George met when they were both living in the Bournemouth area that Graham said to George that it was nice to see his face from the front. George replied that he had still got Graham's 'autograph' marks on his legs from his debut game. In fact whenever Graham and George would speak on the phone George always mentioned the 'autograph' on his leg. Obviously a painful memory of his debut game.

It is ironic that the Manchester United league fixture following the death of George in November 2005 was at home against West Bromwich Albion. The three ex-pros from West Brom were guests at Old Trafford as it became the epicentre of the world's tribute to the young lad from Belfast who as a footballer 'had everything' and as a person was 'a really nice guy'.

Graham, Tony and Bobby all took part on that emotional Saturday as the world paid tribute to the genius of George. Tony's emotions got the better of him when the whole of Old Trafford, in respect of George's life, raised a well-known and favourite picture of George. Bobby's thoughts were that the fans – both Manchester's and West Brom's – were brilliant in showing respect for the greatest. Graham's thoughts were two-fold as he stood paying his silent respects to George. The first was relief that George's suffering was over, and the second was a mix of grief and pride that they were standing in acknowledgement of losing someone as great as George.

IT JUST WASN'T TO BE FOR A YOUNG GEORDIE LAD!

By 1965, an English winger named Stanley Matthews, nicknamed 'The Wizard of Dribble', had been stunning defenders with his crowd-raising dribbling skills for many, many years, but it was in this particular year that he decided to hang up his boots and retire. This was also the year that Stanley became Sir Stanley, receiving his knighthood, and was awarded the Football Sword of Honour.

When George Best first began to dazzle on Manchester United's left wing, contemporaries cast around for the former player he most resembled, and dubbed him the 'new Stanley Matthews'. By the year of retirement of one dazzler (Stanley Matthews), the new dazzler (George Best) had been making first-team appearances for United for two years. George was beginning to show that he was not only a skilful and agile wizard of the dribble, but also a prolific marksman with a physical vibrancy and style of his own.

The football pitch wasn't the only place George Best was beginning to dazzle. Video clips show that on the pop music television programme of the day, *Top of the Pops*, in 1965 George can be seen dancing along with the others in the studio audience in step to The Rolling Stones' 'This Could Be the Last Time'. Although on viewing this it seems his rhythm, pace and footwork had far more star quality on a football pitch than on the dance floor, he did have a pretty lady dancing by his side instead of a challenging centre-half as he was becoming accustomed to.

1965 was also a good year for Newcastle United as, through a mixture of young talent like David Craig and Frank Clark, they returned to top-flight football as the then Division Two champions. Their promotion meant that the club and supporters alike were looking forward to the new 1965/66 season, particularly when the fixtures were announced and the first on the list was Manchester United at home.

What an anticipated fixture that was, particularly for a 12-year-old Geordie lad, Ian Trevethick, who just couldn't wait for September to arrive. Not only was his team now in the top flight and living on the glory of being Division Two champions, the first match of the season was at his beloved St James' Park against another United, but from the North

West rather than the North East. But the North West
United had in its squad the young talented and skilful
young and much-talked-about Irishman – George Best.
What more could a 12-year-old wish for and look forward
to throughout his school holidays? (Incidentally, Ian was an
excellent goalkeeper himself and, as with thousands of other
young hopefuls, he dreamed of playing professionally. He
made semi-professional, but went on to be a PE teacher and

George in action against Newcastle Utd.

encouraged many other young hopefuls into football and other sports.)

Imagine how Ian felt when his mother informed him that they were going on holiday the week before the first match of the season. Horrified! But he wasn't that put out as he knew that they would return from their Hastings holiday on the Saturday morning – so, no problem.

But things didn't quite work out the way Ian had planned. On arriving home to Newcastle, Ian thought that there was just enough time to get to the match, but he was stopped in his tracks by his mother who said he couldn't go.

To this day, he can still remember how he felt missing his team's first match back in Division One. Bad enough for a 12-year-old but he also missed out on watching George Best work his magic on the football pitch: to see how strong and courageous, despite his slight build, George actually was; to witness him controlling the ball effortlessly with both feet as he left defenders foundering; to perhaps see just what an accomplished header of the ball George was and to witness how he was capable of scoring goals from all areas of the pitch with a powerful shot, often with a touch of impertinence. Perhaps he may even have seen one of George's favourite tricks, to play the ball against the legs of opponents to take the rebound like a one-two pass. But it wasn't to be.

Ian's first memory of seeing George Best was watching him on television one Saturday on *Match of the Day*. It was a Saturday-night ritual in the Trevethick household; Ian would make sausage sandwiches for his mother and himself just in time to sit down and watch the footie on the telly. This particular day George was in his green football top (although of course it wasn't colour television in those days,

The programme from the abandoned match.

but the badge of Ireland was clear to see) playing for Northern Ireland against Scotland and Ian recalls how, having watched him on television, he desperately wanted to go and see him play in the flesh.

Ian had to wait a whole season for Manchester United to visit St James' Park again, but it was worth the wait as he loved to watch the interaction between Best and Bobby Charlton – of course with Bobby being a North East lad himself. After that Ian had the pleasure of watching George on many occasions, but he still wonders just what it would have been like to see his team in their first match of the season back in top-flight football, and against Man U with George Best displaying his pure genius. This is one experience that got away and Ian could do nothing about it.

Two years later, our Geordie lad was disappointed on another occasion when Newcastle were due to play Manchester United. He recalls looking forward to seeing his team beat Man United. Ian was then 14 years old and went through the usual routine he and his friend Brian Crow went through prior to a home game. They would meet in town – Ian armed with his paper-round money – go upstairs in the Northumberland Arms, somehow get served with a pint and sink their teeth into a Monster Pie (ham and eggs) – the best you could get, so Ian remembers.

Our unlucky Geordie boy recalls feeling gutted, in fact sick as a parrot (and not from the Monster Pie). He just couldn't believe it when he heard that the match he and his friend were looking forward to had been called off; he was so disappointed, particularly as he couldn't wait to see the skills of George Best on the park again. Still, at least he'd had his pie and pint!

FRANKIE GOES BACK TO THE 1960S

When, in 1966, Ray Davies wrote the words to 'Dedicated Follower Of Fashion', he did so hoping that George Best would record the memorable 'Oh yes he is' lyric and become a chart-topper in the music world. 'But United manager Matt Busby put an end to that idea,' recalls Ray. 'Busby stepped in and told Best to concentrate on his football and forget any notion of becoming a pop star.' Amazingly this was one occasion when George listened and responded to the advice of his manager.

Until the late 1960s, men's fashion had been restricted to sharp suits and shiny shoes – unless you were a pop star or a DJ. But someone the increasingly fashion-conscious men of the decade have to thank is Harold Tillman. He was the first fashion entrepreneur to recognise the cross-over power of celebrity and was responsible for marketing the first sports star as a fashion icon with his clothing ranges for footballer George Best. (Nowadays, Harold Tillman is owner of iconic British fashion brand Jaeger, as well as Allders of Croydon, the UK's third largest department store.)

Little did those heady, fashion-blasting days of the 1960s, which included the George Best range of fashion clothes, realise just how much their innovative fashion designs would still be influencing fashion in the 21st century.

Frankie Johns was someone who was influenced, so much so that he has established a thriving Vintage Urban Village business to house his enthusiasm for keeping alive the designs of the 1960s, '70s and '80s.

Frankie has for many years been collecting items of clothing, records, furniture and whatever he can from those decades. He is an avid collector of 1960s clothing and music and enjoys listening to the music of Small Faces, The Who and probably The Kinks! Being a Mod of the

1970s/'80s he always wanted to meet mods from the 1960s and to hear all the stories from the scene, how it all started, what they wore and which scooter they had. Frankie found this very hard to do and couldn't seem to find anyone really into it all.

Then one of his friends who knew of his love for the 1960s introduced him to an 'old Mod' who had unfortunately fallen on hard times. Frankie's new-found Mod lived and breathed the Mod scene back in the 1960s, had a scooter, had clothing, plus he had seen almost every group of the day. Frankie must have felt that he had died and gone to heaven as their first meeting lasted three hours and more.

The result of the trip down Memory Lane ended with the old Mod asking if Frankie wanted to buy some of his gear – including an original Parka, hundreds of records plus lots and lots of clothes. What a treasure chest for a man who must feel that he was

The blazer in question.

born out of time! Finally the old Mod brought out his pride and joy, a George Best special boating blazer that had cost him a whole month's wages. The quality of the cloth used to make the stylish boating jacket and the eye for detail even down to the design of the buttons was equal to the quality and style of the man whose name was on the label. A class of its own – just like George!

Frankie had always wanted to own a piece of George Best clothing, so what a find it was for him. It didn't fit him, but did he care? Not one bit – he was so pleased to be the proud new owner. Not only did he have a piece of fashion from the 1960s, it was a genuine piece of George Best fashion – what more could he ask for?

George Best may not have taken up Ray Davies's offer to record 'Dedicated Follower Of Fashion' but he certainly lived some of the phrases. He always wore trendsetting clothes and his unprecedented celebrity status would, in the end, 'make or break' him. How prophetic Ray was in writing those lyrics.

Eventually, Ray Davies rescued the song before it landed in the bin, took it to the other Kinks (his brother Dave, Pete

Quaife and Mick Avory) and they decided if George (aka 'El Beatle', so dubbed by the press following snaps of him after the astounding 5–1 Manchester United defeat of Benfica in Lisbon in 1966 wearing a huge sombrero) wasn't allowed to record the song then they would do it themselves. Which they did – and it turned out to be a massive hit for them and is probably for sale in Frankie's Urban Village.

To quote another footballing icon, 'It's a funny old world', isn't it?

SWINGING MANCHESTER

As George Best rode on the crest of the 1960s wave, what else could he do but think about using his popularity and diversify into some kind of business venture? His football was the natural part of him, the part he didn't really have to think about because of his quick mind, skilful footwork and just having that special something that everyone loved to watch. But unlike today, when top-flight footballers are automatically expected to endorse this and that, invest in something else or more than likely bring out yet another fragrance of aftershave, for George Best it had never been done before.

United won the league championship and were back in the European Cup. By now George had become the first showbusiness footballer. He was receiving 1,000 fan letters a week. He was dubbed 'the fifth Beatle' because, in the days when players had short hair, his mop resembled those of the pop group. The boutique, modelling assignments and personal appearances were booming for Best.

It's hard to imagine that only six days after the Benfica game George and his close friend Mike Summerbee (Manchester City player) opened their trendy and very fashionable male boutique, Edwardia, in Sale, Manchester. Fans flocked to the opening, of course mainly girls! So many wanted to get a look in through the shop window that the combined force of them all almost pushed the window through. George saw the shops as something different to do, and of course it attracted a ready-made stream of lovely ladies.

Both Mike and George made regular visits to London, seeking out manufacturers in Bond Street offices, finding out the best of the new styles. Football was still their main job but they didn't want to be sleeping partners in business.

George Best and his friend Mike Summerbee posing outside the shop.

Best was to meet his toughest challenges off the pitch, and he made no secret of his enjoyment of Manchester's growing club scene and the charms of the legions of women who pursued him relentlessly. He not only opened his own boutiques, he also modelled for catalogues and endorsed an array of products from sausages and eggs to aftershave. He became a living commodity! All this was established before George had even reached his 21st birthday – he was also still a regular in Manchester United's first team and in the Northern Ireland XI.

On a roll in the business world George opened two nightclubs in Manchester, in the late 1960s, one called Oscar's and the other called Slack Alice's (which later became 42nd Street). He continued with the fashion boutiques and launched his own clothing brand, in partnership with Mike Summerbee. He also opened Bestie's Beach Club (now called The Underground after the London subway system) in Hermosa Beach, California, United States, and lived in the city throughout the 1970s, '80s and '90s.

According to Jim White, writing in the *Daily Telegraph*, 'At the weekends, Best used to patrol the queue outside the club [Slack Alice's], checking out the top lookers and inviting them inside. It was, those who saw it recall, an astonishing parade of the North-West's most beautiful women (Germaine Greer, then working at Granada Television, was also a regular at the club). Dave Haslam, in his book about the city's cultural development, *Manchester England*, recalls meeting a chap who was dating, by common consent, the best-looking girl in town. He took her along to Slack Alice's one night, was invited inside by Best, and the three of them spent the evening chatting over the champagne. At the end of the night, he left alone; she stayed on with the host. Haslam asked the spurned boyfriend

27

if he had minded being cuckolded so publicly. Not at all, came back the reply, it was Bestie; it was an honour.'

The following extract from *The Fashion of Football: Best to Beckham* by Paolo Hewitt and Mark Baxter gives a clear insight into the fashion world George had got himself into:

'I ended up having a stake in three shops,' Best told writer Joe Lovejoy. 'Another one just off Deansgate and the third in the Arndale shopping precinct in Manchester. Summerbee and I were partners but it was Malcolm Mooney who ran the set-up. Mike and I didn't really have much to do with them; we used our names to promote them and popped in once in a while. Just another way of pulling birds I suppose.'

Clothes for the young were the obvious tool in the selling of Georgie. He was soon being photographed carrying boxes of what he termed 'our new "Mod" stock' into the shop. He was also photographed posing in a white button-down shirt, Prince of Wales checked trousers and waistcoat, looking very Modish. 'I enjoy it and it's good for business,' he stated.

Best often posed with his partner, Mike, and that was good for business as well – United and City for once joined at the hip. Everyone welcome. In one memorable press shot, they wore suits made from 'kid mohair, with satin-faced lapel and cuffs. The trousers are slightly flared with satin-bound side seams. The price: about £42.'

The copy line also says that this is George's one and only suit. 'He always teams jackets with trousers but won't buy a suit.' George's attitude to suits is instructive. At that point in his life, suits to the young symbolised authority and were worn only by the staid, those who would keep talent such as his at bay. Suits were for squares and Best wanted nothing to do with the creaking world the suit represented at that particular point in Britain.

With the shop came further photographic demands: Mike modelling a checked umbrella for men, 'one of the first to break away from the traditional black umbrella image', and George sporting a double-peaked rainhat made by Edward Mann and costing 35s 11d. 'Thank heavens for a bit of imagination,' George's quote runs. 'Men tend to be so dull about accessories. They wear floral ties and things, why not stripes and zigzags on umbrellas or caps like this, instead of outdated trilbies?'

As on the pitch, so in the wardrobe. Best yearned for the new. The new coloured the world and created a brave new future. It was the decade's strongest belief, designed to instigate the complete breaking away from the stiffness of the 1950s, the years of austerity, the years of kowtowing to the upper classes.

George Best was a definitive part of the growing Swinging Sixties and he certainly helped to put Manchester on the map; he helped to make it swing. For a time in the 1960s, George Best was so hot the whole of Manchester sizzled in his wake. John Peel claimed that he only got his first break in radio in the United States because the station controller assumed that, as he hailed from near Liverpool, he must know the Beatles. Likewise, for an entire generation of Mancunians, George Best was the passport to cool.

Although things looked quite good on the surface and there was much said and written about the young Irishman becoming a shrewd investor, unfortunately George's talents were more notable on the pitch as his businesses had little success.

I WAS BESTIE'S BALLBOY!

Saturday, 6 May 1967. Once again Manchester United had become part of the European Cup by being confirmed the Football League champions for the fifth time since World War II. And what a way of becoming champions: by annihilating the West Ham side at Upton Park with a significant 6–1 win, courtesy of Charlton, Crerand, Foulkes, Best and Law.

The fourth goal was competently taken by Best who upset the defence when, in the 25th minute, he took up a pass and scored. After Law scored from a penalty, the rest of the game was no more and no less than an exhibition of United's supremacy, controlling the pace and speed of the game until the final whistle of relief for West Ham.

1967 was also a significant year for 10-year-old Steve when his grandparents moved to Haig Road, Stretford, the gardens of which backed onto United's Canal Training Ground. Due to family commitments, Steve lived on and off with his grandparents and would regularly watch the team training. Tuesdays and Thursdays were the days United used the training ground so there were obvious reasons why Steve was often late to Saint Theresa's Primary School on those days – or even why he didn't make it at all.

Steve's first recollection of George Best is seeing his Granddad telling Bestie off for his bad language when at the foot of their garden as the ball shot over their iron railing fence and George was sent to ask for it back. After all – bad language is bad language even if you are a whizz kid on the pitch!

One of the autographs collected by young Steve.

Even as a youngster, Steve instinctively knew that George was something special – he just couldn't take his eyes off him as he created poetry with the ball.

Steve cannot remember how many times he climbed the iron railing fence to stand at the back of the nets watching Best, Charlton, Law and the rest of the magnificent Manchester team as they drove their shots. He would run and fetch the ball whenever he was needed and was nick-named 'Titch' by Bestie and the others. He was often told off by Jack Crompton for not being at school – but who in Steve's class would have not swapped places with him? Imagine being Bestie's ballboy – fancy putting that on your CV! It's not surprising that George would show some term of endearment to Steve as, in his heart, he was very much a family man. 'In fact he is mad about kids of any size and shape,' an old magazine reported.

Not only was the Canal Training Ground a place to have the most desired unpaid job as a 10-year-old, it was also a

George outnumbered by Derby players.

great place for collecting autographs, which Steve did on numerous occasions from many of the great names, autographs that he cherished for many years and was the start of his collecting from the great and the mighty.

Steve's Bestie ballboying days only lasted for a couple of

years until 1969 when the first team started using the Cliff Training Ground in Salford. Unfortunately, the Canal Training Ground fell into decline – today a line of poplar trees mark the boundary but the rest is unrecognisable. If only those playing fields could talk and recall the many magnificent Manchester greats training and practising – perhaps even Law practising his penalty shots with skills that clinched the fifth goal at Upton Park, and Best gliding and swaying swiftly past the defence. No, the playing fields cannot recall any of these, but the young boy of 1967 can and nothing can take those precious memories away from 'Titch', as he was Bestie's ballboy.

Manchester may have made it to the European Cup but perhaps the feelings of 10-year-old Steve as he watched and helped his footballing heroes would be equally as important and memorable.

THREE TEENAGERS AND A TURNSTILE

On a weekday evening in late April 1968, a charged atmosphere encompassed the whole of the Hawthorns Stadium, the home of West Bromwich Albion F.C. The sheer noise and volume of the crowd reached out and overwhelmed each and every one of the 43,412 spectators, creating an atmosphere that was awe-inspiring. So what had caused this electrifying experience for teenage fan Keith Slater? Quite simply it was being in the presence of a genius at work on the football pitch!

Getting into the ground to gain this lasting memory was another matter. With their money ready and the game about to kick off, Keith and his mate Alan Wade ('Acker') made their way around two or even three turnstiles but all were locked. For the first time ever in Keith's (then) short lifetime he couldn't believe that they were locked. The two lads instantly got down on all fours and crawled under the turnstile. Keith recalls that, if he had stopped to think about it, he doubts that he would have had the nerve! Stopping for nothing they ran through the 'brick wall' and up into the stands at the Birmingham Road End, not looking back to see if they were being hot footed, and mingled with the crowds and the volume of noise across the Brummy Road End and ended up at Woodman Corner.

So why was it so important to both Keith and Alan to get to see this particular game? Why were they willing to risk being caught and possibly escorted briskly out of the ground having had their collars felt? Two reasons. Firstly, as they both played football themselves on Saturdays or on Sunday mornings, the chance of watching league matches only occurred on weekday matches and as this was an evening match they had the opportunity to watch their team, West

Brom. But even more than that, Manchester United and, more importantly, George Best were in town – and this unforgettable evening was in fact Keith's first time seeing him play live.

Some particular memories of the game still live with Keith today. He recalls it was possibly Denis Law's last chance to prove his fitness before the European Cup Final, but that he ended up being taken into hospital after the game. During the match, however, Law picked up the ball, ran through towards the goalmouth and was about a yard off goal at the Birmingham Road End. All other players were behind him, and instead of kicking the ball into the net he chose to flick it. And flick the ball he did right over the cross bar and into the delighted West Brom fans. Keith recalls Law's expression of absolute horror and how he held his face, hiding it from the Man Utd fans, and probably from his team-mates too.

Keith's clearest memory was when George Best picked up a ball passed through to him from the halfway line. Best's long, dark, layered hair bounced as he majestically controlled the ball. The noise of the crowds sent goose bumps up and down Keith's back. The excitement and thrill of the crowd when Best was on the ball was an experience in itself. George didn't score in this match – imagine what the noise level would have been if he had.

It's quite interesting that one of the authors of this book was also at the same match in 1968 and can vouch for the tremendous occasion and experience of the game – particularly as West Brom won! The difference being that she paid to go through the turnstiles and legally cheered her team on while being appreciative of the most handsome Belfast boy at the same time. This particular match was also the first time she saw George Best in real life instead of

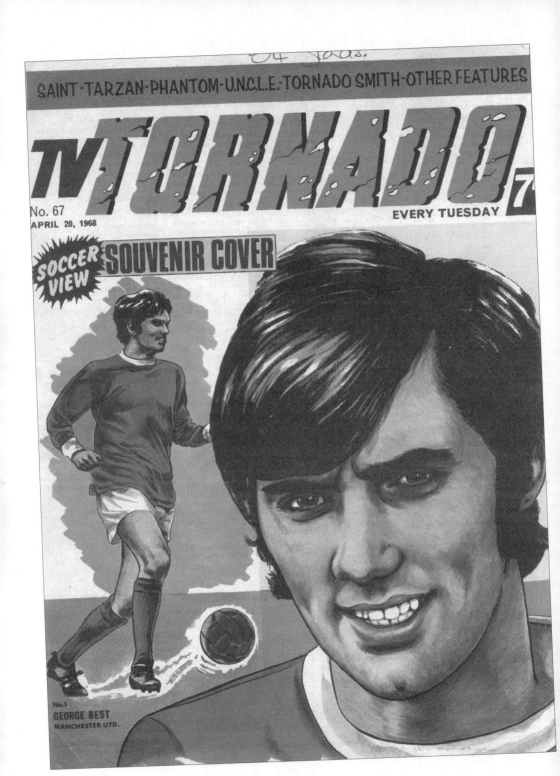

A magazine from April 1968, the same time as the three
teenagers all witnessed the skill of George on the pitch.

having to make do with his picture pinned to her bedroom wall. What an experience that was for a teenage girl in 1968!

Coincidentally, just a few matches away for both teams were respective cup finals; West Brom played Everton in the FA Cup Final just four days before the history-making European Cup Final between Manchester United and Benfica.

Both teams that played that spine-tingling league match at the Hawthorns on 29 April 1968 won their respective finals. The iconic centre forward Jeff Astle's extra-time winner saw off Everton and George Best's early extra-time goal set the stage for Manchester United to go on and win the European Cup Final.

So what a night was had all round on that April evening in 1968. What memories were born and what stories can be told from just an ordinary league game. Three people, two who were friends and slipped into the match under the

STAR ACTION

MANCHESTER UNITED
versus
WEST HAM

George Best, Manchester United's little Irish wizard, must be one of the most photographed of all soccer stars. But then the wee wonder is "always in the picture" whenever or wherever he plays. He loves football and plays with the enthusiasm of two ordinary players. Here he is in flying action against West Ham United at Old Trafford last season, as he leaps to head a fast centre. George Best is the sort of player that defenders need to watch and mark very closely, whether the ball is on the ground or in the air. The players in this dramatic picture are (left to right) Best, Alan Stephenson and Bobby Moore, West Ham half-backs; Billy Bonds, Hammers' fine full-back; David Sadler, tall Manchester United star and Martin Peters, the West Ham man-of-all-work. Did you know that George Best has scored 57 League goals in the last three seasons?

Although this picture shows Manchester United v West Ham (not West Brom!) it is taken from one of the magazines in which George was often featured.

turnstiles and a teenage girl who wouldn't have known them if she had stood next to them, all of them drank in the atmosphere of the game.

And yet all these years on, their memories of that evening when at least three teenagers who had the opportunity to see the genius of George in operation on the pitch are able to join together in their remembrance of him and his wonderful skills on the ball, and how he was able to stir a crowd into spine-chilling volumes of noise.

TWO PATHS THAT CROSSED

Anyone who was anyone in the late 1960s and '70s and who enjoyed a good night out would be seen in Blinkers nightclub in the fashionable part of Manchester town centre. This extremely popular place to be was a favourite of celebrities and football stars, including George Best. Self-made millionaire Selwyn Demmy, who enjoyed a champagne lifestyle and was a very good friend of George, owned the club. In fact both Selwyn and George often shared an all-boys holiday with other friends.

Selwyn's day job was being a very successful bookie and he also not only owned Blinkers, he ran it too. It was a place where you would frequently find George with a beautiful girl on each arm along with his man-about-town dashing friend Selwyn who chose to do the same.

During the heyday of Blinkers nightclub, a successful market researcher, Jane Moss, who worked for Pedigree Petfoods in Melton Mowbray dipped in and out of being one of the in-crowd in Manchester. As part of Jane's job she had to travel around the UK visiting wholesalers and retailers. She loved playing lots of sports and she particularly loved to watch rugby union. As part of her travels she would often stay in Manchester when visiting businesses in the North West and she happened to visit Blinkers Nightclub on a few occasions.

On one particular occasion Jane spoke with George and just for the hell of it asked him to sign the Blinkers book of matches – for no real reason. Having such a small piece of folded-up cardboard with the famous Blinkers logo on wouldn't have been worth keeping for sure, but once George had personalised his good wishes to her, followed by the famous George Best autograph, then it was something worth keeping. And that's just what Jane did – for more than 30 years.

Who knows whether George's mate Selwyn was with him at the time of the book of matches being signed – no one can say. But Selwyn has been known to say of his friend George that he was so popular, even hero worshipped, that when people met him they wanted to show their affection for him by buying him a drink. Having a social drink was a hazard of his life as a star and as a really nice guy.

Unfortunately, like George, Jane is no longer with us but the prized possession of a book of matches signed by the 'nice guy' George Best is a small tribute to both Jane and George. Jane's brother, Nigel, has shared this small snippet of a minor occasion in the life of his sister Jane who had the opportunity of meeting George a few times.

Selwyn now enjoys living life at a less hectic pace and now

runs an animal sanctuary in Mottram, St Andrew. He said:
'George Best once had the world at his feet and in his feet.

He was magic to know and I will never forget him. He loved life and he lived life to its full.'

Both Nigel and Selwyn can share memories of those close to them whose paths crossed in a nightclub in Manchester sometime in the late 1960s or '70s. They could also join together in saying that they will both be remembered with fondness and will be sadly missed... but curiously linked together by a signed Blinkers book of matches.

BESTIE BREAKS THE MOULD

For many people in England in the 1960s, New Zealand took its place in a geography book, a television programme or perhaps a place referred to as small islands close to Australia, where many were choosing to emigrate to gain a better life. That 'far-away' place of New Zealand was the home of a young boy who, during the 1960s, received what was to him quite a strange gift from a relative back in England. A gift that he didn't really realise the significance of.

At this particular time in the 1960s, football was beginning to become a religion to many fans and their football idols were edging towards pop-star status in terms of the adoration they were attracting, the lifestyles they were living and the wages they were receiving. England winning the World Cup in 1966 put football well and truly on the map for the majority of the country, with those people who had no interest in the game before becoming engaged in the euphoria of being football's world champions. Football fans no longer just wore the scarf of their team, sometimes a rosette of the team colours, or celebrated a goal or a win with the clacking sound of a rattle. More and more items were being manufactured which celebrated either England's footballing squad of heros, or the iconic players of the top teams in the country. Marketing was becoming more than just attracting high numbers to a football game, it was necessary to have the right merchandise to satisfy these fans in the beloved colours of their team.

Keymen figures were just one of the pieces of merchandise that became extremely popular. They were 3-inch-high 'men' in a footballing stance painted in specific football team colours. Many that were sold were of England's footballing stars in the beloved England strip – a momento of winning the World Cup. Quite an unusual name for the memorabilia, Keymen, but they were so called because they were painted by inmates of Liverpool Prison who were under lock and key – consequently being known as 'key-men'. Although these little figures have the appearance and weight of being made of lead, they are actually die-cast.

Another chosen footballer for a Keymen figure was George Best in a Manchester United strip and in his international Northern Ireland strip. George in his Manchester United strip was the strange gift that the young boy in New Zealand received back in the 1960s. A bizarre gift to him because as a New Zealander his game was rugby, and so the gift had little or no impact, and it ended up being placed in a drawer for several years.

It was only after the news of George losing his life that this particular Keymen figure saw the light of day again – in perfect condition, as it was when put away all those years ago. The once unwanted, unappreciated figure with the red and white football strip of Manchester United painted on by some unknown prisoner in a Liverpool jail has now travelled back to its homeland of England and is in the possession of a keen George Best fan.

As for the Keymen figures being die-cast, those casts are probably not in use any more. But one thing is for sure: when George Best became part of this earth and displayed his absolute genius on the football pitch with his wonderful talents, the mould really must have been thrown away. In the football world, there may have been 'greats', there may currently be 'greats', and there may even be 'greats' to come – but the mould has tragically been broken on the greatest – George Best.

WHY A ROSETTE?

In 1968, Tim Warne's dad proudly wore a red and white rosette (the first team colours of his beloved Manchester United) adorned with the face and signature of the incredibly talented George Best. Tim's dad was one of the 100,000 spectators lucky enough to get a ticket for the European Cup Final at Wembley in May 1968, when United beat Benfica and raised the cup in triumph, becoming the heroes of the hour in English football.

The origin of the rosette worn on a lapel actually goes way back to the Legion of Honour award. Napoleon Bonaparte established this in 1802 particularly to show recognition of praiseworthy service. The Napoleonic rosette was much, much bigger than the ones seen today, and was the mount to display the Legion of Honour award.

By 1850 the rosette took on a much different design; it was made smaller and could be worn on clothing, much as it is today. It was, however, the Americans in 1877 when the Military Order of the Loyal Legion of the United States used the lapel rosette in the way it is commonly used today. But today the rosette is used for many things other than military recognition, such as for the ordinary people to 'nail their colour to the mast' for their favourite team. That's why Tim's dad wore his rosette with pride on that history-making day in 1968, and why his treasure was passed on to his equally United-mad son, whose favourite player was George Best.

Tim was just eight years old when his dad wore the colours of United on his lapel, and at the time of the

European Cup Final was living in Tregony, Cornwall. While his dad was part of the United multitude at Wembley, Tim was watching the match on the TV with his uncle, another United fan – to this day he has no idea how his dad managed to get hold of a ticket.

Later on in life, Tim (a red forever) lived in London and had more opportunities to watch his beloved United and indeed George Best, as it was easier to travel to Old Trafford and around the country. He particularly remembers seeing George play at White Hart Lane, and being the proud owner of some George Best football boots with the newly fashioned side lace-ups.

As a young boy, Tim was given one of the George Best Keymen, painted by the inmates at Walton Prison. The same coveted little piece of memorabilia made in cast is to this day still in pristine

Bobby Charlton and George Best celebrate.

condition, wrapped up and in its original box – and even now has the packer's number inside the box in case of the need to return.

So thank you, Napoleon, for having the foresight to present the Legion of Honour all those years ago. Football supporters all over the world adorn themselves with miniatures of your idea in the colours that they hold so dear and with the face of players they worship and adore.

45

George Best certainly fits into the category of being one of the Legion of Honour. He is definitely commendable for what he brought and gave to football – the thrills and delights that many hold as memories of the genius on the football pitch and the genuinely caring and kind man so many loved and miss today.

1968

It was the year the mini skirt had reached such heights that dry cleaners charged by the inch, the musical *Hair* made its statement of youth to flocking crowds and The Bonzo Dog Doo Dah Band's 'I'm The Urban Spaceman', Donovan's 'Hurdy Gurdy Man' and Herman's Hermits' 'Sunshine Girl' were the must-haves on the record shelf … 1968. Oh what a year in many ways. Whether due to the marvellous invention of the epidural, the death of the comedy maestro Tony Hancock, Rod Laver winning the first open Wimbledon or Martin Luther King being tragically assassinated, 1968 was definitely a memorable year.

It was in this year, as the dulcet tones of Canned Heat's 'On The Road Again' echoed from radios around the country, that Manchester United was also 'on the road again', heading for the European Cup Final against Benfica.

Just two years before, in the summer of 1966, England's football success in the World Cup had dominated headlines. But, for George Best, it was a time of recovery after having a cartilage operation; a time that did him good as on the opening day of the season Best – now established on the right wing – scored against West Brom in the first minute. Man United went on to win the Championship that season, ending with a glorious result of 6–1 over West

Ham. This placed the mighty reds in a good position to focus on the European Cup the following season.

During the rounds towards the final, Man U looked fragile at times, but Busby told a journalist, 'I feel this is our year.' They went to the second leg of the semi-final against Real Madrid with a 1–0 lead but by half-time they were 3–1 down – dreams were fading quickly. George Best commented, 'You can just imagine the state of the dressing room at half time. Just 45 minutes to go, two goals needed at least and a packed house of 120,000 screaming the brilliant Spaniards on.' Man U fought back and phenomenally finished with a 3–3 draw. They had made the final!

29 May 1968 was the ultimate end of the road towards Manchester United becoming European Champions. Wembley's crowd of 100,000 and an estimated 250 million TV viewers waited with anticipation. The two teams, the

The programme from the European Cup Final in 1968.

George celebrates.

Red Devils of Manchester (who chose to wear their blue away strip) and the Red Devils of Lisbon (wearing their red first strip), made their way on to the hallowed turf to 'let the game begin'!

The first half was quoted as being 'uninspiring', and 'a flurry of fouls'. George Best was having a tough time, 'finding myself out of the action, but one moment when I did break free I wasn't needed'. However, the second half saw an opening rare header from Bobby Charlton as he picked up a David Sadler's cross to open the scoring. George 'had an awful feeling that if we were not more careful they would score. Sure enough they did...' and, with only 10 minutes to go, Benfica scored an equalizer as United's defence left Gracia unmarked.

The final whistle went – extra time was looming!

Just two minutes into extra time George Best took the game 'by the scruff of the neck'. 'We had barely been playing two minutes over the 90 when I scored. A long ball was played out of defence to me and hit the centre half. I gathered it quickly and raced for goal with their keeper coming out. I was sorely tempted to blast it, but told myself I must make sure.' George drifted past his marker with his characteristic swerve, foxed the keeper, left him standing and gently tapped the ball over the line.

George said, 'I used to dream about taking the ball round the keeper, stopping it on the line and then getting on my hands and knees and heading it in the net... when I scored against Benfica in the European Cup Final I nearly did it. I left the keeper for dead, but then I chickened out. I might have given the boss a heart attack.'

Brian Kidd and Bobby Charlton both scored during extra time making a victory 4–1 for Manchester United who became European Champions, and the game one of the most emotional nights of British football.

'The dressing room was so full of joy. Everyone was so happy for Mr Busby.'

Above left: George on the ball.

Above right: A beaming George proudly holds his trophy.

Below: Bestie holds aloft the European Cup – the picture is signed by the man himself.

Although part of the winning side, George felt a little disappointment. He had promised himself that he would do well, that he would play great for the club, but he was tripped and kicked all over the park. It was obvious that Benfica's plan was to close George down as he had destroyed them with a hat-trick two years earlier in Lisbon. Their concentration on George Best allowed Bobby Charlton free range.

The European Cup marked the highlight of Matt Busby's career at Manchester United and he later received a knighthood. For George Best it was the highlight of his footballing career. 'There was also one major personal award for me in our European Cup-winning season. I was made Footballer of the Year. This thrilled me more than words can express.'

1968! What a year! The year when the black-gloved, clenched-fist salutes of American 'Black Power' athletes embarrassed the US Olympic Association, the first sextuplets were born in Britain and Bobby Kennedy was shot was also the year that Manchester United became the first English club to win the European Cup and Matt Busby had finally achieved his lifetime's ambition.

'Yes, it was a great season for me [George Best] and for Manchester United.'

Material quoted from *The Best of Both Worlds* by George Best

THE LIFE AND TIMES OF A PAIR OF FOOTBALL BOOTS

Take a stroll back in time to some 15 years ago. Place yourself in the hustle and bustle of Brick Lane Market, East London. Ease yourself through the side streets to see where they lead to, where you just might be able to pick a jewel out of the junk. It won't take you long to get side-tracked by the many stalls of collectables, as the aroma of the bagel bakeries almost clothes you. You may have something in mind that you are searching for, but expect to find anything: from fruits to furniture, kitsch to kitchenware and bangles to old boots.

A couple of friends, somewhere in their twenties, decided to experience the delights of Brick Lane, and were enticed by the good old cockney rhetoric to take a look at what exactly was on offer. Both were out to grab themselves a bargain of some sorts as a trophy of their visit 'down the lane'.

Just imagine how these bargain-hunters felt when their eyes fell upon a small pile of Stylo 'George Best' football boots! The friends had been told to 'be amazed at what you

"It's only the best for me and Georgie"

When George chose his soccer shoes everything had to be just right. He wanted comfort, lightness but most of all he wanted soccer shoes he could wear with confidence when dribbling, passing, tackling and shooting. That's why George chose Stylo Matchmakers and why he recommends you do the same.

Ask your local sports shop for Georgie Best Matchmakers.

Send for Free Colour Brochure

STYLO Matchmakers

Products of Stylo Matchmakers International Ltd. Matchmaker House Clarence Road Leeds LS10 1TX

can find down the lane' but never in their dreams could they have imagined falling upon what was, to them, such treasure.

Prior to the 1960s, football boots had been more or less the same design, but started to move more upmarket with different colours of leather, various branded stripes with the designs beginning to be named – either after players (like Puma Pelé) or with a suggestion of what skills the player could display while wearing them (Puma Hat-Trick).

By the late 1960s and early '70s boot designs were becoming more innovative – including the production of the Stylo 'George Best' boots that had the look of a pair of bowling shoes, but with the laces on the side of the foot allowing more precision when kicking the ball. And, of course, the noticeable signature of the footballer himself was also on the side of each boot.

How, one must ask, does a pile of such prestigious football boots, that had been the desire of many a young (and older) football fan, end up on a market stall in Brick Lane? That question may never be answered, but what is for sure is that the two footballing friends couldn't stop themselves from buying the whole lot of boots – that still had the famous George Best labels on them – and carrying them back home as their triumph of the day. Once home, they divided the spoils and kept them as a momento of the great man himself, George Best.

A few years later, one of the friends had the pleasure of being best man at his brother's wedding. Best man duties always seem to hinge on the speech, when every guest looks forward to seeing if nerves kick in as the orchestrator of the day takes the stage.

Sure enough, the guests at this particular wedding were not disappointed. The best man had taken time to really think about him and what he would say when his 'spot' arrived, and decided to paint a picture of his brother through three of the bridegroom's loves. One was the

Lambretta scooter, another the darling 'Moggy' Morris Minor and the third was his brother's love of football. This love of football didn't only consist of watching his favourite team; he was also a talented footballer, one that local teams were keen to have play for them. Good as he may have been, he could never have been as good as his footballing idol – George Best.

It was at this part of the best man's speech that a pair of the Stylo 'George Best' boots purchased from Brick Lane Market were presented by the best man to his brother as a token of the bridegroom's love of football. Just imagine the reaction of the guests and picture the look on the bridegroom's face while being presented with the boots that reminded him of his passion and of the footballing genius of George Best.

Since George's sad departure, a pair of Stylo 'George Best' boots have become valuable and are increasing in value as time goes by. But perhaps not equal in value to the feeling of pride and pleasure as the bridegroom received this thoughtful gift from his brother on his wedding day. Perhaps his thoughts went back to childhood days, his adoration of George Best, and echoed the words of the poet

George poses with his boots.

Nell Farrell as he dreamed of being like him: 'I was like you then; flying down the wing, ball glued to my feet…'

Then, one overwhelmingly sad day in November 2005, the world lost the working-class boy from Belfast, the gifted and talented genius footballer, George Best. Those boots no longer only hold the value of memories – from that moment they began to increase in financial value too. No matter how valuable those boots become, no matter how much of a prized possession they are, they will never match the joy and excitement their namesake gave to so many with his skills

The boots presented at the wedding.

and magic on the football pitch. They may just be a pair of football boots – but what a journey they have had. He too may just have been a boy from a council housing estate in Belfast – but what a life journey he had, what drama he played out in his tumultuous time on earth, and, by all accounts, what a pleasure it was for those who knew him.

FOUR FAB MUSICIANS AND A
FAB FOOTBALLER

It wasn't in Penny Lane, Blackberry Lane or even Strawberry Fields that the artist chose to include George Best alongside John, Paul, George and Ringo. It was to the now famous and internationally known cover of the Beatles' *Abbey Road* that an image of George Best was added to produce a much-sought-after photograph that includes 'the fifth Beatle' – perhaps fitting to include the Best alongside the best!

Abbey Road is a street located in the borough of Camden and the City of Westminster in London. Although there are many other roads of this name, including over 20 in London alone, the Abbey Road best known to most people is the road running roughly northwest to southeast through the affluent north London suburb of St John's Wood, where the Abbey Road Studios are located.

Before the decision was made for the title of the 1969 LP, at some point the album was going to be named *Everest*, apparently after a brand of cigarettes. If that had been the case, the cover of the album would have the Beatles in the Himalayas. But by the time the photograph had to be taken they had decided to call it *Abbey Road,* and to take the photograph outside the studio – which they did on 8 August 1969. The photographer was Iain MacMillan. The cover photograph has since become one of the most famous album covers in recording history, and it only took 10 minutes to shoot. It shows the four group members, John, Paul, George and Ringo, walking across the zebra crossing located just outside the studio entrance; it was later that the fifth Beatle, George Best, was added to the piece of artwork.

Although George was added to the famous front cover

'El Beatle'

-George Best, Lisbon 1966

Printed in a Limited Edition of 150 of which this is registered No. 7

picture later, what was he doing at the time of the album's release? In the summer of 1969 George Best was in his early twenties and alcohol was beginning to be ever-present in his life. Describing his own lifestyle, he famously said: 'I spent a lot of my money on booze, birds and fast cars – the rest I just squandered.' Best was sent off for fighting in the World Clubs Cup against the South American champions Estudiantes of Argentina. United's league form was poor and they finished the 1968/'69 season in 11th place. They got as far as the semi-finals in the European Cup, but, at the end of the season, Busby retired.

When Busby stepped down from Manchester United management in 1969, Best's tendency to fall to temptation increased and he began to drift... and drink. At this time George Best was becoming a problem, continually flouting the rules and getting into various disciplinary troubles.

However, George Best was undoubtedly and undisputedly a star footballer of the 1960s. He was a naturally gifted, naturally balanced huge footballing talent who had enormous popularity and his long-haired good looks and celebrity lifestyle made any female take a second look. With his Beatles-style moptop haircut, George was perhaps the sporting figure that so epitomised the feel-good mood of the Swinging Sixties.

The Beatles are the most critically acclaimed and commercially successful pop-music band in history. Their innovative music and style helped to define the culture of the 1960s. Their music was rooted in the sounds of 1950s rock 'n' roll, but they explored many genres including psychedelic rock, and they became the best-selling pop music act of the 20th century.

George Best could have held a mirror up to the 'fab four' during the 1960s and indeed the early 1970s. George has been decreed by the most influential in the sporting world as the best player in the world, whose innovative and natural talent on the football pitch left people on the same pitch standing and those on the terraces, astonished at such capacity on the ball. His gifts were rooted in the age-old

way of kids playing on the streets and he developed an inimitable swerving style when on the ball. George became the football player everyone wanted to promote their merchandise, such was the attraction of the man.

It seems totally fitting that George Best has been included on the most famous album covers of all times, alongside the most famous four of all times. To have the fifth Beatle included on the tourist-attracting zebra crossing, controlling the ball with such ease and accuracy, is the most natural thing to have taken place. To have such a

compilation of the ultimate talents of four famous and talented musicians and an exceptional and gifted footballer all together in one piece of art is clearly out of this world – and we have the pleasure of being able to see it.

GEORGE STEPS ONTO THE PROPERTY LADDER

George Best had never left his home town before but, at the age of 15, he left his family home on Burran Way in the Cregagh Estate just outside Belfast and took the now famous journey to Manchester – only to return very swiftly because he was homesick. Soon after he left again, only to return to the family home for visits. On the outside of that same house today is a special plaque informing onlookers that George 'lived here' and was the eldest child of Dickie and Anne and brother to Carol, Barbara, Julie, Grace and Ian.

George relaxes with a cup of coffee in his state-of-the-art home.

George had to be coaxed back to Old Trafford, where he was placed under the maternal supervision of a sympathetic landlady called Mrs Fullaway. George left his landlady in a house nominated as suitable by Manchester United for a young footballer who had grown up on a council estate in Belfast, and moved to one he designed and built in a leafy, upmarket Cheshire suburb.

It was in 1969 that George had built a futuristic house near Bramhall, Cheshire, at a cost of £30,000. The modernist split-level design was encased in glass with a flat roof and had all the latest hi-tech gadgets. George had come to a point in his life where he had a desire for independence, but the change in his lifestyle could not have been more marked.

He commissioned an architect, Frazer Crane, who also designed Best's city-centre boutique. It took a year to build the bachelor pad on a plot of land in the stockbroker belt, Blossoms Lane near Bramhall. All Best stipulated was that it should have a sunken bath and a snooker room. What he got was a glass-encased futuristic fantasy, with a dizzying variety of gadgets.

Leading from the games room was a concrete disc surrounded by a moat. It was faced in small white tiles and you could sweep down the drive into the underground garage. A short walk down the garden was the swimming

George poses outside the Goldfish Bowl.

pool. The Goldfish Bowl could have come straight out of one of the latest design magazines – not one from more than 30 years ago. It had all the latest gadgets, hot-air heating pumped underfloor by a huge boiler, a television that disappeared into the chimney, remote-controlled curtains and garage door and intercom security.

If it looked more like a goldfish bowl than a home, it certainly began to feel like one as fans besieged George. He suffered fans continually surrounding the house and eventually sold it after only three years. George was really proud of its modern design, and was reportedly very hurt when he read in one newspaper that it resembled a public lavatory. The attention George received was relentless and

George insisted on a snooker room in his home.

overwhelming. George had to suffer fans continually surrounding the house and a ten-foot-high fence was built all round to keep out prying eyes.

Frank Farrell was quoted as saying, 'The worry is not so much for George today, he is still young, he has his looks and his celebrity and no doubt he will be able to make some sort of living outside of football. But I worry about him in the future, when he has lost those looks, when he cannot be fit again, and then I wonder how he will feel.'

As we know from other stories in this book, within a

couple of years or so George was back in his old room at Mrs Fullaway's but, by then, the fault lines were appearing, father-figure Busby had gone and Best's relationship with United had been undermined by a series of incidents that made front- and back-page headlines. George sold the house for £40,000 before being banished back to his Chorlton-cum-Hardy landlady for breaking club rules.

FROM ONE BELFAST BOY TO ANOTHER

Imagine being a football-mad young boy in Belfast during 1969. Who would be your idol? There could be none other than George Best. Imagine that certain young lad being picked from a local Belfast boys' club and having his wildest dream – to be a ball boy at the Northern Ireland v Wales match – come true one day at Windsor Park, the home of Northern Ireland football. How must he have felt? I guess his shoulders were pushed back with pride as he walked out onto the turf alongside his idol, George Best.

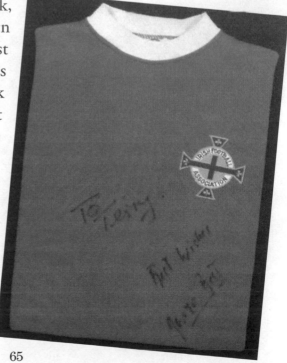

George told the young fan to take the shirt and run home as fast as he could.

The game itself was nothing to shout about, in fact it was pretty dull and unexciting, but nothing could take away the delight of the young fan – so much so that, at the end of the game, he

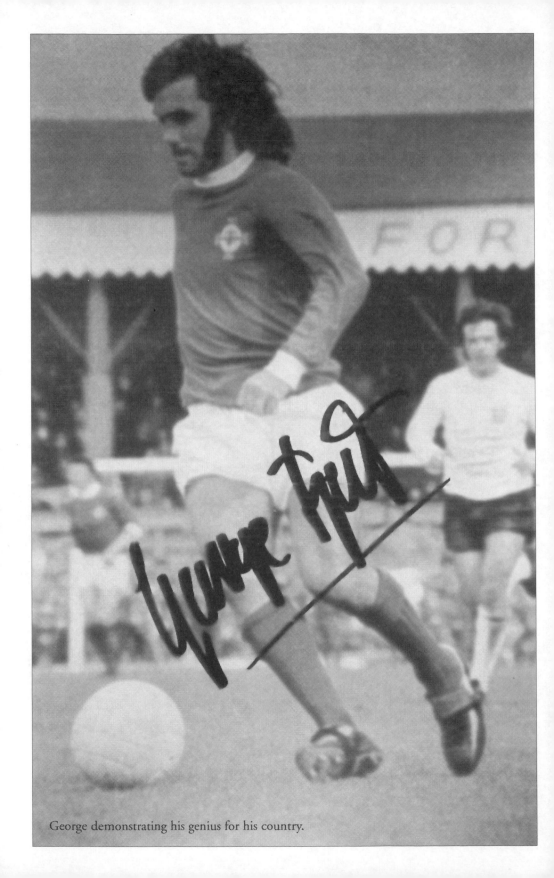

George demonstrating his genius for his country.

boldly walked up to George and asked him for his shirt. Best looked at him and just walked off – obviously quite amazed at the cheek of the boy.

Undeterred, the ball boy weaved his way through the throng of players and officials and waited patiently by the changing rooms. Seeing him waiting for so long, some of the stewards asked him why he was waiting – to which he replied with quick thinking, and a bucket full of cheek, that he was waiting for Best's shirt.

Was it bravery, impudence, courage, nerve, over-confidence or absolute cheek? It didn't matter to him when, five minutes later, George appeared out of the dressing room with a plastic bag, smiled at the boy and told him to run home with the bag as fast as he could.

It may have been just another football shirt to George Best (even if it was an international shirt) but to his young admirer it was so out of this world, just like George's footballing talent.

Perhaps our imagination can be excused for going yet another step and thinking that George would have known just how much the young boy would have treasured the shirt. Maybe thinking about it as he got changed, he decided to reward the lad's patience and determination to get his prize – the Northern Ireland green number 7 worn by the Best.

NEVER ABOVE HIS STATION

In the 1960s, '70s and '80s, over 58,000 people could pack into Old Trafford football ground. However, in the early 1990s, after the Hillsbrough disaster, the Taylor Report stated that all of England's top clubs had to have all-seater stadiums. Since the early 1960s, the plan had been to redesign Old Trafford in a kind of bowl shape. This kind of design would have reduced the ground's capacity, though, and, with the team increasing in popularity, the new design would not have been able to accommodate the growing number of fans.

Manchester United's success in the late 1960s secured an extremely large following and began to draw national and international support. Letters appeared in the *Manchester Evening News* and *Chronicle* drawing attention to the growing United support in London, Dublin and other parts of the UK.

Social developments throughout the 1960s had an inevitable effect on football fans and, while many still supported their local teams, for an increasing number of people, in particular the young, football began to be an expression of the developing national culture of 'freedom' when decisions on which team to support were influenced by how good, how fashionable and how visible the club, team and players were.

By the late 1960s George Best and Manchester United were more and more becoming a 'brand'. George's footballing genius was ogled by the masses and covered the back pages of national and regional newspapers, while his good looks, perfect athlete's body and trendy fashionable style made front-page news. The genuinely shy Belfast boy found it difficult to be anywhere without being recognised and sometimes hounded by his fans.

The book that Ray Wyatt had with him when he met George on the train.

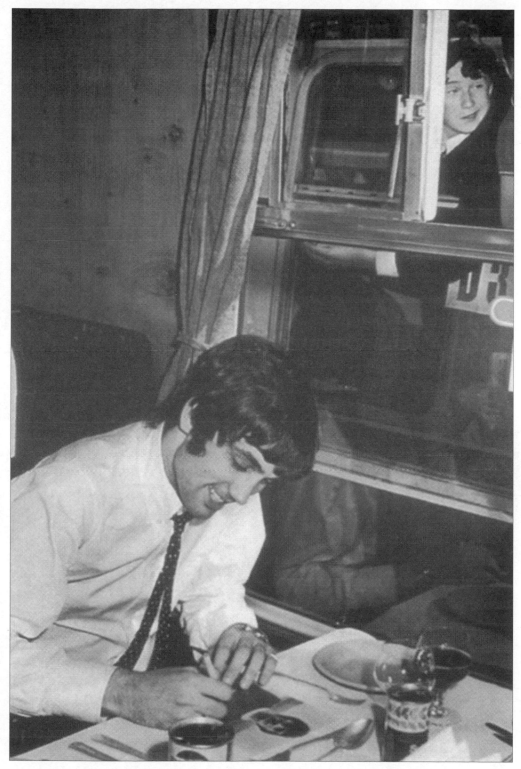

George often caught the train back to London after matches. Notice the fans at the window.

Even with all this as a backdrop, George never felt himself above anyone and still found time for the individual – and one such person recalls how George Best made him feel very special.

Ray Wyatt, a United fan living in London during the late 1960s, recalls how he and his friends would regularly travel to Old Trafford from London to watch United play. They would make their return journey on the 5.30 or 6.30 p.m. train from Manchester – depending on extra time or crowds getting to the station.

The then young George Best would regularly catch the same train and often engaged Ray in conversation – depending on what kind of game he'd had or just how he felt. Imagine these fans having travelled from London to watch their beloved Man U, then to share the journey home with George on a regular basis. That in itself must have been worth the train fare!

On one particular journey Ray had two copies of the book *Matt, United and Me* by Jimmy Murphy and George

George signed photos from the book for Ray.

took the time to autograph three of the pictures in the book. Two of the signatures are still in the book, while one was carefully taken out and kept in Ray's autograph book to remind him of the day he shared a carriage on the Manchester to London train with George Best. This famous footballing genius, who was to make 361 League appearances for Manchester United scoring 137 goals, took time to chat with him and to leave him with lasting memories of the Manchester to London train. What a guy!

CAROLINA'S SUMMER OF '69

When American astronaut Neil Armstrong became the first man to walk on the Moon, he stepped onto the Moon's surface in the Sea of Tranquility at 0256 GMT, nearly 20 minutes after first opening the hatch on the Eagle landing craft. Armstrong had earlier reported the lunar module's safe landing with the words: 'Houston, Tranquility Base here. The Eagle has landed.' As he put his left foot down first Armstrong declared: 'That's one small step for man, one giant leap for mankind.' When Brian Trubshaw made his first flight in the British-built prototype of Concorde,

the 22-minute flight left from a test runway at Filton near Bristol and landed at RAF Fairford in Gloucestershire. Concorde completed its first supersonic flight later in the same year. These memorable events happened in 1969.

During the same year, US units were withdrawn from Vietnam, the fifty-pence coin was introduced in Britain, Pele scored his 1000th goal, *Monty Python's Flying Circus* was first broadcast on British TV and Woodstock 'happened'.

All of this and indeed much more happened in 1969, but for five-and-a-half-year-old Carolina Eastwood, the summer of 1969 was even more unforgettable – although at the time she probably didn't know just how memorable it would be.

Carolina's mum had an apartment in San Agustin, Majorca, not far from Palma Nova beach; it was on the part of the beach in front of LaBaraka Bar. Back in 1969,

LaBaraka had sunbeds lined up, and was home to celebrities of the day together with those into the nightclub scene. Many among the in-crowd on the beach and by the bar were owners of, or visitors to, the nightclubs of Birmingham and Manchester.

On one particular day during Carolina's 1969 holiday, she was crying and so upset while on the beach, having stood on a cigarette stub in the sand that was still alight. Ouch! Carolina's knight in shining armour was none other than George Best, who was also holidaying on the Palma Nova beach. Kind-hearted George, who always admitted to having a soft spot for kids, picked up the crying Carolina and took her to her mother, who was soaking up the sun on a sunbed. Although so young, Carolina was aware that George was a famous footballer.

The mishap with the lighted cigarette stub, although painful for Carolina at the time, was the start of a special adventure with George and his friend George Harrison (no, not the Beatle). Carolina's memories of 1969 are to do with the friendship she had with George Best, and she recalls them with some fondness. So just what are those memories?

Carolina remembers going for car rides in George's open-top SL Mercedes car, and of course that the two Georges always asked Carolina's mum if they could take her with them. On many occasions Carolina went fishing and crabbing with George, getting the little creatures out of the cracks in the rocks. She remembers George telling her off if she left the crabs in the heat of the sun; he always encouraged her to put them back into the water.

Carolina with her knight in shining armour. It was a summer to remember for her.

She went on their speedboat and had some lovely meals with them; it was quite a good feeling for the young Carolina as George, and his friend George, felt like her big brothers taking care of her, and she felt like their mascot. How lovely for the young girl.

It probably goes without saying that Carolina played football with George, but she remembers how hard it was as, try as she did with all her might, she just couldn't get the ball off him and he certainly never made it easy for her – forever the competitor, George!

Carolina could quite easily sing along with Bryan Adams about the summer of '69, that she wished the summer could have gone on forever, but it couldn't. In fact Carolina didn't see George again until she met him on the same beach when she was 22 or 23 years of age in 1986/87. Carolina did approach George who was with Mary Shatila on the beach and chatted to him and recalled her happy memories of the summer of '69, but unfortunately he didn't recall their time together. Much different for Carolina who remembers it all quite clearly.

George can probably be forgiven for not remembering Carolina, particularly considering everything else that was happening to him in 1969. He was crowned European Footballer of the Year that year, and he was still only 12 months on from being part of the winning Manchester United team in Europe in 1968. An *Observer* article of November 1969, 'Best's Private Thoughts', noted that 'he is, without question, exposed to more formidable distractions than any other British footballer in history.' So thank goodness Carolina remembers making friends with George Best in 1969 and that she is pleased to share those happy childhood memories with us.

THE BALLS, THE BELLBOY AND THE PHOTOGRAPH

Everyone must have heard of Chinese Whispers and perhaps have played it as a kid's game just to have a laugh. There is a well-known example of how a message can be distorted when information is passed from one to another: in World War II, the command was sent down the line 'Send reinforcement, were going to advance.' By the time the command got to the end of the line the message was heard as 'Send three and four pence I'm going to a dance.' I wonder what the Enigma Code would have made of that?

The same kind of thing can happen within the world of football and the press. Rumour had it that Bill Shankly had broken down in the Mersey Tunnel and was offered a tow by Alan Ball's father. (Incidentally when Alan had just signed for Everton, Shanks was heard to say, 'Don't worry, Alan. At least you'll be able to play close to a great team!')

The reply to Mr Ball Senior's offer came from Shankly: 'You've gotta be jokin', can you imagine the headlines in tomorra's *Echo*? "Shankly pulled out of the Mersey Tunnel by the Balls."'

Best and Ball on the pitch together.

However, that could be just one of the tales of the Balls in the tunnel. Another story was that it was George Best's car that had broken down in the Mersey Tunnel following the Everton v Manchester United game on 31 August 1971. The whisper goes on that it was Alan Ball, accompanied by his wife, who stopped and actually did tow George's car out of trouble in the tunnel. Quick-witted George said to the towing couple that he could imagine the headlines in the following day's *Manchester Evening News*: 'Best pulled out of the tunnel by the Balls'.

The programme from the Everton v Man Utd match.

It makes you wonder if George had got into the habit of writing his own headlines by that time in his life, doesn't it?

While we're on the point of what is 'truth', what about the infamous bellboy that uttered that questioning, but strangely ambiguous phrase to George Best as he entered the five-star hotel bedroom to deliver the chilled champagne? He viewed the tens of thousands of pounds scattered on the king-size bed alongside a scantily dressed Miss World, and said to George, 'Where did it all go wrong?'

Again, this did actually happen, but details of the location are murky. Some stories suggest it was in Birmingham following a Manchester United match against Aston Villa, while other sources suggest it took place in Manchester.

Another story that has different details attached to it depending on what you read relates to that moment-in-time photograph of George Best alongside Sir Matt Busby, both seated in Old Trafford with George's arm around Sir Matt as he wipes a single tear from his eye. One story suggests that the photograph, taken by Robert Aylott, was in 1990 while Ralph Sweeney claims that it was in 1993 when Manchester United claimed the league title for the first time in 26 years.

It doesn't matter what the 'truth' is really on either one of these stories about George Best, but wouldn't it be good to really know what happened, where, when, why and how – or will the truth be lost forever in newsroom and editorial corridors?

The photo of George and Sir Matt – will we ever know the true story behind it?

HAVE YOU HEARD THE ONE ABOUT THE WELSHMAN AND THE IRISHMAN?

It's not one of those notorious jokes, but you may wonder what a Welshman can have to say about an Irishman, particularly about the beautiful game of football. Well, quite a lot actually, particularly when the Welshman is Alan Latham, retired secretary of Carmarthen Town Football

Club, and the other, the one and only Irish international George Best.

After 25 years of loyal service to Carmarthen Town F.C., at the end of the 2002 season Alan gave up his secretary duties but still remains an avid supporter. The club felt that Alan's unending store of footballing stories could not and should not be missed and he kindly agreed to write something for every home-game programme. He was thought of very highly by

The programme from the Wales v Ireland match.

the club and his contribution to it was immeasurable. Full of humour and wit, his column in the programme kept the supporters informed and often in stitches.

For the programme of 26 December 2005 Alan chose to dedicate his whole column to George Best, and he would like to share his thoughts with others:

The festive season, the purpose of which, of course, as far as Christians are concerned anyway, is to celebrate the birth of our Lord, is nearing its end. So you might find it slightly inappropriate that my subject today relates to the recent sad demise of George Best. His life story has been well documented throughout the media in recent weeks but nevertheless I thought I might give some views on the great man, although I only saw him in live games twice, to which I will refer later.

What impressed me immensely from what I regularly saw on television in the '60s and '70s and of recent footage of Best was his superb attitude on the field of play. Often a victim of some heavy attention from such renowned individuals as Ron 'Chopper' Harris, Norman Hunter, Frank McLintock and such like, George never feigned injury, never reacted whilst lying injured nor took a dive at the first opponent's touch to try to cheat the referee, which was admirable and much to his credit, especially as he had become such a role model for youngsters.

His individual ball skills were unquestionable, of course, but there was a slight criticism that, with partners such as goal scorers Bobby Charlton and Denis Law in the Manchester United line-up, his individualistic approach was sometimes questioned in so far as that his illustrious team mates did not always receive the ball when in a better position to score. But still in his teens, on one occasion, in a game against West Brom at Old Trafford, he upstaged the iconic Charlton and Law when moving away

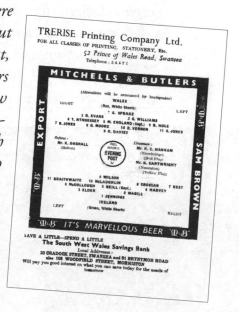

The team sheet from the same match.

from goal in the penalty area, he spun in an instant and fired a shot without pre-meditation into the roof of the net from 20 yards. 'What time was that?' a prosaic journalist enquired. 'Never mind the time just make a note of the date,' a colleague replied.

As I mentioned earlier, I saw the great man on just two occasions – both at the Vetch Field in Wales v Northern Ireland British Championship matches. The first in April 1964, when George, virtually unknown, made his debut for his country. We lost 3–2 and, incidentally, the Welsh scorers were Brian Godfrey who played for Preston North End and Aston Villa, and Ron Davies, the Southampton striker. The attendance was on the 10,000 mark, which was the norm for Wales v Northern Ireland in those days.

The second occasion, however, was a different kettle of fish. Quite simply, by then, George was considered by many to be the most talented player in the world and 30,000 people crammed into the Vetch Field in April 1970.

What struck me on that occasion were the girls who had turned up in their thousands to see this most eligible bachelor. Although I was not aware of it at the time, Best had to be smuggled in and out of the Vetch Field or risk

serious bodily harm from the female fans. On that occasion it was a great day for Wales as they beat the Irish 1–0, with Ronnie Rees of Coventry scoring the only goal and George being well shackled for much of the game by a tight Welsh defence who marked him very closely indeed. That year in fact Wales shared the Championship having drawn with both England and Scotland in the previous two games of that tournament.

In George Best's poignant last interview this year he claimed that he would like to be remembered as the greatest footballer of all time and when that day comes they won't be talking about the booze and fast cars, etc., but about the football. Well, a tribute like a state funeral in Belfast was ample proof that his wish had been granted. I will end by referring to what I think is this very articulate individual's funniest proclamation. 'In 1969, I gave up women, alcohol and fast cars. It was the worst 20 minutes of my life.' And on that note I would like to wish you all a Happy New Year.

Alan recalls that on both occasions George's football performance didn't really stand out. But he remembers the 1970 game as if it were yesterday, not only because Wales won, but how the gate was a total sell-out and that, included in the vast numbers, it was amazing to see the high number of females all wanting to get a look at the good-looking Irishman. Some may probably never have gone to see a football match before but did so on that night, just because George Best was there. They probably never ventured through any turnstiles again! Such was the popularity of the man, the genius, the handsome, shy and unique George Best as he played for his country Northern Ireland in the principality of Wales.

CHOPPER'S MEMORIES

'He was the best player I had ever tried to kick in 21 years' is how ex-Chelsea defender Ron 'Chopper' Harris would describe George Best. But this is not the only memory that Chopper holds of his late football colleague, and mate; there are many more which Chopper is only too pleased to share with others about George Best who would, in his opinion, be described as 'the best ever player'.

George Best's and Chopper Harris's paths first crossed during the 1964/65 season when Manchester United played Chelsea. Both George and Chopper were perhaps the lesser-known players of the game that day, but none the less both

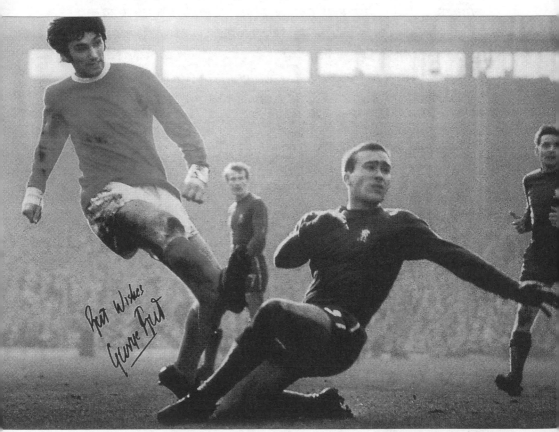

went on to make names for themselves within the football society, making headlines on their unique approach and footballing techniques.

Their careers had kicked off around the same time and, up until just 18 months before George passed away, George, Chopper and another well-known footballing personality from the same era, Jimmy Greaves, were doing theatre shows around the country and were a phenomenal success. Jimmy suggested that in reality it was probably George who was the draw to the many thousands who turned up to listen to them. For example, during the latter part of the tour they visited Birmingham where 1,500 packed into the Symphony Hall to watch and hear their heroes talk about their lives and experiences.

It would be impossible to think about George Best and Chopper Harris without at least mentioning that tackle on 28 October 1970, in the Football League Cup fourth-round match at Old Trafford between Manchester United and Chelsea.

Chopper himself recalls, 'When I look at it on video I just cannot believe I missed him! People often talk about referees of today and the decisions they make on intent. Let me tell you, if I had caught him I would have been jailed for life. Today, players would have gone down and rolled over three or four times to get the free kick, and to get me sent off – but not George; he rode the tackle and left me – not standing, but on the floor.'

The *Guardian* newspaper reported the next day:

Chelsea, playing some brilliant football, had equalised Charlton's goal and they were set fair to do even better. Then in the 70th minute Best, who was just inside the Chelsea half, called to Aston to give him the ball. Aston is not one to ignore such a request and he put through a perfect pass.

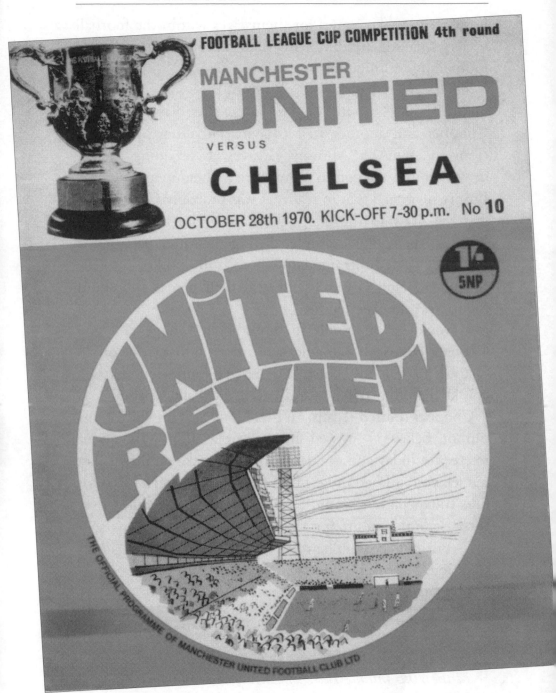

The programme from one of the Man Utd v Chelsea matches where the great striker and defender would have met.

Off went Best with the redoubtable Harris in stern pursuit. Twice Harris tried to bring him down from behind and twice Best eluded the tackle. Best next rounded Bonetti, stopped briefly to have a word with Hinton, who had appeared smartly, and then tapped the ball into the net. Insolence gone mad!

In those days there was no place in British football for players of a nervous disposition. If any were fainthearted there was definitely nowhere to hide on the football pitch. Any player of the day could recall that a visit to Highbury revealed Peter Storey to hound you, Anfield had Tommy Smith on the lookout, Elland Road had Norman Hunter (fantastic!) and at Chelsea 'Chopper' Harris clattered all who stepped in his way.

But it is the incidents that people recall instantly that still arouse the emotions, like that tackle by Chopper Harris in 1970, and the follow-on incredible goal scored by George Best against Chelsea. After riding the fierce, lunging tackle from Chopper which literally knocked him sideways and which, if committed in today's game, would have earned the notorious Chelsea hard-man an automatic red card, George then beat the goalkeeper and nonchalantly crossed the ball over the line to gain the winning score line.

No, Best didn't go down under the tackle, but regained his balance and his composure to go on to score with such admiration exuding from the crowds. This was surely a demonstration of George's almost supernatural talent that made him so elusive.

United went on to win the match 2–1, but it was Tottenham that went on to win the cup with two goals from Chivers against Aston Villa on 27 February 1971.

Like so many others, Chopper Harris only has good things

to say about George Best. He was 'kind-hearted', 'a lovely person', 'free-hearted' and always the first to offer to buy someone a drink and socially such good company. Chopper recalls with such affection how he loved to listen to George as he had a certain way of explaining things, and how he always had time for anyone who went up to him and would stand talking with them, never disregarding them.

He remembers how intelligent George was and could talk about almost everything, but what he keeps in mind most is how George spoke highly of everyone and didn't like to put people down or make negative comments about them. Chopper remembers in particular, with a smile, how George would often say that there had been 52 action pictures taken of himself on the ball and that Chopper was in 50 of them.

George Best could play everywhere on the park, he could dribble, pass and score with both feet, tackle as well as any defender, and was great in the air. He was just as fast running with the ball as he was without. His balance and co-ordination was out of this world, players like Chopper would try to crush him but George stayed on his feet and never lost control.

Chopper recalls how, although he had played against many good players and had seen some excellent goals scored, the one person he had played against who scored the most fantastic goals was George Best. Many of these incredible goals were shown on television programmes following George's passing. One thing in particular that Chopper loved about George's play were those incredible goals when George went clean through and was one on one with the keeper. George wouldn't try to chip the keeper or wait for the keeper to go for the ball, inevitably George would, in his famous way, dribble round the keeper and safely put the goal away – can't you just picture him doing that now?

SIX GREAT GOALS

Have you ever been asked, 'Where were you when Kennedy died?' Countless people have and so many have vivid memories of exactly where they were and can give almost a minute-by-minute account of their recollections. The question next in line in 1970 is probably 'Where were you when Manchester United beat Northampton Town 8–2?' Not only was it the talk of the nation in terms of describing the game, relishing the triumph and celebrating the record-breaking six goals from the mighty George Best, but it has been stored in memories all over the country and in some cases the world.

For the goal-scoring victor George Best, it was unforgettable too. 'Now I can't remember ever having played on Northampton's ground before. And if I play there a thousand times in future, I wouldn't be able to forget this particular game in which we walloped the Cobblers by eight goals to two. And I got six of those goals,' stated George during one of his many interviews following the FA Cup fifth-round match in February 1970.

Cobblers' skipper Frank Rankmore won the toss, giving them the advantage of playing with the sun and the wind at their backs in the first half. George Best was only just back from a spell on suspension and it was, for him, a comeback and he obviously wanted to do well. George had something to prove as he knew that there had been whispers around the game that maybe the mighty reds would be better off without him. Knowing this must have added a bit of an edge to his game.

The kick-off whistle was blown and for the first few minutes it was a close-run thing between the two teams with both sides having chances as they tried to get the better of each other. Then the goal scoring began:

George with his trademark arm-in-the-air celebration.

27 Minutes: Goal scored by **George Best**
36 Minutes: Goal scored by **George Best**
51 Minutes: Goal scored by **George Best**
61 Minutes: Goal scored by **George Best**
70 Minutes: Goal scored by Brian Kidd
72 Minutes: Goal scored by **George Best**
76 Minutes: Goal scored by Brian Kidd
81 Minutes: Goal scored by Dixie McNeil
88 Minutes: Goal scored by **George Best**
90 Minutes: Goal scored by Frank Large

'You can't predict six goals, of course,' said George. 'In fact in this day and age it is unusual for anyone to do just that... Now I can almost hear some of you saying: "Ah, but it was only Northampton Town and that's nothing like as big a deal as getting say three against Liverpool." But the FA Cup never did run like that. There's nothing predictable about it...' Best admitted that the whole of the Manchester team played beautifully that afternoon, that it was probably true that Northampton were under a lot of pressure from the fans, but that Manchester went straight into top gear.

But what about the fans' memories of that day? One fan proudly wore his Northampton Town rosette given to him by one of his teachers, who had received them from a Northampton official. That fan was Kevin Tarbox of Guisborough Secondary Modern, Northampton, who remembers it well.

'I was playing football in the morning for my school against another school. We had been given free tickets for the match and were supposed to meet the Manchester United team before the match, but they turned up late.

The programme from that memorable day.

'We waited around by the main stand where we were told we would be sitting, but when our teacher got the tickets we had to go round the Cricket Side, and most of us couldn't see a thing because we were just standing in pallets.

'I remember the Cobblers having two penalties. The ground was taken over by Man U fans. I can remember a Northampton flag appearing in the Hotel End and it vanishing in a big red swarm. I also remember Ray Fairfax saying in the local newspaper that he was not going to give Bestie an inch – he was the player chosen to mark Best. One thing that sticks out the most is Bestie jinxing and making Kim Brook fall over, and just flicking the ball in the net. Then George put his arms out to the crowd and taking a standing ovation – but how he appeared to feel sorry for the keeper – yes I was there! What a player!'

As 15-year-old Nigel Hart strolled down Abingdon

Avenue towards the County Ground, he sensed an upset in the air. On the face of it, little Northampton Town didn't stand a chance against the might of Manchester United in this fifth-round FA Cup clash.

But maybe, just maybe, United's team of superstars wouldn't be up for it!

Ninety minutes later the dream was over for Nigel and his mates, watching from the terraces as a rampant George Best smashed in six goals in the famous 8–2 victory.

Nigel recalls, 'I can remember it as if it was yesterday, me and a few mates used to go and watch the Cobblers every other week and when they drew United in the cup there was a huge buzz in the town. We'd just witnessed the side going from the old Fourth Division to the First Division and all the way back down again, so the people needed a bit of cheering up.

'It was a really nice day, blue sky and white fluffy clouds. There were about four or five of us, all wearing Northampton scarves and hats and even carrying purple and white rattles.'

Nigel was just out of school and earning four pounds a week as a storeman. He insisted the Cobblers had United on the rack early on.

'Frank Large had a good run and everyone thought he was going to score. Unfortunately he put his shot wide and then George took over.

'It was the only time I saw George Best play and to watch a legend like that perform in a tiny, three-sided ground was unbelievable. One goal in particular stands out – the one where he chipped it over the goalkeeper, but his overall performance was mesmerising.

'Having said that, Northampton were by no means disgraced – after all they were playing the team that had won the European Cup two years earlier. Bobby Charlton, Denis Law, Brian Kidd, they were all there and Northampton got a big round of applause afterwards because they'd managed to score two goals against them.'

Despite his affection for the Cobblers, Nigel admits he also had a soft spot for United at the time and was not too disappointed by the result.

'To be honest, when George scored his sixth goal, I shoved my Northampton scarf in my pocket and started supporting United,' he confessed.

George Best's name didn't appear in the matchday programme because he had served a six-week suspension and his place in the United line-up was in doubt right up to the morning of the game. After such a long lay-off, it was clear that George was 'cruising for a bruising'. George recalls that there were several things that stuck in his mind apart from the goals, one of which was the sporting way in which Northampton took their walloping – and that it's not easy to accept when you're playing in front of your own supporters.

George in a
Northampton
sweater.

It was almost as if George was on a personal mission and Northampton's Richard 'Dixie' McNeil admitted, 'There was a genius playing that day'.

But what about George's lasting memories of that day? He recalled, 'The six goals at Northampton did a lot for me in terms of restoring a feeling of confidence. Things had not been going right for me, and I needed to make a big splash on my return to the game.' But even in the glory of the super-six George admitted that he could only score goals if his colleagues were helping out. That, that afternoon in Northampton taught him again that it's very important to be a team man, not just to play for himself.

The gate on the day was 21,711, all of whom watched six of the best in the history of the County Ground and also witnessed ten international players on duty; but despite George Best's haul of six goals on that day he failed to score in any of the other seven FA Cup ties he played in that season.

Graham Felton, the Cobbler's right winger said, 'I lined up opposite my hero George Best, I looked around and saw Bobby Charlton, Pat Crerand and Alex Stepney. I was in awe of the whole situation.'

So many can remember events of the Saturday 7 February, and the match itself moment by moment. Memories that meant different things to different people whether it is from the schoolboy supporters or the genius of the man himself, George Best. There is no doubt that the town of Northampton and the City of Manchester were united in history on that momentous day. A day when George Best exploded on to the County Ground in Northampton, giving those who witnessed it – and those who have read about it since – some magical memories that will never be erased from their minds.

Stories courtesy of BBC Sport. www.bbc.co.uk/sport

A VILLA FAN REMEMBERS...

February 1970 brought incredible headlines for Manchester United and in particular George Best when he scored the record-breaking six goals in the FA Cup fifth round against Northampton Town. The day following this incredible score line, George Best was the toast of Fleet Street as the pundits waxed lyrical over his superlative skills.

By December in the same year headlines such as UNITED RECALL SIR MATT TO HALT THE SLIDE were becoming all too familiar. So just what had happened?

For more than 20 years under the keen leadership of Matt Busby, United were expected to receive honours and silverware. Wilf McGuinness had only been in the job 18 months but had failed to deliver; although they had reached two League Cup semi-finals and an FA Cup semi- final, this clearly wasn't good enough. This may have been acceptable at other clubs, but United fans had come to expect more.

The 1970/71 season hadn't started well and by the end of November they had only five wins under their belt and were taking a nose-dive into the relegation zone. Sighs of relief were heard all around Old Trafford when United were drawn against Aston Villa for a place in the League Cup Final, but an unexpected 1–1 draw at Old Trafford threw even that prospect into doubt. United poised themselves for a replay at Villa Park on 18 December.

While United fans were holding their breath and crossing their fingers – and everything else they could cross – hoping that a win at Villa Park would kick-start their season, Villa fans were dusting down their claret and blue scarves, rattles, hats and anything else they could find as they prepared for the second leg of the League Cup semi-final against the mighty reds.

The programme from the match day.

Bottom right: The cover of the programme and entry ticket for that unforgettable Villa day.

Below: Jim and his friends looking like the Blues Brothers.

One such fan was lifelong supporter of the Villa Jim Weaver along with three or four of his friends who were also claret and blue through and through. They couldn't wait!

They decided to get to Villa Park as early as possible to get a good spot in the famous Holte End – towards the back and near the middle. Jim remembers that Villa went 1–0 down to United but he and his friends never got downhearted as they joined in with the Villa crowd, urging the team on. He recalls that George Best was his usual self on the pitch, but that he was wearing the number 8 shirt for some reason. He didn't get the chance to put the ball in the back of the net, and if he placed the ball for someone else nothing came of it. Jim does admit that every time George got hold of the ball he secretly held his breath just in case – you just never knew with Bestie.

Still 1–0 down and the second half kicked off. Villa got two goals that were ultimately enough to take them through to the final where they met Spurs. On the final whistle everyone in the Holte End went deliriously mad and as Jim made his way down the stone stairs his feet hardly touched the floor.

Things were so different for the United fans who were part of the almost 59,000 gate. Even the skills of George Best weren't able to carry United through to an away win to put them in the League Cup Final, and to ease some of the pressure that was currently on the club and in the dressing room.

For the Blues Brothers lookalikes in their dark sunglasses and Villa caps, it wasn't sufficient that they had actually witnessed the remarkable win over United – they managed to get home in time to watch and revel in the highlights again on television.

For the United team and fans alike, it must have been a long journey home to Manchester.

HIDDEN TREASURE

With George receiving up to 10,000 fan letters a week, it seemed obvious that there was need of a George Best fan club. It also seems obvious that the reputed 10,000 letters were from individuals who idolised Best and wanted him to know that. One such individual was 12-year-old Nigel Cavill who, in 1971, became a member of the illustrious GB Fan Club and received his certificate, authenticating him as a true member, plus letters, special promotion offers and everything else a fan-club member could expect to have.

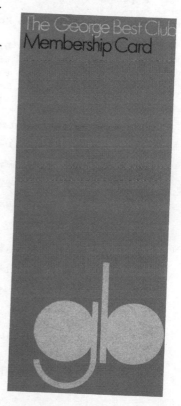

Along with many thousands of youngsters during the '60s and '70s, Nigel collected everything he could to do with George Best – in fact he didn't throw anything away, whether it was a receipt from George's shop in Manchester (where George actually served him and ruffled his hair), an envelope, anything from the GB Fan Club, comics or the now much-sought-after 'Manchester United: European Champions' carrier bag. You name it, Nigel kept it.

What happened to the treasure-trove of George Best and Manchester United memorabilia? After being married for 17 years, Nigel's wife, Carol, decided to assail his mum's attic that had, since the '70s, been the vault holding the treasures. To her amazement she really did find a cache of treasure relating to George Best and Manchester United that Nigel had kept, including his own Manchester United scrapbook that

For many years I received hundreds and hundreds of letters every week, many of which were asking about a Fan Club. Despite the numerous enquiries, I resisted the temptation to start a Fan Club without first ensuring that there was the organisation available to run a successful Club.

January 1971 (but delayed because of Postal difficulties) saw the launch of The George Best Club through which Members can get to know more about me and what I'm doing. Sometimes you may feel a lack of contact and this is where The Club will help. It will, I hope give you a channel for making contact with me and providing a personal touch between you, your friends and myself.

The first mailing to Members includes the following:-

> Distinctive Membership Wallet
> Diploma of Membership
> Personal Club Emblem
> Detail-Packed Personal Profile
> Large Colour Poster

In addition to the above enclosures, Members receive the first of the quarterly bulletins, through which they can make more contact with me. For those who join during the middle of a year, the first mailing will also include the year's past quarterly bulletins which they have missed, plus many other offers and surprises already mailed to existing Members.

On Thursday March 11th 1971 a draw was held at my new house, and Terry McDonagh was the one out of thousands to be drawn as Number 1 Member. He won a trip to Manchester to meet me, and a week-end in Paris.

I look forward to welcoming you to my Club, and hope you have lots of fun from it.

All the best,

George

The letter received by members of George's fan club.

provided a place for those special memories. The more Carol looked into the attic, the more she found, and the more she found the more memories began to be unearthed of those thrilling days back in the '60s and '70s.

In the year that Northern Ireland beat England 0–1 at a Home International at Windsor Park, Belfast (still one of the highlights of George's career, even though it ultimately counted for nothing), 12-year-old Nigel was storing away his treasures. Now the treasures have been rediscovered and brought back into the daylight for other fans to enjoy and carry on securing the future for such memories.

The George Best Club

CHRISTMAS COMPETITION

My answers to the questions are as follows:-

Question A ....

Question B ....

Question C ....

"I think The George Best Club is Fun because

....

....

...."

NAME ....

ADDRESS ....

....

....

.................Membership No. ....

If you have collected the signatures of 30 full international players, place a tick in the square

An entry form for a fan-club competition.

Nigel and Carol, together with their family, still attend the matches at Old Trafford – what else do avid Man U fans do? Perhaps their children will be carrying on their dad's tradition by collecting their memories of Giggs, Ronaldo, Ferdinand and Rooney for future generations to enjoy and look back on Manchester United's players of the 21st century.

FROM WEST BROM TO WOLVES

Following a two-week suspension in January 1971 – the maximum penalty for failing to report for training at Old Trafford – George Best met with Sir Matt Busby for half an hour and it became quite apparent, as they emerged from

The souvenir programme from the celebrations surrounding the opening of the Football Hall of Fame.

George Best is mobbed by fans.

their meeting smiling, that they had agreed for the sake of Manchester United to start all over. George had told Sir Matt that he had been 'bitterly disappointed with the team's performances in the past months: it was the main reason I staged my protest. I certainly do not want to leave United – I want to see them at the top again.'

Neither George nor Sir Matt could have realised just how pleased a particular 10-year-old Midlands lad was that George had decided to stay with United. Not because he was a United fan, but for the reason that he was looking forward to the West Bromwich Albion tie against Manchester United at the Hawthorns in March of the same year, and in particular to seeing George Best.

Young Graham Pick remembers, with great enthusiasm, watching with wonder from the Smethwick End of The Hawthorns, and realising why everyone just loved to watch George Best in action. West Brom beat Manchester United 3–2 on that occasion, but, not long after witnessing this win, Graham had what he calls a Damascus Road experience and deserted West Brom for another Midlands team just a few miles away, Wolverhampton Wanderers. Graham really doesn't know why he did this, but he is still a Wolves supporter to this day, in fact a very proud season-ticket holder. Strange really that George Best in his younger days was also a Wolves supporter – perhaps even stranger than Graham swapping his allegiance from West Bromwich to Wolverhampton.

In the year where George Best was making headlines for many things, when he was having to talk over personal and private problems with Sir Matt, as well as professional issues he had on and off the pitch, he was still able to wow the crowds with his exceptional talents and to etch those memories in the mind of a 10-year-old Midlands boy.

BERNARD'S LITTLE TREASURES

People collect so many different things; they hold them very dear and look at them from time to time, have conversations about their collections and secretly hope that maybe one day their collection might just be worth something. Football is an obvious favourite to those magpies amongst us, no matter what age, whether it's collecting match-day programmes and tickets, club paraphernalia or even those much-sought-after autographs scribbled on anything close to hand or collected in a specific book, or on a team shirt of an individual's choice.

Bernard Flynne holds his hands up and admits that he was a collector of football items and in particular of books and mass-produced football collectables. But things didn't come that easily to Bernie, for whenever he decided to collect something he had to save his money in order to buy them.

Bernie collected a selection of things such as 'My Favourite Soccer Stars' football cards presented free with the

Tiger, *Lion* and *Thunder*, *Buster* and *Jet*, and *Scorcher* and *Score*. In fact he was able to collect the whole series and still has them proudly stuck into the colourful books produced for collectors to keep. One of these Soccer Stars football - card books has a picture depicting the seconds just before that famous disallowed goal George Best scored against Gordon Banks in the England vs Northern Ireland international game.

Another collection that Bernie set his heart on was the series 'Giants of Football', a Hall of Fame Book, produced by Wolfe Publishing. This series was not given away with anything, but had to be purchased at the local shop, and Bernie remembers well having to save up to get the first one in the series which was, of course, on George Best. Bernie was able to collect all in the series including number six, on Chelsea's Peter Osgood.

These compact books hold such interesting facts and information about the chosen giants in football, facts that any football fan would love to spend time reading and embedding in their minds.

Here is just a flavour of some of the material used in the George Best book:

'Unlike many further away from Best, Crerand is convinced of his [George Best's] deep commitment to the game, his sincerity about it, and his willingness to run himself into the ground on the training pitch…. He says, "There is a lot of rubbish talked about George; a lot of misconceptions. I know he's had a few escapades, but what young man hasn't? There just isn't a shred of doubt about George's enthusiasm for the game."'

It's interesting that this particular comment faces an exceptional black-and-white photograph of George playing 'Cricket in the street with fans'. Just to observe the look on the young boys' faces in the photograph as George takes a swing with the cricket bat is a delight.

The write-up continues, 'Perhaps we demand too much of him [George Best]. Perhaps we should just be happy that at Manchester United there is a player who can do things like no one else in English football.' Perhaps, just perhaps, whoever wrote the series of 'Giants in Football' was right.

NORTHERN IRELAND'S GENIUS

Ask any young person as they play kick-about with a football in their local park and they will probably all say that, apart from playing for their chosen football club they support, they dream of playing for their country. And George Best, who had been kicking a ball since he was 18 months old and was rated as the most talented footballer ever to walk this earth, would have said that that his dream was to wear the emerald-green jersey for Northern Ireland.

It is no surprise that that's what he achieved and in fact George was capped for Northern Ireland 37 times and scored nine times.

Two particular matches are much talked about by his Irish fans and indeed the majority of all football fans and pundits. One of these occasions was when George scored what is arguably his cheekiest and perhaps the most famous non-goal of his career in the game between Northern Ireland and England at Windsor Park, 15 May 1971.

Gordon Banks, in goal for England, was about to kick the ball downfield and dropped the ball towards his left foot ready to lunge it forward. George, always one step ahead of the game, predicted Banks's move and with his right foot kicked the ball in the air before Banks could kick it. The ball went behind Banks.

The two famous footballers scrambled towards the ball. George outpaced Gordon and headed the ball towards the net. Imagine the delight of the home fans as they increased the noise levels in celebration of what they thought was such a mischievous goal.

It is reported that the referee had his back towards the ball at the time of this happening, but still disallowed the goal due to 'ungentlemanly conduct' – indeed! Although the goal was not allowed, still to this day it is talked about over the odd pint, but nothing can take away the embarrassment Gordon Banks experienced by being outwitted by George.

George's finest hour in Northern Ireland green was the home game at Windsor Park, Belfast, against Scotland on Saturday, 21 October 1967.

Just one year before, George had been a part of the European Cup quarter-final against Benfica and this was reportedly the best George Best performance that Bobby Charlton had ever witnessed. However, many (including George's dad, Dickie) who observed the 1967 Northern Ireland v Scotland Home International match agree that it was this match that was definitely George's finest moment.

With the exception of England/Scotland matches, Home Internationals were usually the chance for England to show off their footballing mastery, but on this occasion it was different. George was in control right from the first whistle. This wasn't a great team performance inspired by one man – this was a one-man show, the man being George Best.

The ball seemed to be tied to George's feet, except when he let rip and fired so many shots at Ronnie Simpson's Scottish goalmouth, and it really didn't matter where George was on the park, right wing, left wing or mid-field.

There had been a number suggesting that their star player hadn't been showing the commitment to his country that he was showing to his club (most noticeably in the Belfast press), so clearly George was out to prove something to his countrymen. That's just what he did – and it's not as if Scotland had sent out a weak side. They had Denis Law and Jim Baxter and were the first team to beat World Champions England at Wembley that year.

The sting felt on Ronnie Simpson's hands from an early 30-yard shot from Best lasted so long as he watched Best go on his way again, past two and three players before cutting inside and delivering a right-footed cross that Derek Dougan couldn't quite connect with. 'On another day,' said George, 'I might have scored three or four myself but their goalkeeper Ronnie Simpson, who was only winning his third cap, played a blinder. He was unbelievable. I was hitting shots that were flying towards the top corner and he was suddenly appearing from nowhere to tip them over.'

An eyewitness account from *The Times* said, 'He [George] caused as much trouble as three men with some exhilarating runs and shots of quite remarkable force from such a slight frame.' They still call the game the 'George Best International' – and if Ronnie Simpson hadn't been on such fine form the score line could easily have been more convincing.

Eventually George whipped in a perfect low cross that bounced off a defender; Clements controlled the ball well and struck it past Simpson for the winning goal.

With only 20 minutes to play, Northern Ireland were keen to keep the game closed down and hold out to keep the win in their pocket. But George Best wanted to play football. Terry Neil remembers Pat Jennings holding onto the ball with that look on his face that he intended hoofing it out of play to waste just a few more seconds. But George shouted, 'I'll have it! I'll have it!' With lots more running still left in his wiry legs, and an appetite that had been with him since his days playing out after dark on the Creagagh Estate.

What did George Best think of his finest hour? 'This was my game for Belfast, showing them, perhaps for the only time, what the boy from Burren Way could do when the mood took him. People still talk about it as the greatest individual performance in an international.'

The following year George was to begin to experience superstar status when he achieved the well-deserved English Footballer of the Year Award. He was also Manchester United's top scorer that year with 28 goals, not to mention being part of the European Cup-winning Manchester United. But for George Saturday, 21 October 1967 was special for him, for those that had the privilege of watching him and for Northern Ireland.

In modern-day football it is rare for a footballer to wear the United red shirt as long as George Best did, with some notable exceptions: Ryan Giggs, Gary Neville and Paul Scholes were at United for over 15 seasons and David Beckham was there for 12. George played ten seasons for them his life suggests that of a wayward genius. It has been suggested that this wild self-destruct button that George was able to press also gave him his almost eccentric qualities and the creative and fantastic qualities very few possess.

As the days closed in on George's life his request was that 'People will remember me for my football', and certainly matches such as the Northern Ireland v Scotland

International are where he put his football centre stage for all to see the beautiful talents he possessed.

We don't have the pleasure of ever being able to watch those skills in action again, but through modern technology we can certainly relive the magic of those moments when George Best came alive on the football pitch. We can continually be amazed at his superior quality and skills that just had to be God given.

ABSOLUTELY 'FAB 208'

When the dedicated followers of fashion were drifting into the 1970s towards the tiered-skirted gypsy look, full of frills, layers and complicated trimmings or wearing the tightest hotpants a girl could squeeze into, Fabulous 208 wasn't only the number on the dial to turn to for all-day music on Radio Luxembourg. In fact, *Fabulous 208* was also the hottest-selling weekly magazine that was a must-have for every teenage and early-twenties female.

Fab 208 had everything, including David Cassidy writing to the readers each and every week; Lulu giving agony-aunt advice to readers' letters; the latest fashion and beauty; news and gossip 'from Jenny in Hollywood'; the Two Sues back-page cartoon strip; short stories to while an hour away; facts, opinions and the necessary colour pin-ups; the latest in pop gossip and music and of course the regular 'Best Days of the Week' column written by none other than George Best.

In this weekly slot, George would answer questions sent to him by readers, or write something that he wanted to share about his likes and dislikes. Many times he would give advice and, although he did try to avoid football comments, they did creep in from time to time.

In one particular article he recalled how 'The only way for Georgie to play soccer was by playing truant!' He remembered how his school satchel was a giveaway to his being caught outside of school during school hours. George hit on the brilliant idea of hiding the offending satchel

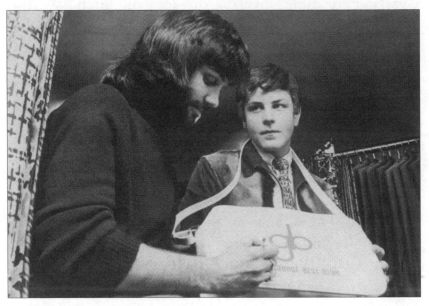

George signs one of his kit bags for a fan.

behind the dustbin on the porch of his aunt's house. But his deceit was discovered one afternoon – his mum got to hear about it and warned, 'I'll see you later.'

George's game of football that day went on and on, even to the point of every one of his mates going home and leaving him to play solo football, whacking the ball against the fence and catching it on the rebound – anything but go home.

Eventually, so the article goes on, his sister was sent out to find George and escort him back home where a nasty-looking stick was waiting for him. His dad said at a later date that he didn't really get the full swing at George because he was as slippery as an eel – he'd already learned how to dodge trouble!

Readers were also interested in how and where George wrote the column each week. George revealed that he certainly didn't use a typewriter as he said, 'I'm hopeless with a typewriter, so it has to be jotted down with the old ball-point and later on I get my secretary to type it out neatly. She's about the only person who can understand my scrawl.

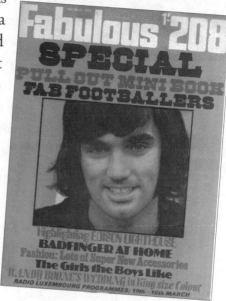

'It's been written just about everywhere: in a hotel room, in bed, on a huge jet plane, even on one occasion in the smallest room in the house!'

While George Best's behaviour on and off the pitch was increasingly becoming front- and back-page headlines, his incredible talent was still evident when he made contact with a football. His popularity was also clear from the mounting number of letters received by the *Fabulous 208* office. His fans wanted to know more and more about the acclaimed superstar who never really saw himself as anything other than George who just loved to play football.

GEORGE'S PUZZLE

'Who needs a friend like George Best?' you may have heard Mike Duffy of Mike Duffy Associates saying in the 1960s. He may have had cause for these sentiments then, but he certainly didn't when George was fighting for his life in 2005, as he prayed for his recovery. But what was Mike's association with George, and just what didn't work between them?

The jigsaw didn't sell very well and many copies of it were destroyed, but at least one is still in existence.

Mike had known George from the time he arrived in Manchester and had seen his rise to fame as a teenager, and witnessed first hand some of the headlines George had made on and off the pitch. Mike recalls that George's only real flaw was not being able to handle the fame at the tender age of 17, but as a footballer he was among the greatest names throughout the world.

It was in the 1960s that Mike Duffy Associates decided to produce the very first George Best jigsaw puzzle. This was among the multitude of other Best memorabilia around at that time. Mike recalls deciding with George which pictures to select to create a montage of pictures depicting various areas of George's life, and both were pleased with the results of the first official George Best Jigsaw Puzzle.

What could go wrong? A marketable personality loved and worshipped by many either for his sultry good looks or for his footballing magic – or even a mixture of both. The product – a jigsaw puzzle – that would appeal to all ages and the actual picture designed and agreed by the producer and the main man himself, George Best. All, it would seem, was on course for making a hefty profit. So what happened?

At the same time as the launch of the

One reason why the jigsaw did not do as well as hoped was due to negative headlines about George at the time. Here he is being sent off for spitting at the referee.

112

first official George Best Jigsaw Puzzle, George himself was making a series of negative headlines around his antics on and off the pitch. He was sent off playing for Northern Ireland for spitting at the referee and went on record during a newspaper interview claiming all English girls were 'scrubbers'. Not the kind of pre-launch publicity the new product needed. Overnight, Mike recalls, George went from being the biggest commercial name in Europe to one less than commercial. Consequently, Mike Duffy Associates didn't sell too many jigsaws. In fact, Mike had to burn the best part of the 10,000 print run to satisfy the tax office who were demanding he paid three shillings per unit in sales tax. But at least one has survived and is safe and secure in England.

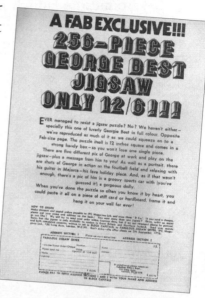

Adverts for the jigsaw.

Mike now lives and works in Australia and is creating headlines as a journalist for the *Adelaide News*. He last saw George when he visited Australia in the 1980s. At this meeting they both had a good laugh about their youth in Manchester – and perhaps the bonfire made up of jigsaw pieces.

No, Mike Duffy didn't question George's friendship. He saw him as a person who had a tremendous sense of humour and was always loyal to his friends –

but also as someone whom too many people took advantage of and would gladly help him spend his money. One thing Mike could have questioned George about was his timing – they will never know just how profitable the jigsaw venture could have been because of the incidents culminating around the launch. It's one of life's coincidences for which no one has the answer, but perhaps reflects in some way the puzzle of George's life.

To: THE SECRETARY,
THE FOOTBALL ASSOCIATION,
16 LANCASTER GATE, LONDON, W2 3LW

I (*name of player in full*) GEORGE BEST

of (*address*) 9 Aycliffe Avenue, Chorlton-cum-Hardy, Manchester 21

desire the cancellation of my registration as a Professional for the

MANCHESTER UNITED Football Club.

Signature of Player

Date 13th May 19 74

On behalf of the MANCHESTER UNITED Football Club

I agree to the cancellation of the registration of

(*name of player*) GEORGE BEST

as Professional for this Club. **The Certificate of Registration is returned herewith.**

Signature of Secretary

Address Old Trafford,

MANCHESTER M16 ORA

Date 13th May 19 74

SECOND HALF

SHOULD AULD ACQUAINTANCE BE FORGOT...

George Best famously 'retired' to Marbella in 1972, before coming back again and eventually leaving Manchester United for good in January 1974. George Best's United career deteriorated during the 1970s and, after a series of on-off retirements and a dip in form, he left United for good on New Year's Day 1974 after his final game against QPR. Many aspects contributed to the eventual and, some would say inevitable, day that George Best left United for good.

George 'retired' to Marbella in 1972.

In December 1972 other exits were being enforced at Manchester United. In fact, the *Guardian* suggested that 'Manchester United's most momentous day since the Munich disaster in February 1958' was when United's manager, Frank O'Farrell, and chief coach, Malcolm

Musgrave, along with chief scout John Aston, were dismissed just before Christmas 1972.

This 'momentous' decision was taken during a morning board meeting when chairman Louis Edwards released a statement: 'In view of the poor position of the club in the league, it was unanimously decided...' Also decided at the same board meeting was that George Best was to remain on the transfer list as 'it is felt that it is in the best interests of the club that he leaves Old Trafford.'

However, when Les Olive, United's secretary, arrived at Old Trafford in preparation for the afternoon's board meeting he was handed a typed letter from George who, so far as was known, was unaware of the board's earlier decision:

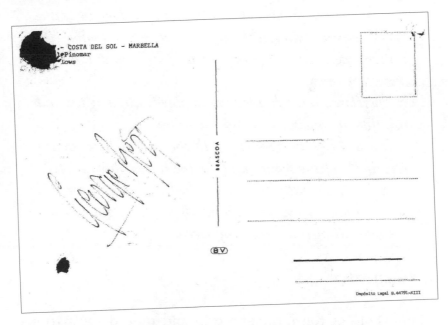

I had thought seriously of coming personally and asking for a chance to speak at the board meeting, but once again I am afraid when it comes to saying things face to face, I might not have been completely honest. I am

afraid from my somewhat unorthodox ways of trying to sort my own problems out I have caused Manchester United even bigger problems.

I wanted you to read this letter before the board meeting commenced so as to let you know my feelings before any decisions or statements are issued following the meeting.

When I said last summer I was going to quit football, contrary to what many people said or thought, I seriously meant it because I had lost interest in the game for various reasons. While in Spain I received a lot of letters from both friends and well wishers – quite a few asking me to reconsider. I did so and after weeks of thinking it over I decided to give it another try. It was an even harder decision to make than the original one.

I came back hoping that my appetite for the game would return and even though in every game I gave 100 per cent there was something missing. Even now I am not quite sure what.

Therefore I have decided not to play football again and this time no one will change my mind.

I would like to wish the club the best of luck for the remainder of the season and for the future, because even though I personally have tarnished the club's name in recent times, to me and thousands of others Manchester United still means something special.

George Best

The whole of the football world and indeed the national and international press were focusing on the increasingly wayward behaviour off the field and alcohol-related problems that had impaired George's health and ultimately shortened his career. A rift had developed between the club and player as off-field problems and the pressures of super-stardom took their toll.

But George walked out on the club on a number of occasions. After he ran off to Marbella, he returned to Manchester United in September 1973 but finally broke both Tommy Docherty's and Manchester United's patience when he failed to turn up for training in January 1974. His final league match for United had been in a disappointing 0–3 defeat against Queens Park Rangers on New Year's Day 1974.

The match programme from George's last game for Manchester United.

And so it was over.

On Tuesday, 1 January 1974, against Queens Park Rangers, George Best played his last competitive game for Manchester United. George Best, who started his professional career in 1963 at the age of 17 with Manchester United, made an immediate impact on the game. In full flow with the ball, he was a hypnotic blend of litheness and movement. He invited and evaded tackles like a matador taunting a bull. He would score goals beyond the imagination of ordinary players.

It would be interesting to know if George joined in with 'For auld lang syne my dear for auld lang syne… We'll take a cup of kindness yet for auld lang syne' that New Year's Day in 1974, and, if he did, who he was singing it with, or to.

FROM TYPHOO TEA TO
WORCESTER COLLEGE XI

There is a great temptation to offer a spot the difference on two pictures of football teams shown here. So what's the link?

Just a few years before the Worcester College picture was taken, a young boy was entranced by Manchester United and, in particular, George Best. Nothing unusual! The young boy patiently collected tea-packet cards so that he could send away to Typhoo Tea to obtain his very own 10" x 8" colour photograph of his beloved Manchester United – a photo that was 'suitable for framing' as far as Typhoo Tea was concerned.

That young collector was in fact one of the authors of this book, Bernie Smith, who remembers collecting with such enthusiasm the 12 precious cards needed to send away for his then prized possession from the Famous Football Clubs, 2nd series, Colour Pictures.

The reward for being so diligent in collecting the cards has been kept safely for a number of years.

But what of the photograph that's not Manchester United?

This was taken when the same boy was a little older and had moved away from home to experience higher education and obtain a teaching qualification. In his spare time, Bernie was playing for Worcester College where he was studying. Quite a change from the young boy collecting tea cards but still with a passion for football, Manchester United and indeed the skills of George Best.

Perhaps the test is to identify the George Best lookalike that at this time in his life tried to emulate his hero both on the pitch and in how he looked!

WITH THE COMPLIMENTS OF Ty-Phoo LTD., BIRMINGHAM 5
TEA

MANCHESTER UNITED F.C.
Back row, L to R: Brennan, Stiles, Dunne (T.), Dunne (P.), Foulkes, Crerand
Front row, L to R: Connelly, Herd, Law, Charlton, Best

NORTHERN IRELAND
APRIL 1964 – OCTOBER 1977

15/4/64 Debut v Wales, won 3–2
14/11/64 First Goal v Switzerland
21/04/71 Only International Hat Trick v Cyprus
12/10/77 Final International Game v Netherlands, lost 1–0

International Record
13 Wins – 8 Draws – 16 Losses

Appearances	Goals
37	9

THE GREATEST PLAYER NEVER TO PLAY
IN THE WORLD CUP

Written by **Mike Gibbons**, an aspiring young journalist from the UK who has followed the World Cup with passion from an early age.

If the World Cup has one Achilles heel, it is this – you can become one of the best players in the game, one of the few in the world that excels in your position, yet never have the chance to prove yourself on the biggest stage in sport. Sometimes you can be derailed by injury, that can happen to anyone, or you can simply talk yourself out of World Cup football like Bernd Schuster. How frustrating it must be though if, because of the geographical circumstances of birth, you will never have the team-

mates to help you qualify, no matter how good you are yourself. Former European Footballer of the Year George Weah, who even funded the efforts of Liberia out of his own pocket, will pay testimony to that.

When the old argument of who is the best player never to play in the World Cup rears its head, two names above all others are invariably mentioned. One is Alfredo Di Stefano, who as a naturalised Spaniard missed out on qualifying in 1958 (despite being in a team alongside those other well-known Spaniards Kubala and Puskas) then was selected in the squad for Chile 1962 but did not play through injury and/or disagreements with the coach, whichever you believe. The other passed away after a long and inevitably doomed battle with alcoholism just last Friday – George Best.

Anyone who knows football will know the name and the myths surrounding this magician of a player. I won't launch into an extended eulogy on how good he was –

these are numerous from team-mates and opponents alike, especially this week – I will just say that coming from the British Isles we have never produced a more gifted footballer and that, if we can transcend borders for a second, he is one of the greatest players of any nationality ever to pull on a pair of boots. That he pulled these boots on for Northern Ireland, however, meant that getting to a World Cup

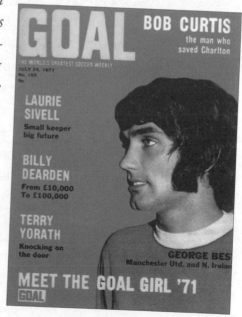

Finals, which during his career only accommodated sixteen teams, was a monumental task.

George made his debut for Northern Ireland against Wales in 1964, the same day as another debutant, the outstanding goalkeeper Pat Jennings. Unfortunately, these were the only two players in that team of international class. For Best there was no outfield player to act as a foil, no one remotely like a Didi, Garrincha or Tostao afforded to Pelé, not even a Valdano, Burruchaga or Cannigia that aided Maradona. Compared to the other home nations, Northern Ireland were very much the poor, distant cousins, memories and heroes of that epic run in 1958 now slipping away, but how quickly that can change with a genius in your team. In the qualifying cycle for the 1966 World Cup in England the Northern Irish played above themselves, the teenage Best inspiring them to a position whereby they only needed a win in Albania to qualify for a play-off with Switzerland for a place at the finals.

And they blew it. An awful 1–1 draw in Tirana ended their hopes and sent the Swiss through to the finals by a point, an utter disaster of a result with the World Cup waiting just over the Irish Sea, in stadiums the players knew so well and that Best was starting to illuminate. As if to prove what a loss he would be to the tournament, in the spring of 1966 Best turned in perhaps his greatest ever performance, scoring twice for Manchester United in a 5–1 European Cup victory over Benfica in the Stadium of Light, the Benfica of Eusébio, European Cup finalists in four of the previous five seasons. Best was christened 'El Beatle' and the legend grew and grew until it inevitably spiralled out of control.

The qualifying cycle for the 1970 tournament in Mexico put the Irish in a tough group with Turkey and the USSR. When the qualifying started in 1968 Best was at the very apex of his powers – Footballer of the Year in England, winner of the Ballon D'Or for the best player in Europe and in the May of that year scored perhaps his most famous goal which effectively decided the match as Manchester United finally won the European Cup 4–1 against Benfica. He was so far removed in terms of ability from his international team-mates at this stage he may as well have worn a different kit.

Certainly other teams had marked him out, Estudiantes showing the roadmap to dealing with Best by kicking the living daylights out of him in the Intercontinental Cup Final. With both the Irish and USSR brushing Turkey aside they essentially contested a two-legged play-off to reach Mexico. The teams fought (literally) to a stale-mate in Belfast in September 1969 and one month later met for the showdown in Moscow. Crucially Best was out injured, with him went the hopes of Northern Ireland and inevitably the Soviets won 2–0 to qualify.

And so the dream was over. He made sporadic appearances in the 1974 and 1978 qualifying tournaments but these were as infrequent as his appearances were becoming in club football. Having first quit football in 1972, Best's career and life went into a steady decline and he would never be the player he was again. Like Garrincha and Maradona, his fall from grace was at times sad, tragic, and horrifying, but when you fall from that height it is a long, long way down. Northern Ireland finally made it back to the World Cup in 1982 whilst 37-year-old Best was going through the motions with AFC Bournemouth. One of the stars for them in Spain that summer was a 17-year-old prodigy called Norman Whiteside, a Manchester United youth player discovered by Bob Bishop, who a generation earlier had sent a telegram from Belfast to Matt Busby with the legend 'I think I've found a genius' upon his sighting of one George Best.

So is he the greatest player never to play in the World Cup? Probably. Maybe. Oh what the hell, definitely. Sorry, Mr Di Stefano, but I'm planting my flag firmly in the Best camp. Of course it's personal bias, but my choice is made on what I have seen of both players from the archives, and other than Diego Maradona I have never seen a player with so many weapons in his armoury, so many options of how to beat his opponent or quite simply the capacity for me to jump out of my seat in amazement.

He reminds me why I love football so much. People will continue to dwell on his self-destructive nature that curtailed his career and eventually his life so early, but to paraphrase the man himself, they should remember the football. And what football it was. That he never played in a World Cup is not his loss, it's ours.

Acknowledgements to Planet World Cup webpage where this article first appeared.

MORE THAN JUST A GAME OF TWO HALVES

For those of us that have experienced those unspeakable feelings of seeing the winning goal brush into the goalmouth netting with that delightful, almost echoing 'whooshing' sound during the final minute of extra time; or indeed the reverse feelings of wretchedness as the opposing side are awarded and execute a penalty kick that wins them the game – have you ever wondered just what it is that touches our emotions in such a way?

That, of course, is from a fan's perspective, but what about those on the pitch? Why do they act and react the way they do? Why do some managers strut the technical area shouting limitless instructions, and on occasions provide the crowd with war-dance tendencies, when other managers, chewing their favourite gum with arms strategically folded, lean against the dug-out stanchion following every move of every player?

Then again, why is it that usually dignified human beings become chanting, outspoken, demonstrative beings,

Why do fans become tribal when they enter the football ground?

and players who are normally shy, reserved and non-challenging citizens become war-like when in their club's strip, part of a team kicking a ball around a piece of grass? What happens? Is there some kind of metamorphosis that takes place when either fans pass through a turnstile, or players and managers make the transition from dressing room to football pitch?

If, as Karl Marx suggested, 'Religion is the opium of the masses', and football undoubtedly takes on religious proportions, can we then suppose that an intoxicating tribal mentality can also be intrinsic in all associated with the game of football?

'Some people think football is a matter of life and death. I can assure them, it is much more serious than that.'

Bill Shankly

'Some people think football is a matter of life and death. I can assure them it is much more serious than that' is a famous quote from the great Liverpool legend Bill Shankly, but are we really to believe that football is anything more than simply 'a game of two halves'?

If, as some would suggest, Britons everywhere are elevating the beautiful game to religious status, then are the players to be described as gods, the stands as the pews, and the football songs passionately sung by tens of thousands which can be heard for miles around as hymns?

Football provides the ritual for weekend and sometimes weekday evening gatherings for the truly committed. To actually see first hand thousands of people singing their hearts out, hands held high to, in their opinions, greater beings is quite an emotional experience.

Football clearly demonstrates the tribalism associated with religion. It brings together the young, the old, the rich and the poor. It even has its fundamentalists, the hundreds of foolish hooligans that think violence is the best illustration of their devotion. Whatever the comparison, football engages people in a mass emotional display of their selected 'faith'.

In 1977 Desmond Morris became a director of a professional football club. As Desmond is a student of human behaviour, he became fascinated by the way a simple ball game had risen to become the 20th century's most widespread and popular sport. In his book *The Soccer Tribe*, he writes about football as if he were an explorer visiting a fascinating native tribe for the first time. He suggests that those involved in football, including players, managers, directors, officials, supporters and fans, have rituals and beliefs just as remarkable as those of any remote culture on a far-away island.

Desmond Morris, author of *The Soccer Tribe*.

Morris explores the idea of how football players are 'shaped' and become tribal heroes. He looks at how football has shifted from players once coming from affluent public- school backgrounds to when the game became a profession and was rapidly taken over by the industrial world of Victorian England. He suggests that 'The factory workers filled the grandstands and it was their sons who performed on the pitch.'

Most of today's great stars kicked their first football in a back alley or a side street. As Pelé recalled, 'Our field was the street where I lived… and our goals were the two ends of the street… Our sidelines were where a kerb might have been had the street been paved.' Equally Danny Blancheflower would 'kick a ball at every opportunity in the streets of the housing estate where I lived, in the school playground, under the railway arch and beneath the lamp-posts on dark evenings'.

Young football superstars nowadays have support and advice – these were not readily available when George became the first footballer to become a celebrity.

The passion became so intense that small boys became ball-jugglers and appeared to be magicians of leg movement and balance, with the football becoming almost a part of their anatomy. As George Best said, 'In those days when I was a kid the only thing I shared my bed with was a football. I used to take a ball to bed with me. I know it sounds daft but I used to love the feel of it. I used to hold it, look at it and think, "One day you'll do everything I tell you." I only lived for football.'

But it's not all about being a 'tribal hero', the personality of these 'heroes' have to incorporate competition and cooperation. Morris suggests that, 'The role of tribal hero involves basic conflict. To succeed he must be intensely competitive, but he can only achieve success by behaving cooperatively as a member of a team.' So our football player must be aggressively self-centred and to some extent egotistical while also being self-effacing and helpful. Morris explains, 'This fundamental contradiction goes a long way to explain the personality of the modern soccer player.'

And of course it's not only players and managers that have tribal characteristics. Mark Dowd, a television football commentator and lifelong Manchester United fan, investigated the question of the religion of football in a Channel 4 documentary *Hallowed Be Thy Game*. He interviewed players, managers, fans and religious authorities and others in a programme packed with footage that captured the fervour the game inspires all over the world. His film showed how the ritualisation of football not only echoes that of religion but also increasingly converges with it. A Portsmouth fanatic whose home and tattooed body are shrines to his club told Dowd: 'It's not just a religion, it's a way of life.'

For Dowd, 'The passion for football builds on a void at the heart of our existence in a society of fragmenting communities, where more people live than ever before… The sheer power, noise and rhythm of the crowd, I can both marvel and yet feel a deep unease. That which grips man's soul has the potential both for enormous good, and yet can unleash tremendous tribal violence.'

Desmond Morris suggests: 'In essence, then, the personality of the soccer player must contain a lust for victory that is powerful but controllable. There is no question of "art for art's sake" – playing for the fun of playing… His professional world is one of ambitions and those seeking of rewards – the winning of glory, money and status.

'To satisfy these aims, the player must have inherent toughness of character and a strong romantic streak. Publicly, he must be down-to-earth, even cynical and self-mocking to protect himself from ridicule, but privately he must dream of glittering prizes and great triumphs. He must have a powerful ego, but one that is prepared to suffer to achieve its goal – in both senses of the word.'

It would be interesting to unearth plenty of other unions between football and religion: the Catholic–Protestant hostility that taints Rangers–Celtic matches; the fact that many funeral directors now sell coffins in team colours. What would a 21st century Marx make of it? Regimes, dictatorships especially, including religions, have seized on football's potential to divert attention from divisions dogging their society. For example, the Brazilian team unifies the nation more effectively than the Catholic Church. If religion as Marx perceived it, stripped of its spiritual trappings, is little more than a powerful agent of social control, he'd probably say that football functions are effective substitute.

Football is tribal. The smaller tribes are clubs; the larger, nations. Football can unite us more than it can divide us, and today's beautiful game can also channel tribal emotions along peaceful paths.

It doesn't matter the colour of your skin, where you come from, your political ideology, your educational background, even your primary religion; football belongs to every person. 'The great thing about football is that it can attract the sort of emotion and passion that becomes a sort of religion in people's minds,' says Manchester United boss Sir Alex Ferguson.

So how can we account for what happened to one soccer tribe hero and genius, George Best? It has been recorded and stated many, many times that he was football's first superstar. George said himself that what happened to him off the pitch had never happened before, no one really knew what to do or how to deal with all that his stardom entailed. And so George was metaphorically left to the devices of wolves, in whatever form: the press, 'friends', money, women, lifestyle and in the end alcohol.

Unlike Ryan Giggs who, according to *Giggs: The Autobiography* by Ryan Giggs and Joe Lovejoy (Penguin Books), 'is comfortable with fame because, from an early age, he was sure it would become part of his life, he prepared for it. When he was a child he used to practise his autograph… he had always had an ambition to be on the cover of *GQ* magazine… With preparation like that, when fame arrived, he wasn't surprised or wrong footed by it; and now it's attached itself to him.'

But not so for George Best! The genius of George was placed at centre stage with nothing and no one within the tribe who had either the foresight or the experience to put in place a mechanism to protect him. He made many mistakes and was criticised publicly for whatever he did. But, except for a few true friends, did anyone consider giving him the support he needed?

Was January 1974 when George finally handed in his United red shirt for the last time a time of reflection for him – or perhaps his own personal 'half-time'? Perhaps the blushes he displayed during his brief encounter with the 14-year-old fan Mary at Manchester Airport (see page 140), when she approached him for his autograph, was truly a part of his musing on releasing himself from the tribe that he had been a part of for 11 years.

Desmond Morris theorises some of the tribal pressures encountered by those within, such as tribal territories, taboos, strategies, tactics, gatherings, the central rituals of a tribe and so on – but George Best experienced all of these tribal pressures, and far more.

Consider, just for a moment: did George Best realise at the end of the European Cup Final, even with all the euphoria, the delights, the celebrations, that he could go no higher within this tribe? He didn't join in the festivities of the evening following the record-breaking win, he went off somewhere on his own. Did the tribal pressures cause him to just want to escape it all at some point, and was part of that escapism his reported womanising, clubbing and drinking? Was it in 1966 after the Benfica game that he first became that tribal god? Were the elders in the tribe getting just too old to go out and battle on the green turfed war-zone, but not have the experience of super-stardom to pass on any words of wisdom to the younger tribe members? In the Northern Ireland tribe, were the other members of the tribe lacking enough skill to work and battle along with the Best?

Desmond Morris suggests 'The Tribal Hero's attitude to

sex involved the classic double standards. When he marries he is typically a loving husband who cares deeply about his wife but, when some players are single, they tend to treat girls like crude sex objects, to be bedded as quickly and as often as possible.'

So the handsome, fashionable, fine figure of a 1960s guy, George Best was not only a 'Tribal Hero', he was also a sex god to many. His only complaint about the easy availability of sex was that, in the end, it became too much for him: 'It got on my nerves. I'd open my curtains in the morning and there would be a line of young birds looking through the window... It was incredible. I never had to take them out to dinner or any of that crap. They'd ring me up or hang about the boutique and straight upstairs... They used to fall over themselves to get into bed with me... I know a lot of them just did it to say they had slept with George Best... just as they were going to climb into

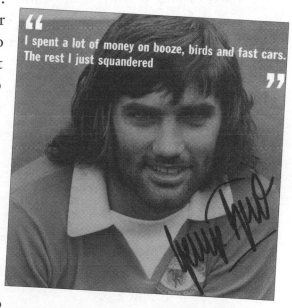

bed with me they'd say, "I hope you don't think I'm doing this just because you're George Best..." I didn't mind so long as I enjoyed myself.' Was George Best's exit from the United tribe a time for him to shut the curtains on the tribal groupies awaiting their tribal god to choose them or had it, in the words of the hotel porter, 'all gone wrong'? The offer from the United States gave George the opportunity to be a part of a new tribe and did George need the offer to try to reinvent the warrior within himself?

Today's highly organised game does not merely channel tribal-national emotions into relatively peaceful paths, with clear limits, well-enforced rules (on the pitch, at least) and handshakes at start and finish. Now, any fame or stardom that goes unprotected is taken very seriously and, if an individual is left to fend for himself, it can have a detrimental effect on his life. It has put in place the much-needed – but all too late for George Best – mechanism to protect those extraordinary individuals who transcend all barriers and become true world stars, but who are, more often than not, just young lads off the streets where they were brought up, who just want to play football.

Dunstable Town
August 1974 – October 1975

12/8/74 v Cork Celtic

5/9/74 v Manchester United Reserves
(won 3–2, George was mobbed)

29/10/75 v Luton
(New Floodlights)

Appearances	Goals
0	0

THAT'S WHAT FRIENDS ARE FOR!

'When he's off the booze he's a wonderful guy. He'll do anything for you' was the heartfelt comment of 28-year-old Barry Fry when he was player-manger at Dunstable Town F.C. in 1974. And that's exactly what George Best did: Best did his best for his old Manchester United team-mate Barry Fry.

George hadn't really done anything football-wise since February of that year; in fact, Julie Welsh in the *Observer*, July 1974, suggested that 'football had been granted an unconditional divorce from George Best'. So why had George decided to reunite with the love of his life – football?

In simple terms, he was helping an old friend out, someone who had been given the job of managing and playing for Dunstable Town F.C. and who, under a new chairman Keith Cheeseman, had been given the job of putting the club on the map.

Barry had been on the books of Manchester United just a short time before the genius of George had been spotted in Belfast and subsequently signed by the mighty reds. Barry Fry recalled that the happiest legacy of his time at United was an enduring friendship with another youngster who out-dazzled even the bright lights of the big city.

One of the programmes from when George turned out to help his friend Barry Fry at Dunstable Town F.C.

'I'd been there a year when Bestie came, and he soon leap-frogged me. He was obviously a genius. The lads used to moan in training because he'd beat six men, then go back and beat them again, but Matt Busby and Jimmy Murphy said, "Leave him alone, he'll learn to pass" – which of course he did.'

When Fry commenced management with humble Dunstable Town in the Southern League, he invited George Best to make a guest appearance. 'George was still with United, but he'd fallen out with Tommy Docherty and was refusing to play. When I told Tommy Doc that he had agreed to play for Dunstable, he said, 'Right, I'll bring a team down and you can play against us.'

Barry's first match as manager of Dunstable Town had been played in front of 34 spectators. For the next match, 43 turned up. But, when George Best played against a Manchester United XI, amazingly Dunstable's gate exceeded 10,000. 'That put us on the map. Then we signed ex-West Brom and England centre forward Jeff Astle and, having been bottom of the league for nine years on the trot, we scored 105 goals and won promotion. George has been a real good friend to me.'

On Wednesday, 29 October 1975, the match, Dunstable Town F.C. versus Luton Town F.C., celebrated the official opening of Dunstable's new floodlights. The programme on the night featured the late, great George Best guesting for Dunstable. On page 3 of the programme Barry Fry wrote: 'I welcome players, officials and supporters of Luton Town F.C. and would like to take this opportunity of thanking Harry Haslem and his Directors for sending his 1st team to officially open our £10,500 floodlights. I also welcome George Best back to Dunstable and thank him for guesting for us once again. I am sure that everyone is in for a very entertaining evening with plenty of goals...'

George and Tommy Docherty had fallen out.

Some may say that that's what friends are for, to call upon in a time of need. For Barry Fry and indeed Dunstable Town F.C. it meant far more. Barry said of George, 'How can you put into words what it means getting George Best at Dunsatble? It'll be a bigger boost for the club than having Frank Sinatra sing at half-time.'

For Dunstable in 1974 something far better than having Old Blue Eyes happened, the brown-eyed genius – who may have been edging towards the end of his footballing career – made just three appearances as a favour and in support of an old mate. As Barry Fry said, 'He's a wonderful guy. He'll do anything for you.' And he was right, George didn't let him down.

MARY'S STORY ... MEMORIES OF MR 'G'

In March and April 1974, George Best was living through the nightmare of being accused of stealing Miss World Marjorie Wallace's fur coat. He had received £2,000 conditional bail not to contact Miss Wallace directly or indirectly, to which the magistrate said, 'Well, he would have a job to do that. We can't contact her ourselves.'

George kept bail conditions and was accompanied to court by his friend Michael Parkinson in April. He was cleared of the charges of stealing property from the flat of Marjorie Wallace. Although Miss Wallace didn't make any court appearance, George made three and Mr Kenneth Harrington, the magistrate, told George, 'You are dismissed and I think I should add, as this matter has received a good deal of publicity, I should emphasise that you leave this court without a stain on your character.'

It was with all this behind him that George happened to be at Manchester airport – as was 14-year-old Mary who was living in Willenshaw at that time. George was obviously waiting for a flight, but the airport was the place that Mary and her friends would often be found hanging out on weekend afternoons. They used to do a spot of people-watching and dream of far-away places like the United States and Las Vegas – imagining boarding the plane and being waited on as they flew off to some exotic destination. The airport was also the place to get a tasty cup of hot chocolate from the vending machines!

It was on one of these afternoons in May 1974 that Mary and her friends spotted George Best waiting in the airport. Being Irish herself, even at the tender age of 14, Mary was so proud of George and how he had literally put Ireland on the inter-

Mary and her friends used to like hanging out at Manchester airport.

national map, and she had seen him play and display his talents at Old Trafford over the past two years.

Mary wanted so much to go over and ask George for his autograph, but her friends didn't think it was a 'cool' thing to do. Although usually a very shy person, Mary felt so confident that her Irish countryman wouldn't shun her that she calmly walked up to him and asked him for his autograph.

Mary was so surprised at George's shyness and how he even blushed. Unfortunately for Mary, she had a pen but nothing for him to write his autograph on – so George took from his pocket a takeaway menu from a Chinese restaurant and began to sign his name. The pen didn't work! George managed to write the letter 'G' but that was all. Now blushing even more and almost stuttering George apologised and gave Mary the menu for keeps.

Mary went back to her very jealous friends with the 'G'-signed menu that she kept in her memory box alongside other precious things such as a letter from her first boyfriend and another letter from her mum when she first left home. She kept that menu for years and only recently threw it out during a mega clear-out – but the memory of Manchester airport in May 1974 still lives on.

Young Mary treasured her takeaway menu bearing George's initial!

The court appearances relating to Miss World's fur coat had caused George to be humiliated and it had embarrassed him; it had inconvenienced him and subjected him to adverse publicity.

The embarrassment of the dried-up pen stopping him making a 14-year-old girl's day in Manchester airport later on in that year would not have been the same for sure. Even without the autograph the pen had stopped him from writing, George was able to make memories for his fans and supporters – such things never made the headlines but are kept in the archives of the memories of many.

Jewish Guild
May 1974 – June 1974

Appearances	Goals
0	0

GEORGE'S SOUTH AFRICAN JOURNEY

In 1974, George Best played as a guest for the Jewish Guild F.C. in Johannesburg. He did so as part of a lifestyle that included playing a total of five games for the club and drinking, gambling and living the high-life – he was allegedly paid mega-bucks for the privilege. Not much is recorded about George in South Africa, but we do gain some insight into his time there in a tribute article written by Sy Lerman for the *Mail and Guardian* online newspaper around the time of George's death:

BEST WAS 'BASICALLY A SHY PERSON'
Sy, Lerman Johannesburg, South Africa
26 November 2005

The image of soccer genius and legend George Best as a compulsive extrovert and womaniser was refuted by two South Africans who knew the soccer genius and legend better than most.

Best, who died on Friday (25th November 2005) at the age of 59 of a lung infection to his alcohol-ravaged body, which had required a liver transplant four years ago, played several games as a guest for Jewish Guild in the old National Football League in the 1970s.

He was described by former South African and Highlands Park midfielder Martin Cohen as 'coming from the salt of the earth – a very rare player and a very rare human being'. Cohen played alongside the Manchester United icon when they were both with the Los Angeles Aztecs in the United States in 1977.

'He was basically a shy person behind all the glitz and publicity,' said Cohen, 'and cultivated the outspoken, bravado image and sharp tongue as a tool against what he perceived a cynical, unprincipled media whom he despised. I remember the phone ringing once,' said Cohen, 'and the caller announcing himself as John Smith of the Sun. *"This is George Best of the Earth," replied Best, "so just f*** off."'*

Cohen said women flocked to Best like moths to a flame – 'but it was not because he chased them. Rather, it was because he was so good-looking and had such a magnetic personality they found him irresistible. I met him in London five years after we played together in America,' said Cohen, 'and he treated me like a long-lost brother. That's the kind of guy he was.'

Lawyer Itzey Blumberg, who was a director of Jewish Guild when Best played briefly for the club and who was his constant companion in South Africa, described him as a 'gem – a very unique person'.

'I owned a beaten-up old Toyota at the time, with the passenger seat only prevented from collapsing by an old hockey stick,' reminisced Blumberg. 'The Guild directors

sent a fancy limousine to take George to the Rand Stadium, but he insisted on travelling in my jalopy.

'He spent most of his time in South Africa partying and only showed his rare talent for the first 10 or 15 minutes of each game. But one shot from almost the halfway line at Balfour Park rocketed against the crossbar and was the best of Best.'

Blumberg introduced Best to controversial stripper Ultra Violet, who was one of his clients, and the pair raised more than a few sparks. 'But he was never happier than in the privacy of his close friends,' said Blumberg, 'and I still cherish a vintage wine bottle we polished off together at one such meeting with a couple of friends.'

Through what appears to be an honest report of George's time in South Africa, it isn't difficult to see through all the drink, glitz, women and money to see that underneath it all George was still a normal guy with a terrific gift, and someone who people enjoyed being with.

Stockport County
November 1975 – December 1975

10/11/75 v Stoke
Friendly with 8000 fans

28/11/75 v Swansea
League debut. Scores. 9230 fans

12/12/75 v Watford
5055 fans

26/12/75 v Southport
6321 fans

Appearances	Goals
3	2

Cork Celtic
December 1975 – January 1976

League of Ireland
28/12/75 v Drogheda (H)
11/1/76 v Bohemians (H)
18/1/76 v Shelbourne (A)
19/1/76
Sacked for lack of enthusiasm

Appearances	Goals
3	0

SIMPLY THE BEST FOR STOCKPORT
AND CORK CELTIC

In 1975, George Best signed with Stockport County, a Fourth-Division club that would be the equivalent of a single-A baseball team in the United States.

Still in the shadow of his reputation of being one of the finest footballers Britain has ever produced, George resumed his football career as he stepped out onto Edgeley Park for a fundraising game against Stoke City – incidentally, Stoke was desperate to sign George at t his time.

As you would expect from a player who had been off the top-flight scene for 20 months, George took things tentatively but occasionally produced some magical moments such as a fierce drive from 50 yards that dipped just wide of the post. He also displayed some exquisite passes and incomprehensible changes of direction – something he never lost.

George never lost his magnetism. The fundraising game attracted an 8,081 gate, almost four times the normal attendance at Edgeley Park.

It had been rumoured that George would play for Stockport in a league match against Swansea on 28 November. As the rumours came true it was reported that Stockport were extremely grateful that he was a part of the team on that day as they would have found Swansea too much.

The following article is from the Stockport County website and gives a clear idea of George's return:

Roy Chapman was only manager of Stockport County for nine months, but he'll always be remembered as

147

the man who brought George Best, arguably the greatest footballing talent produced in the British Isles, to Edgeley Park.

It was November 1975, with the Hatters involved in a real battle to avoid re-election, that Chapman, amazingly, persuaded the Irishman to weave his magic before the Edgeley faithful.

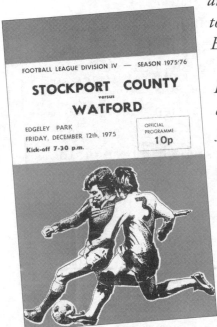

A crowd of 2,789 was present at Edgeley Park to witness a 1–0 defeat at the hands of Huddersfield Town in the previous home game before County crashed out of the FA Cup, 3–0 at next Saturday's opponents, Hartlepool.

Without George Best, the attendance for County's next game, against Swansea City on November 28, would have probably been under 2,000. With Best, the attendance was recorded at an incredible 9,240! And the mercurial Irishman didn't disappoint the admirers.

19 minutes: County 1 Swansea 0

George scored with his third successive in-swinging corner from the left. The first two had the defence in such a tizzy that goalkeeper Steve Potter could only help it into the net.

55 minutes: County 2 Swansea 0

Best with heart-warming artistry beat three men, held another three off and glided the ball into the path of a young Lee Bradley to crash the ball past a now bewildered defence.

72 minutes: County 3 Swansea 0

The piece de-resistance! George started the move with a pass to Ian Seddon. The cross was headed on by McNeill, and Best, with his back to the goal, perfectly balanced, swung and volleyed the ball into the net with tremendous power. The noise from the crowd shattered the night air!

Swansea pulled back two late goals through Alan Curtis and Dave Bruton, but Best was not to be denied as County hung on for two valuable points.

The George Best bandwagon pulled in another 5,055 fans for his next appearance, against Watford on December 12, when another marvellous goal from the genius helped the Hatters pick up a point from a 2–2 draw. Another Northern Ireland international, Ian Lawther, was the other County marksman.

Best didn't score in his final game wearing blue and white, against Southport, but his presence again attracted a bumper 6,321 crowd and also inspired Chapman's side to a 1–0 victory thanks to a goal from Micky Hollis.

Without argument, one of the world's greatest ever footballing talents had certainly put the club in the headlines and, although he was being well paid on a match-to-match basis, he must have kept the Hatters' bank manager happy by pulling in over 20,000 supporters in just three appearances.

Without Best, County continued to struggle and they went into the final game of the season, at Scunthorpe, needing a victory to guarantee finishing outside the dreaded bottom-four. Anything less could see Swansea climb above them if they won at Rochdale.

Older fans will remember that Scunny used to kick off at 3.15 p.m. not the traditional 3.00 p.m. so County still had 15 minutes to play when news filtered through that the Swans had gone down 1–0 at Spotland.

The massive travelling army immediately burst into song: 'Rochdale 1 Swansea 0, hallelujah!'

Knowing that County's result at the Old Show Ground was now immaterial legendry keeper Alan Ogley got down on his knees to conduct the Hatters' faithful who were now bouncing behind the goal!

Locals then watched on in astonishment as the final whistle sparked a huge party amongst the travelling hordes who had invaded the pitch.

Notable Former Players
- George Best
- Geoff Hurst
- Bobby Tambling
- Uwe Seeler

Cork Celtic F.C. crest

The following day's News of the World reported: 'At the end of the game hundreds of Stockport County fans invaded the pitch and from the noise they were making you'd have thought they'd just won promotion, not avoided re-election.'

The man George Best was back. Perhaps not fully fit and still with his unpredictable personality off the pitch, but nothing could take away his delightful talent – something Stockport was thankful for even if it was just for a short time.

Later, George played for an Irish club, Cork Celtic, and was let go after three games. Out of shape and 30 pounds overweight, he had become a parody of himself to serious soccer fans, but he still had the talent and instincts to dominate any football match he was a part of.

www.stockportcounty.premiumtv.co.uk

Fulham
September 1976 – November 1977

12/8/76
Signs contracts

2/9/76
Registered to play

4/9/76 debut v Bristol Rovers
Scores on 71 seconds. 21,127 in crowd

3/9/77 v Blackburn

12/11/77
Last game, lost at Stoke 2–0

29/11/77
Suspended for not training. He was in LA

Appearances	Goals
47	10

Los Angeles Aztecs
April 1976 – June 1978
Signed late December 1975

20/2/76 Arrives in the USA

17/4/76 Debut v San Jose Earthquakes

18/7/76 Hat trick v Boston Minutemen

20/5/77 First game of season v Portland Timbers

25/8/77 Last game of season v Seattle Sounders

2/4/78 First game of season v Houston Hurricane

20/6/78 Last game v Washington Diplomats

Event	Appearances	Goals
Regular Season	55	27
Play Offs	6	2
Total	61	29

George Best –
a footballing legend.

Above: Accepting the European Footballer of the Year trophy in 1968.

Below: The Best in action.

Playing for the Aztecs in LA.

With his
son, Calum.

Above: Three Manchester United greats: George with Sir Bobby Charlton and Denis Law.

Below: Best and Beckham – both decided to promote football and play soccer US-style in Los Angeles.

Arguably the two best footballers ever to have lived – Pelé and Best.

George enjoys a football match at Portsmouth FC – it was rumoured at the time that the club had a role lined up for him.

On 16th March 2006, the world remembered one of its greatest footballers at Manchester Cathedral.

Fort Lauderdale Strikers
June 1978 – July 1979
Transferred for LMA

24/6/78 debut v New York Cosmos
Scores 2 in 5–3 win

23/8/78 v Tampa Bay Rowdies
Lost, last game of the season

31/3/79 v New England Strikers
First game of the season, win 2–0

25/7/79 v California Surf
Last game of the season, away win 6–3

Event	Appearances	Goals
Regular Season	28	6
Play Offs	5	1
Total	33	7

San Jose Earthquakes
April 1980 – August 1981

13/4/80 Signs contract

27/4/80 Debut v Edmonton Drillers
Lost 2–4

1/6/80 v California Surf
Fails to turn up

23/8/80 v LA Aztecs (H)
Lost 2–1 but scored

29/3/81 v New York Cosmos (H)
Lost 3–0, first game of season

22/7/81 v Forst Lauderdale Strikers, 3–2 win
One of his finest games

19/8/81 v Vancouver Whitecaps
Last ever game

Appearances	Goals
56	21

EXIT UNITED – ENTER THE UNITED STATES

On 19 December 1972, Frank O'Farrell, Manchester United's manager, lost his job. In a way it was the end of an era, with Bill Foulkes having retired, Bobby Charlton's testimonial having been held the previous day and George Best retiring on that same day.

Tommy Docherty immediately began to rebuild the side with a series of signings, most notably Lou Macari. United recovered and finished that season in 18th place. George Best came out of retirement once more to sign with the team for the 1973/74 season. United were again caught in a relegation battle and entered the penultimate game of the season needing to win two games and for Birmingham to lose in order to stay in the First Division. Birmingham won their game and Denis Law, now playing for Manchester City against United, sealed United's fate with the only goal of the game. Manchester United were relegated to the Second Division for the first time since 1937.

George with Elton John, who was part-owner of the club in LA.

1976 was a notable year in US 'soccer'. While new names began appearing in many English club signings, favourite footballing heroes were taking the transatlantic flight to fame and sometimes fortune in the North American Soccer League. Rodney Marsh from Queens Park Rangers for US$80,000; former England captain Bobby More was enticed away from Fulham to San Antonio and, finally, Los Angeles, with new part-owner Elton John succeeded where New York had failed a year earlier, signing the elusive George Best – with George, just before his 30th birthday, being the youngest signing of the lot.

The American Bicentennial (1776–1976) was also being celebrated throughout the United States marking the beginning of their third century as an independent nation as well as the 200th anniversary of the American Revolution. Gerald R. Ford, President of the USA, stated:

Two legends together – Best and Pelé.

'For two centuries our Nation has grown, changed and flourished. A diverse people, drawn from all corners of the earth, have joined together to fulfil the promise of democrac... It is about the events of our past, our achievements, our traditions, our diversity, our freedoms, our form of

Aztecs 2: George turns out to the adoring crowd at the LA Aztecs.

government and our commitment to a better life for all Americans... Thus, in joining together all races, nationalities, and individuals, we also retain and strengthen our traditions, background and personal freedom...

As we lay the cornerstone of America's third century, I am most happy to commend the officers and members of the United States Soccer Federation and their Bicentennial Soccer Cup activities...'

The Bicentennial Soccer Cup was organised by the USSF to celebrate the United States' bicentennial as a soccer tournament with three of the strongest national teams in the world: Brazil, Italy and England. It was intended to promote the game to the US audiences at large at a national level, and could easily have been called a mini World Cup; the Brazilians had won the cup three times, the Italians twice and England once. These

157

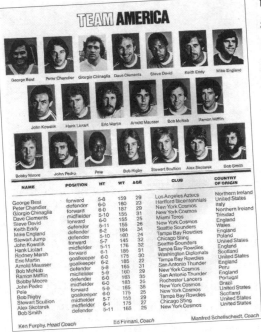

TEAM AMERICA

NAME	POSITION	HT	WT	AGE	CLUB	COUNTRY OF ORIGIN
George Best	forward	5-8	159	29	Los Angeles Aztecs	Northern Ireland
Peter Chandler	defender	6-0	160	23	Hartford Bicentennials	United States
Giorgio Chinaglia	forward	6-0	187	31	New York Cosmos	Italy
Dave Clements	midfielder	5-10	155	31	New York Cosmos	Northern Ireland
Steve David	forward	6-0	155	25	Miami Toros	Trinidad
Keith Eddy	defender	5-11	155	26	New York Cosmos	England
Mike England	defender	6-2	184	34	Seattle Sounders	Wales
Stewart Jump	defender	5-10	160	24	Tampa Bay Rowdies	England
John Kowalik	forward	5-7	145	32	Chicago Sting	Poland
Hank Liotart	midfielder	5-11	176	32	Seattle Sounders	United States
Rodney Marsh	forward	6-1	185	31	Tampa Bay Rowdies	England
Eric Martin	goalkeeper	6-0	175	30	Washington Diplomats	Scotland
Arnold Mausser	goalkeeper	6-2	185	22	Tampa Bay Rowdies	United States
Bob McNab	defender	5-8	165	31	San Antonio Thunder	England
Ramon Mifflin	midfielder	5-9	160	29	New York Cosmos	Peru
Bobby Moore	defender	6-0	183	35	San Antonio Thunder	England
John Pedro	midfielder	6-0	183	25	Rochester Lancers	Portugal
Pele	forward	5-8	165	35	New York Cosmos	Brazil
Bob Rigby	goalkeeper	6-0	175	25	New York Cosmos	United States
Stewart Scullion	midfielder	5-7	155	29	Tampa Bay Rowdies	Scotland
Alex Skotarek	midfielder	6-1	175	27	Chicago Sting	United States
Bob Smith	defender	5-11	165	25	New York Cosmos	United States

Ken Furphy, *Head Coach*   Ed Firmani, *Coach*   Manfred Schellscheidt, *Coach*

three teams competed against an all-star team, called Team America. This was treated as a major event both in the United States and among the world press; over 500 media reporters covered the event.

Team America was made up of a mix of football stars from 12 countries included Pelé, Bobby Moore, Rodney Marsh, Dave Clements and, of course, George Best.

Unfortunately, Team America and the US audiences did not see the delights and skills of two of the players in this particular tournament, as, in a spate of last-minute politicking, George Best and Rodney Marsh demanded that they start all three games, when the coach, Ken Furphy, refused, they walked!

Although both of their names and photographs appeared in the red, white and blue souvenir programme of 1976, neither of them actually wore the red v-neck USA shirt. Who knows, may-be that could be one of the reasons why crowds averaging 45,000 witnessed

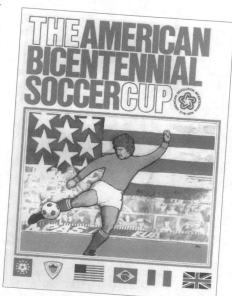

THE AMERICAN BICENTENNIAL SOCCER CUP

Team America only scoring one goal throughout the tournament. Perhaps Ken Furphy lived to regret his refusal.

George with former wife Angie and their son, Calum.

Hibernian
November 1979 – October 1980

16/11/79 Signs for Hibs from Fulham

24/11/79 v St Mirren
Scores on debut in 2–1 loss, 13,670 attend.

9/9/80 v Dundee (A)

11/10/80 Final game v Falkirk (H)

Appearances	Goals
3	0

SCOTLAND WELCOMES BACK
YESTERDAY'S HERO

On a weekend television show in 1979 George Best offered himself to any First Division club in England – not a bad way of telling the football world that you want to play football.

This offer, from such a talented and naturally skilful player, was too much to miss for Stewart Brown (the late *Evening News* writer) who suggested the idea of George moving North to Scotland to the Hibs manager, Eddie Turnbull. Hibernian were suffering the embarrassment of potential relegation for the first time in almost 50 years, and Stewart thought that even with George Best on the team the footballing disgrace couldn't be prevented – but at least the attention would be sidetracked for a short time.

Eddie Turnbull thought it was a good idea and so the

chairman, Tommy Hart, was brought in to the discussions. Tom was equally a supporter of his beloved Hibs as well as being chairman and responded really quickly to the suggestion of George Best being on the books.

Demonstrating his new-found allegiance.

George had not long arrived back in England from the United States and was staying with his in-laws at Southend. He was still registered as a player at Fulham, so Hibernian had to seek permission from the club to talk to George. Within two days Hibs were talking with George and the agreement was made for him and his wife Angie to fly to Edinburgh to 'have a chat' and still be in time to watch the home game against Kilmarnock. Tom Hart met them at Edinburgh airport. But following lunch, as George made his way into the directors' box at Easter Road, over 5,000 fans welcomed him into their stadium.

Eventually, George Best became part of the dressing room at Easter Road and the celebrity image was looked on with caution by his fellow players – particularly as they thought George was on £1,500 a match, funded personally by

Tommy Hart. Hart defused any backbiting by doubling the bonus system the players already enjoyed.

One of the team, Tony Higgins, said at the time, 'We'd heard some rumours that a big name was coming but it was only when George arrived that we believed it. But

despite his reputation, George was a very quiet guy; there was nothing fancy about him. He was down to earth, a professional football player like ourselves.'

George quickly became one of the players but it soon became quite evident that his life was poles apart from the lives of his new team-mates. While others had comparatively normal lives, George would still mix with people such as Rod Stewart, John Lennon and Michael Caine – to name a few. His lifestyle was just so different.

George was still officially a Fulham player when he returned to the UK.

Something that never changed while George was at Hibs was the fact that he was a crowd puller. Where they were used to crowds of around 9,000, some gates totalled 22,000 just because George Best was on the team sheet. Not only did George attract crowds on match days, but the press from other shores would gather outside Easter Road just to get a glimpse of the man himself. The interest the 33-year-old former superstar aroused was absolutely startling. One wonders if the world's press would have been so stirred up if someone like Diego Maradona had just joined a Scottish club! The most ambitious transfer in Scottish soccer history was also proving to be the most intriguing, as Best arrived to an overwhelming welcome.

'He's turned up,' shouted one pressman, obviously still not sold on the idea that Best was, in fact, ready to make his first competitive appearance on British soil for two years.

Best had to push his way through an army of photographers as he took his place on the pitch for the first time in Hibs' green and white shirt, so reminiscent of the Northern Ireland jersey he wore with so much pride when he was in his prime.

The game against St Mirren is now in the history books. Best played well enough, scored a last-minute goal, came within inches of another, but still Hibs went down to a 2–1 defeat.

At the end of the game it looked as though the entire population of China had arrived. The corridor outside the away team's dressing room was bursting at the seams as journalists jostled to get into position. Microphones, cameras and notebooks were at the ready.

The door opened slowly and George, the man who had seen it all and done it all several times before, blinked in utter astonishment. The barrage opened immediately and an avalanche of questions – some in broken English – cascaded down on top of him.

Was he happy with his performance? He thought for a brief moment and said, 'I wasn't entirely satisfied. Ask me again in about six games' time and I will be able to tell you. You'll never see the old George Best though. But I think I still have something to contribute.'

How did he feel? 'Obviously I need to get match fit. I wasn't going to run up and down the pitch like a lunatic in the first half and burn myself out. I had to play myself quietly. It would have been nice to have turned on the old style, but that wasn't the game to do it.'

Was he nervous? 'You can say that again! I said to my wife

Angela before the game that I had butterflies. This is a new experience for me. It was worse than playing to a capacity crowd at Wembley.'

Did he enjoy the reaction? 'The fans were fabulous. The chairman, Tommy Hart, told me there were only 6,000 fans at Love Street earlier in the season when Hibs played there.

George leads Hibs onto the pitch.

Almost 14,000 turned up for my debut match and that pleases me. It was good to see that the gate had more than doubled. I'm happy the fans still want to see me. I knew everyone's eyes were on me in that game against St Mirren and that is why I was a bit nervous.'

Did he still think he could play at the highest level even at 33? 'If I can get back to peak fitness then I don't see any reason why I can't. My legs might not be so fast but my head still works, you know. I can still see moves before a lot of other players.'

George handled the questioning superbly and then stepped into a chauffeur-driven Daimler along with his Scottish-born wife Angela and was whisked off to Glasgow airport where he caught the next flight back to his home in London.

It was very clear in the early stages of the momentous Hibernian signing of George Best that it was well worth it with the crowds that turned up to see him display his genius talents on the park. Tony Higgins last saw Best before he had his liver transplant, describing his appearance as 'dreadful', and reminding him of another footballing legend

Jim Baxter who suffered an early death due to his inability to resist the bottle.

Although an alcoholic, George still had the ability to have a laugh at himself. Tony Higgins recalls, 'I remember playing Rangers at Easter Road when we beat them 2–1. In those days dark holes would open up on the terracing as fights broke out. George went to take a corner and the Rangers fans started throwing cans of beer at him. Rather than react, George picked one up, pretended to take a sip from it and put it down by the touchline. It defused the whole situation, they started clapping him for that touch of humour he had.'

When around 18,000 people turned up for Hibs match against Ayr, Willie Murray was booed when he ran out with the number 11 on his back because they'd all turned up to see George. The night before, French rugby captain Jean Pierre Rives had heard Best was staying in the hotel and insisted that he join the party. Best did so with a vengeance and was the last man standing, albeit with difficulty, at the bar the next morning. Hibs sacked Best but Hart relented within a week and Best would remember the chairman fondly. 'Tommy was just like Sir Matt... always giving me another chance.'

Despite the gulf which existed in their lifestyles, team-mate Jackie McNamara and George Best became firm friends, so much so that he returned to Edinburgh to feature in the Easter Road star's testimonial match against Newcastle United.

Jackie McNamara said, 'George was a lovely, lovely man. There were no airs or graces about him. He was well accepted and got on with all the boys. There was no "Billy Big" about him, he wanted to be part of the dressing-room, although he was earning many times our wages.' And

McNamara believes Best should be remembered for his skill as a football player and the pleasure he brought millions of fans rather than for his well-documented battle against drink that ultimately took his life.

The cosmopolitan George Best was always prepared to share his French lotions and deodorants (£100 a bottle) with team-mates more used to carbolic soap. Gordon Rae recalls:

'The whole team would queue up to splash it all over and we'd all go around smelling like George hoping some of his magic would rub off – with women at least if not on the park.'

The drinking binge at the French rugby party was another chapter in the sad decline of one of football's greatest-ever talents, but there were still glimpses of what Best had been. Chairman of Hibs, Tommy Hart, who gave Best numerous chances, was later to admit he had covered up for his wayward star on each occasion by saying he was injured, photographs even being taken of him on the treatment table to confirm the story.

However, Best's drinking was spiralling out of control and his absences increased. He managed only 13 league appearances, although Hibs did get to the semi-final of the Scottish Cup. They were thrashed 5–0 by Celtic and at one stage Bobby Lennox could be seen consoling a frustrated George Best as once again team-mates failed to read his passes.

Sadly, Best's battle with the demon drink was all too evident to his new team-mates and, ultimately, it led to a series of showdowns with Tommy Hart, who once famously declared: 'The marriage between George Best and Hibernian Football Club is over.'

In hindsight, everyone could say that they had known it would never last, and the day that was confirmed the assembled press were thankful that it had happened at all.

George Best's career as a Hibs player may have been short-lived – but his time at Easter Road was as colourful as the rest of his life. Tommy Hart pulled off one of the greatest signing coups in Scottish football, snapping up the wayward former Manchester United and Northern Ireland superstar from Fulham. But in April 1980 George's Hibs career stopped and his football career started again in San Jose.

But that wasn't the last Hibernian fans were to have the pleasure of George Best's company at Easter Road.

On the evening of Monday, 5 October 1981 a challenge match was played against George's new club, the San Jose Earthquakes – the team he signed for following his stint at Hibs.

In the programme for the match, manager Bertie Auld welcomed the Earthquakes: 'San Jose are the first NASL team to play at Easter Road and this is a reciprocal game for the one we played – and thoroughly enjoyed – in California at the end of last season.

'Any team which contains George Best is bound to be a major attraction and I know that Hibs' fans will welcome him back with open arms after his links with the club in the past two seasons.

'George has been a marvellous player throughout his career and, even at 35, he can produce the magic that's always associated with him...'

Also in the programme were extracts from George's life story *Where Do I Go From Here*.

In the book he confessed that 'I could never see why this important English club [Manchester United] should have any interest in some five-foot-tall weakling who had

been rejected by a Belfast club [Glentoran].' He admitted, 'That was my game for Belfast [when Ireland beat Scotland 1–0 in 1967], showing them perhaps for the only time what the boy from Burren Way could do when the mood took him. People there still talk about it as the greatest individual performance in an international and it pleases me that I could give them something memorable.'

George Best's journey during the early part of his thirties took him from the United States to Scotland and back to the United States again – but the thing that followed him wasn't only his popularity, his skills and obvious talents on the ball, it was also the uncontrollable desire he had to have a drink. And once he gave in to that desire the drink became the master and the ultimate headline maker.

Perhaps in his own way George Best did learn to survive; survive between his own self-destruction combined with those that wallowed in his downfall. George wanted people to remember him for his football and, for those of us that really care, that's what we do and will continue to do. George, when close to death, said that he had no regrets – we will just remember him.

SAN JOSE REMEMBERS GEORGE

Pelé's presence in the North American Soccer League gave the whole set-up something it had always lacked credibility around the world. Suddenly, players who had snubbed the possibility of playing in the United States were queueing up to join the League. As a result, there was a sudden influx of top-quality signings not seen since the first American Soccer League's heyday in the 1920s.

NASL teams, hoping that signing a Pelé-like superstar would boost attendance at home the same way Pelé's presence had in 1975, opened their wallets like never before. Seattle Sounders signed striker Geoff Hurst from England, who scored a hat-trick in the 1966 World Cup Final.

Still, some players came over with their skills intact. Tampa Bay purchased flamboyant striker Rodney Marsh from Queens Park Rangers for $80,000. Toronto signed Eusébio away from Boston. Ward Lay dipped into the family crisp firm's fortune to sign former England captain Bobby Moore away from Fulham for San Antonio.

When George Best entered the US football stage, he had already won everything at club level in England and, by the time he reached the United States in 1975, Manchester United were top of the table in the old Second Division.

But what do the US football followers have to say about him now?

The following is taken with kind permission from the *Metro Silicon Valley* and was written by one of their staff writers as a tribute to George just a few days after the sad news of his death. Gary's loose and laid-back style of writing has a fun tone to what he has to say, but the respect he and others had for George is present throughout the column inches he writes in honour to the Best:

The last professional goal George ever scored was for the San Jose Earthquakes.

BEST IN SAN JOSE
By Gary Singh

GEORGE BEST, one of the greatest soccer players in the history of the sport, is no longer with us. The Northern Ireland native passed away last Friday after almost two months of hospitalization. Even a controversial 2002 liver transplant could not stop him from drinking and he always said that alcohol was the only adversary he could never beat. He was right.

During his heyday for Manchester United in the latter days of the Swinging Sixties, Best was universally known as the Fifth Beatle and fans followed him wherever he went. Thousands of 14-year-old girls screamed whenever he touched the ball. The entire concept of the rock-star-millionaire-womanizing-boozing-sports-figure – Best practically invented it. There had never previously been such a flamboyant persona that combined a show business lifestyle with sheer genius on the pitch. He was the first and greatest rock star footballer. The chicks loved him and he did things on the field that no else could do. He was worshipped by millions. You think Dennis Rodman is an 'outrageous' celebrity basketball player? Well, Rodman couldn't hold a punk candle to George Best's antics in his day. Upon hearing of Best's passing, Prime Minister Tony Blair even chimed in with a tribute from the road.

But if there was ever such a thing as a flawed genius, that would be George Best, and he was often lambasted for squandering his talent and his money over the years. He was quoted countless times as saying that he spent his millions on women, booze and cars – and that he wasted the rest.

By the time Best came to play for the San Jose Earthquakes of the old North American Soccer League in 1980, he was more than past his prime, but he still showed occasional flashes of incomparable genius. In 1981 he scored a near-impossible, bordering-on-frightening goal that people are still talking about to this day. He was called for a questionable foul and booked for verbally assaulting the ref afterward. Clearly angered... he took a pass and then went through six Fort Lauderdale players in 25 yards all by himself and blasted home the goal. He even beat one guy twice. Most who attended that match say it was the greatest goal they've ever seen, and it was the 1981 NASL goal of the year. For those of us who were at that game, we will never forget that goal, and he himself said it was the best one he ever scored.

Best was on hand when the first Britannia Arms opened up in Cupertino in 1981. In fact, he was usually in the bar 30 minutes before the games most of the time. The famous 'George Best Pub Crawl' took place whenever game time drew near and nobody knew where the hell he was. They had to go from bar to bar in search of the guy. Best will be remembered by many locals who are still left from those days, and he had many friends here. But that goal was the fondest memory for so many people. The goal was shown, among several others, in many newsreels after he died.

San Jose was also the place where his first marriage fell apart, due to alcoholism and adultery. In his second autobiography, Blessed, *Best had this to say: 'Even if [Angie and I] had a hope of sorting out our life together, it was not going to be in San Jose, which turned out to be the worst place ever for me, in just about every aspect of my life.' He also says that San Jose is where he really hit rock bottom. 'I hated San Jose and, although we had a nice house, which we filled with beautiful furniture, it was situated in the middle of nowhere. And while I tried to help around the house and get things ready for the new arrival [their son], I soon got bored and would head off on another bender... And nothing was going to stop me drinking, not even when Angie started hiding the car keys and all our money.'*

Angie went on to write a book about it all and their son Calum, who was born here when Best played for San Jose, is now a famous model. After Best left the Quakes, he went back to the UK for the 1983 season, but that was it. The last professional goal he ever scored was for the San Jose Earthquakes.

Clearly, George is remembered with fondness and with honesty about this time of his life in the United States. Gary Singh is very proud to boast that he was 'at that game', in May 1981, the game where 'that goal' was scored. George may have been past his prime in those days and Gary himself was only a kid, but he and his mates will never forget that goal.

Gary Singh is also keen for those interested in George Best to know about Brandi Chastain who is one of the most famous US women's players and is a San Jose native. She played in the kids' game at half-time during the match where Best scored that goal where he went through six players. That experience solidified her decision to devote her life to football, and she mentions that game in her book.

Earthquakes Staff

MILAN MANDARIC

The San Jose Earthquakes were just a dream before 1974, when electronics industrialist Milan Mandaric started building San Jose's North American Soccer League franchise. After the first game, with nearly 16,000 fans at Spartan Stadium, Mandaric knew the game had arrived in San Jose.

Mandaric came to the U. S. seven years ago from his native Yugoslavia, and quickly built Lika Corporation into a leading electronic circuit board firm. He played amateur soccer as well as fielded several strong teams in the Peninsula Soccer League before he brought the Quakes to San Jose.

He resides in Saratoga with his wife, Gordana, and two daughters, Jasmina and Aleksandra.

Gary didn't just write an immediate tribute to George following his death. He also used his column in 'Silicon Alleys' (*Metro Silicon Valley*) one year on from George losing his battle for life to remember him.

Columnist Gary Singh delves into the far reaches of the art, music and counter-culture scenes from Los Gatos and Saratoga to San Jose, Santa Clara and beyond. Each week, Gary delivers a healthy dose of opinion, controversy and insight on the real and surreal. What a tribute to George that he used his column to 'Give the Best' to George:

THIS YEAR, GIVE THE BEST
By Gary Singh

Allow me to furnish some belated thanks now that the turkey day has passed us. George Best, one of the greatest footballers in human history, left this earth a year ago last

Saturday. After a way-too-short career in Europe, the Northern Ireland native wound up with the San Jose Earthquakes during the 1980 and 1981 seasons. He died last year on the day after Thanksgiving, and on that fateful morning I stormed into the office and cranked out a last-minute obituary.

Best's son, Calum, was born at Good Samaritan Hospital while Best played for the Earthquakes and, along with the greatest goal of his career, Calum's birth was one

George enjoying life in the USA with the Playboy bunnies.

of the few good memories of Best's stint here. Given Best's constant falling off the wagon, his then-wife Angie famously recalled the sequence of events that led to her to leave him: 'Calum was a year old, I hadn't seen George for a week and I was taking Calum to the doctor for a checkup. I'm driving down the street in San Jose, it's raining – a really miserable day – and in the middle of the street, between the two yellow lines, there's this creature walking towards me, soaking wet, miserable, huddled over like a homeless person, and I realized it was my husband. I looked at my son and thought: I can't do this anymore. I can't look after two babies. The big one has to go. And he did.'

Now, as I finish this missive on the day after Thanksgiving 2006, I must give thanks to Bestie for all the memories, especially that great goal in May of 1981 when he went past six defenders in 25 yards all by himself.

I was not the only one inspired by that performance, you see. A young girl named Brandi Chastain played in the kids' game during halftime at that match and scored a goal herself. Listening to the crowds cheer afterward, along with witnessing Best drive home that now legendary goal, is what cemented her decision to devote her life to soccer.

'When I started playing soccer, I had no role models to inspire me on the field,' she wrote in her book, It's Not About the Bra. *'No one in my neighborhood, or in my family, played the game. But the very first time I saw the professional team that would become my guiding light, the San Jose Earthquakes, I found my role model. He was George Best, and in my mind, the name fit. Watching him corkscrew bewildered defenders into the ground with his amazing moves and a smile on his face, I said to myself, That's what I want to do.'*

Anyway, back in the '60s, Best vaulted to worldwide stardom as a teenager and, according to Phil Hughes, his manager, Best was never allowed to own his own life ever since. He was constantly thrashing it out with pesky, irritating reporters who hounded him. Whenever he got into a barroom brawl, the media were right there looking for stupid sensational material to feed on. In Scoring at Halftime, *Best recalls a holiday in Cyprus where he became ill, only to have reporters track him down in his hotel room. They wanted to hear that he'd fallen off the wagon again or, even better, if he was dying. They just weren't satisfied that he had a simple virus. The hospital administrator then showed up and told him the reporters wanted to know if he was HIV-positive. Best said, 'Tell them, yes, I am HIV – heavily into vodka. That'll shut them up.'*

There you have it. Why Best isn't in the San Jose Sports Hall of Fame, I'll never know.

The general opinion in the United States was that he was a flawed genius and that they took for granted how lucky they were to actually have seen George play in person. He may have been ridiculed for having to wind up in San Jose after having been on top of the world, but, for those that were fortunate to have seen him play, they 'were blessed'.

WHEN A HERO COMES ALONG

When George Best tells his own dramatic and inspiring story in *Blessed* the blurb explains that 'George Best was blessed with an extraordinary gift; he brought beauty and grace to soccer never before seen. But he was unable to cope with the success and fame his genius brought and his life story is littered with tales of women, sex and, of course, drink.' This was written a few years after his infamous comment, 'In 1969 I gave up women and alcohol – it was the worst 20 minutes of my life.'

As the world said goodbye to George on Saturday, 3 December 2005, *Scotland on Sunday* newspaper reported that 'from among the crowds of people as his coffin was carried out from the flower-strewn Best family home, spontaneous applause broke out among the surrounding crowd. Single red roses were thrown in front of the funeral cortege by women…'

More likely than not, women probably came very high on George Best's list of priorities. Whether it was Alex, Mary, Angie or Susan to name just a few, George enjoyed being with women. And, in fairness to George, women enjoyed being with him. Football gates increased in number including women wanting to get a glimpse of the maestro in his football kit – even though many of them didn't know or weren't even the slightest bit interested in wanting to know about football.

Throughout George's life, the good times, the bad times and the indifferent times, women have been there.

So it may come as no surprise that in 1981 George Best became the influence and role model to a young North American girl when she witnessed his near-impossible goal scoring in action when he was playing for the San Jose Earthquakes.

Brandi, famous for stripping off her football shirt,
was inspired to play football having seen George play.

Our thanks go to Gary Singh of the *Metro News* in San Jose who wrote the following article on the young girl who became a famous footballer in the United States – and all because of George Best.

STRIPPED

Soccer sensation Brandi Chastain gets underneath the underwear episode to the heart of her feelings about sportsmanship and role models.

Everyone's seen the photo. The one where Brandi Chastain tore off her jersey after driving home the winning penalty kick in the 1999 Women's World Cup in front of 90,000 screaming fans at the Rose Bowl. That now famous snapshot of her in a sports bra graced the covers of Time, Newsweek, Sports Illustrated *and who knows how many other magazines.*

The San Jose native's recent book, It's Not About the Bra, *spills her thoughts on sportsmanship, competition, youth sports, leadership, coaching and smiling. It combines inspiring essays from fellow players and friends as well as anecdotes from her long career with the women's national team. She writes about teamwork, finding role models and using sports – especially soccer – as a metaphor for dealing with the ups and downs of life.*

A main impetus behind the project was to tackle the ever-growing violence in youth sports – you know, those belligerent parents who push their kids too far, scream at them, threaten them, or instruct the kids to beat up someone on the opposing squad. Along with co-author Gloria Averbuch, Brandi took the idea and turned it into a declaration to parents and children about the game of life.

'There's a lot of pressure on kids to excel and do the best, and when we ask that of our kids, and we're unrealistic for them, I think we put them in a very uncomfortable, very negative environment,' Chastain said over the phone. 'And I just wanted to make parents responsible for their actions like we ask our kids to be responsible for their actions.'

Chastain writes that her passion for the sport solidified as she grew up attending the old North American Soccer League's San Jose Earthquakes and watching the legendary George Best. In 1981, he scored a near-

impossible, bordering-on-frightening goal that people are still talking about. Angry with the ref for calling a foul and booking him, the Northern Irishman took a pass and went through six defenders in 25 yards all by himself and scored. Brandi was on one of the youth teams that played during half time at that match, and to the crowd's roar, she also scored a goal. George Best became her inspiration and at that moment she realized she was meant for soccer.

'When I started playing soccer, I had no role models to inspire me on the field', she wrote in the book. 'No one in my neighborhood, or in my family, played the game. But the very first time I saw the professional team that would become my guiding light, the San Jose Earthquakes, I found my role model. He was George Best, and in my mind, the name fit. Watching him corkscrew bewildered defenders into the ground with his amazing moves and a smile on his face, I said to myself, That's what I want to do.'

What a terrific tribute and indeed compliment that is to George, who perhaps would never have guessed on that day in 1981 when another one of his wonder goals was scored and recorded in the archives and memories of those that saw him in action, that a young girl took a turning point in her life. At that point, hitherto unknown Brandi Chastain saw her hero George Best on the football pitch and made a life-changing decision to become a footballer and all because he had inspired her to do so.

This clearly wasn't just another female linked with the name George Best, it was one of those moments in his life where doing what he did best (playing football) influenced and changed the direction of the life of a young girl in the United States to whom George Best was a champion.

GEORGE'S HUMOUR TRAVELS
ACROSS THE POND

Ron Gilmore was a clubhouse kid for the NASL San Jose Earthquakes during the time that George Best played for his team. He has many fond and funny memories of George, and in particular the following story of George making sure an injustice was dealt with in his own unique way.

During the 1981 season, I [Ron] was a young assistant who worked in the dressing room working for the kit man. George Best was in his first year with the NASL San Jose Earthquakes. During training sessions, my responsibility among others was to retrieve balls that were spread across the field. In fact, the manager often used my twin brother Rob and I in drills. To be on the same field with George Best during this time was an honor [sic].

George had an outrageous sense of humour and, after training one day, he called Jimmy McAlister, one of the best American defenders at the time, over as the rest of the team were heading into the showers. We were still on the practice field.

Bestie told McAlister, 'Jimmy, $100 says my pal Ron can convert more pks [penalty kicks] against Huey [Mike Hewitt, the starting goalkeeper for the team] than you can!' McAlister laughed out loud and said, 'You're on!'

Best then told McAlister that he had to take all five of his kicks first, prior to any of mine, and McAlister said, 'No problem, Bestie, this will be like stealing candy from a baby!'

McAlister then proceeded to take his five kicks and he converted on three of the five. Then it was my turn. As

180

soon as I stepped up to take my first shot, Huey told me to wait a moment. Huey then bent down and laid down horizontally along the goal line and said, 'Okay, Ron, fire away!'

I then quickly took four shots and easily converted them over the lying-down goalkeeper! I was laughing so hard I could barely do it! Bestie as well was amused, he had tears from laughing so hard coming down his face!

Bestie then told a speechless McAlister, 'F*** it, Jimmy, you don't owe, the look of disbelief on your face is f*****g priceless!'

George then took two $50 bills out and handed one to me and one to Huey who was obviously in on the ruse!

George then put his arm around me and walked with me back to the locker room. He told me to look at him like he was just one of the guys, not George Best from Manchester United. He then stuck his hand out, shook my hand and winked at me! It was a moment that will live in my heart forever!

DREAMS CAN BECOME REALITY

Belfast's Glentoran and Manchester United: what could these two clubs have in common? In reality it's George Best that links the clubs together.

Many former Glentoran players, such as Danny Blanchflower, Peter Doherty, Bertie Peacock, Billy Bingham, Jimmy McIlroy, have gone on to play for teams in England and Scotland, but nowhere is George Best's name mentioned in that roll of honour.

In 1914 Glentoran won the Vienna Cup, becoming the first British or Irish team to win a European trophy. However, Glentoran's finest hour came in a European Cup

THE GLENTORAN GAZETTE

GLENTORAN
v
MANCHESTER UTD.

Saturday 14th August, 1982
Kick-off 3 p.m.

SOUVENIR PROGRAMME 50p

encounter with Benfica in 1967, just one year before the mighty reds, Manchester United, beat Benfica in the European Cup Final in their history-making game at Wembley. The 1967 tie was played over two legs, the first being at the Oval where Glentoran scored a penalty early on and held out for nearly 60 minutes until football great Eusébio equalised. The match ended 1–1.

Glentoran must have gone into the return tie at Benfica's famous Estádio da Luz with some certain Irish confidence. Many thought that the part-timers would crumble under the pressure of the occasion but again they held out for a famous draw. It was only the away-goals rule that allowed Benfica to go through to the next round.

So what about George Best? Yes, he was born in Belfast but what links him with Glentoran?

Let's go back to the young lad from the streets of Belfast. Quite simply, George Best watched Glentoran with his grandfather as a youth and cheered his then heroes on to many a victory, and presumably on a Boxing Day duel between the Belfast Big Two.

Like every boy, George must have dreamed of playing for his team, wearing his team colours with pride, but unfortunately he was rejected by the club for being 'too small and light'. How the club management must have kicked themselves just a few years later.

However, George did eventually make one appearance for Glentoran, in the club's centenary match against, you've guessed it, Manchester United on 14 August 1982. But, the matchday programme doesn't give evidence of that fact – so it's just as well that a supporter who was there recalls that George not only played in the centenary celebrations, he also captained his boyhood favourites against his old club Manchester United.

From the whole match, the greatest memory of the game for one particular supporter was when George gave Ray Wilkins the run-around on the pitch, and was in fact fouled quite painfully by the then hirsute Wilkins. The absolute class of George was still with him: as he picked himself up from the foul, he also picked up the ball and handed it to Ray with an aside, 'There, have it… ' (the ball that is).

The young boy George, who kept his granddad company on many an occasion at the Oval ground in Belfast, watching his favourite players conjure up magic with the ball, had to wait until almost the end of his career to fulfil his boyhood dream. Perhaps he never let that dream go; maybe he often wondered why his team had rejected him. Possibly one thing all of us can learn from George's experience is to always hold on to your dreams and vision and to never let anyone take them away from you. George's life journey took him to the great and the mighty, to fame and fortune, through the ups and the downs of his life, but he returned to his boyhood roots, to where he had at one time been discarded because of his size, to fulfil his dream.

George's great dream was accomplished – to the delight of so many of his fellow countrymen and women watching on the terraces of Glentoran Football Club – but perhaps mostly to the delight of himself.

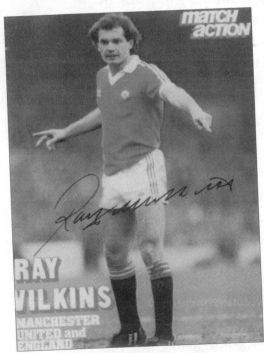

Ray Wilkins

DOWN BUT NOT OUT!

Just in case you ever encounter the question 'What do Henry Ford, Oscar Wilde and George Best have in common?' at your local pub-quiz night, the answer is that all, at some time in their lives, filed for bankruptcy. Instead of Henry Ford or Oscar Wilde names such as Donald Trump, Bjorn Borg and Abraham Lincoln could also be included in the same question. But, for some unknown reason, whenever anything is written about George Best's life (and particularly since his death), his filing, and appearance in court for bankruptcy is always mentioned.

A cheque signed by the man himself.

During the early part of his career, George had everything: good looks, long hair, unlimited money, a white Jag and legions of adoring fans. He exploded onto the football scene with outstanding natural talent, wearing his football shirt outside of his shorts and at times with his socks pushed down to his ankles. George Best was different in many ways. He was the first footballer equivalent to the emerging pop stars of the 1960s, with fan- club branches in Moscow and Tokyo. Whatever he did made the gossip pages. This exposure followed him through the dizzy heights of winning

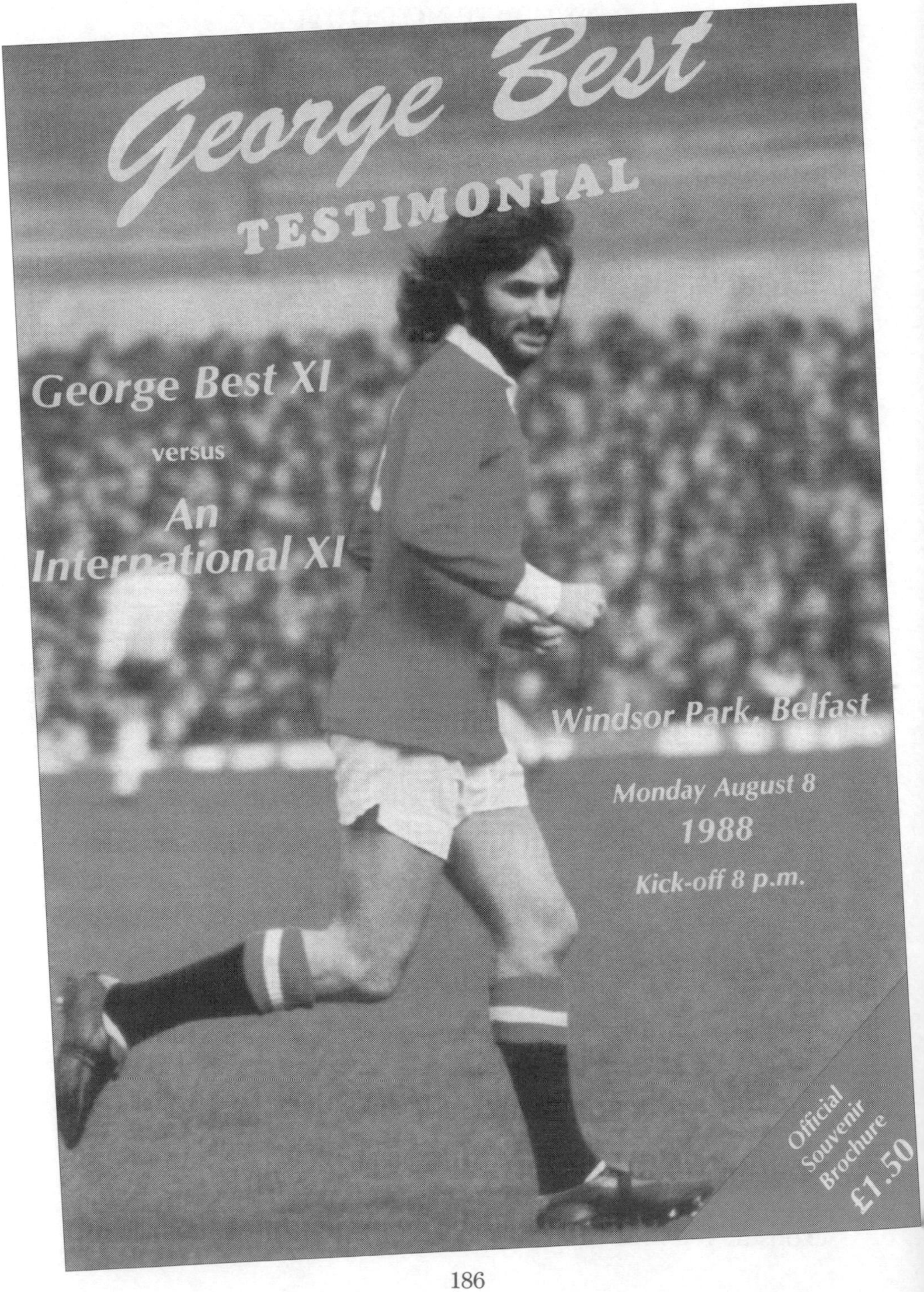

George Best
TESTIMONIAL

George Best XI

versus

An
International XI

Windsor Park, Belfast

Monday August 8
1988
Kick-off 8 p.m.

Official
Souvenir
Brochure
£1.50

cups, trophies and accolades and perhaps even more so through the decline of his career and his departure from Manchester United.

Malcolm Brodie, then the sports editor of the *Belfast Telegraph*, who covered all of Best's games for Northern Ireland, said, 'George had a phenomenal career, he was a fantastic footballer. He was one of the best in the world, up there with Pelé, Maradona, Cruyff and Eusébio. George had everything and some of his performances were outstanding. In 1967, at Windsor Park, he took Scotland apart in a 1–0 victory. I do not think there has been a finer display of football than that day. You could not write a book about his personal life, as it was incident-packed. He often hit that self-destruct button, but he was a wonderful person and was his own harshest critic.'

George auctioning memorabilia.

Frequent and unexplained upheavals with club management were seen at the time as the actions of a fractious athlete. Later, it came to light that Best had a drinking problem. In 1982, while playing in San Jose, California, Best was suspended indefinitely by the club and entered an alcohol rehabilitation programme.

When George returned to Britain in 1982 after his season with the San Jose Earthquakes, he was met with a tax bill for £16,000. He offered to pay £10,000 immediately and the rest in six months, but was told that this was not acceptable. During a bankruptcy hearing in London in

1983, Best told the court, 'I am an alcoholic. My drinking over the last 12 years has been the root of my trouble.'

George and Calum

Just hours after his court appearance for failing to pay back taxes, George was hit over the head with a beer glass in a London pub. On top of all that, for George, the result of the unacceptable £10,000 down payment was a ten-year wrangle that, with the compound interest, cost him more than £60,000 to settle. Just before Christmas the following year, he was jailed for three months for drink driving, assaulting a policeman and jumping bail.

Four years later, with the help of £75,708 raised by a

testimonial match, George began to emerge from the shadow of bankruptcy. Malcolm Brodie said, 'I watched him throughout his career and dealt with him. I helped organise his testimonial, which raised the finance and got him out of bankruptcy. But he was a generous person, not a mercenary, and did a lot for charity.'

George Best was one of many that faced bankruptcy, the famous and the not so famous, but not all have their personal financial embarrassment as headline news. At the time of his bankruptcy George also had to deal with his increasing addiction to alcohol. Every person going through bankruptcy feels alone or that they are the only ones suffering from the stress and strain of financial struggles, and George would have been no different. He would have felt alone in a crowded world where some people feed off the downfall of others, even though it would have been just as easy to give some kind of support and encouragement.

Thank goodness George still had those real people around him who wanted to be there for him. Ultimately, his popularity and skills on the football pitch freed him from bankruptcy. For his testimonial a 25,000-strong crowd, the largest in Belfast for 20 years, braved persistent rain to pay homage to the man George Best.

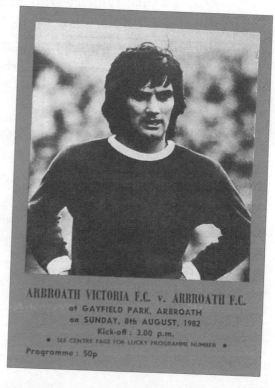

ARBROATH VICTORIA F.C. v. ARBROATH F.C.
at GAYFIELD PARK, ARBROATH
on SUNDAY, 8th AUGUST, 1982
Kick-off : 3.00 p.m.
• SEE CENTRE PAGE FOR LUCKY PROGRAMME NUMBER •
Programme : 50p

THE BEST IN SWINDON

Sounds a bit dramatic, doesn't it? George Best: The Swindon Connection. As if the lovely Wiltshire town had some sort of clandestine effect on the career of arguably the world's greatest footballer. As if Swindon made a difference in the life and times of a soccer legend – it's not that! It's that Swindon saw the very best – and at times the worst – of George Best during his life. For 40 years, he both thrilled Swindonians on the pitch and, once or twice, frustrated them off it. But that was George.

Heather Hewlett Fundraiser 1982

George Best's last playing appearance in Swindon earned him the then princely sum of £300. That was the amount the *Evening Advertiser* stumped up to secure the services of the former European Footballer of the Year at a special game in aid of Heather Hewlett, the widow of speedway rider Martin Hewlett, who had died earlier that year.

It was an all-star game that not only included some of football's best-known names (Channon, Rogers and Summerbee) but also other sporting celebrities such as cricket's Viv Richards and Swindon's own champion jockey John Francome.

Best's show helped boost the attendance to over 7,000, and contributed in swelling the charity's coffers by over £5,000. The 36-year-old Best even ended up on the winning side, triumphing 12–9! He scored five goals.

On stage
George Best & Rodney Marsh
Questions and Answers at
The Wyvern 1992

When George Best arrived in Swindon in November 1992, his playing career was well and truly at an end. He hadn't played since turning out for lowly Bournemouth AFC in 1983, and it was the theatre and after-dinner circuit that was paying the bills (or tax demands, depending on whether the Inland Revenue were in touch or not).

He had formed a formidable partnership with former team-mate Rodney Marsh and they had sold out venues across the country with their question and answer show 'An Evening with Best and Marsh'. It was two hours of brilliant entertainment. Best at his charming best; and Marsh contributing with equal verve in what one person who attended described as 'a dream night for any football fan'.

Both amusingly recounted their halcyon days at Fulham in the 1970s, and at Manchester United and City during the Swinging Sixties. Never ones to finish a good night at 10.30 pm, Best and Marsh then continued their comedic partnership in the bar at the Thistle Hotel afterwards as well, signing autographs and enjoying a drink with fans like Swindon was their home town. By all accounts they finally called it a night at 4 am. Vintage Best!

Premiership Forum 1994

As part of Sky Sports coverage of the Premiership in 1993/94, the television channel held an 'Experts Forum' at the venue of their Monday night 'Live' game, and on 4 April 1994, the one and only George Best was a guest panellist at the County Ground alongside Swindon Town F.C.'s Don Rogers.

Both reported on another disappointing defeat for Swindon, who lost 1–0 to Sheffield Wednesday in front of 13,927 fans. Diplomatically, Best did try to put a positive shine on the Robins' performance, but even he couldn't hide the fact that Town were staring relegation in the face – and leaking too many goals.

It was such a dismal game that it could have driven anyone to drink. Not George! He surprisingly looked sober all night.

FA Cup Thrashing 1977
Fulham Fall-Guys: Bobby Moore, George Best and Rodney Marsh

This was almost Swindon Town versus the Harlem Globetrotters. An FA Cup mismatch if ever there was one. Swindon had John Trollope, Ray McHale and errr... no one else we can remember. Fulham had George Best, Rodney Marsh and England's World Cup-winning captain Bobby Moore. Except these footballing legends hadn't managed to see off the Swindon Town boys in the first match. It had ended 3–3 at Craven Cottage on a chilly 8 January 1977. Moore and Best were so confident of victory they'd been out 'til 5 am the night before.

Three days later, though, Fulham's long-toothed galacticos got the thrashing of their lives – 5–0 in the replay! Swindon Town ran riot! Best, Marsh and Moore didn't run at all.

Whether they had been on another of their famous King's Road pre-match warm-ups, no one knows, but, while Swindon Town fans celebrated, the three amigos trudged off never to feature in the FA Cup again.

In a sad bit of symmetry, Best had started his career with an historic youth team win over Town in 1964; and he ended it here with a performance that was so off-key some Town fans can't even remember him playing.

De Vere No Show 1996
Gone AWOL: George Best

Over 200 guests had paid £50 to hear him tell humorous tales of scoring both on and off the pitch. All had dressed up in their best bib and tucker. George Best, footballing icon, was the star guest at a special Sportsman's Dinner at the De Vere Hotel, Swindon, in spring 1996. Even his manager had calmed the organisor's nerves by confirming that she had bid farewell to her sober client at Paddington Station at 6 pm.

Except he never arrived! What he found on the 125-Intercity train to Swindon that distracted him no one will ever know. The usual suspects Johnny Walker and Jack Daniels were the hot favourites, though. Strong rumours of a beauty pageant taking place in Swansea were also blamed.

At 10.30 pm, with George un-contactable, the miserable decision was finally made to announce that the main attraction wasn't coming. 'Unforeseen circumstances' was given as the official reason for Best's no-show.

The evening was partially saved by free drinks at the bar and a quick routine by a comedian. He even quipped that George had been delayed launching a ship – but that the vessel had gone seven miles out to sea by the time they got the bottle of champagne out of Bestie's hand!

Mike Summerbee – the 1960s
Best Buddy: Mike Summerbee

George Best's glorious heyday was surely the 1960s. Christened 'El Beatle' by the Press, he lived a superstar lifestyle where he somehow managed to fit booze, birds and boutiques in between scoring magical goals for Manchester United. He well and truly lived the playboy dream, and his best friend during these heady times was none other than former Swindon Town legend Mike Summerbee.

After playing over 200 games for the Robins and becoming a firm fans' favourite at the County Ground for six years from 1959, Summerbee swapped the quiet life of Swindon for the bright lights of Manchester City in 1965.

And then he met George Best!

Immediately they became the best of friends, and almost inseparable in their quest to sample everything Manchester's nightlife had to offer.

In 1966, they opened a boutique together called Edwardia as they enjoyed the bachelor lifestyle to the full. 'We were both single and basically had the time of our lives,' Summerbee said. George even helped Mike meet his wife, when he introduced the pair at a nightclub in Manchester. The partying only ending in 1969, when Summerbee married. George was, of course, the best man.

And so there you are! What does a '60s icon, who was a footballing genius and national superstar, have to do with the pretty town in Wiltshire? Quite easy really, Swindon's loose connection with the talent of a genius was none other than George Best.

Many thanks to Phil Poulton for the use of some information from Swindonweb.

AFC Bournemouth
March 1983 – May 1983

24/3/83 Signs contract

26/4/83 Home debut v Newport
Crowd of 9,121

16/4/83 Final away game v Southend
Crowd of 4,275

11/10/80 Final home game v Wigan
Crowd of 4,523

He was 15 days short of his 37th birthday

Appearances	Goals
5	0

THE CHERRY ON AFC BOURNEMOUTH'S CAKE

'Love him or hate him George Best certainly fires the imagination of fans and reporters alike' was the club comment in the programme for the last ever match he played for AFC Bournemouth. George essentially finished his legendary soccer career in San Jose, scoring 21 goals in 56 games from 1980/81. After returning for one last season with AFC Bournemouth in the Second Division, Best retired for good in 1983 at the age of 37.

It is interesting to note that Northern Ireland finally made it back to the World Cup in 1982 while 37-year-old

Best was with AFC Bournemouth. Ironically, one of the stars for them in Spain that summer was a 17-year-old prodigy called Norman Whiteside, a Manchester United youth player discovered by Bob Bishop, who a generation earlier had sent a telegram from Belfast to Matt Busby with the legend 'I think I've found a genius' upon his sighting of one George Best.

But how did George end up with the Cherries?

The very last programme to have the legendary George Best as part of a football team was when AFC Bournemouth played against Wigan Athletic, 7 May 1983. In it was an explanation of how and why George graced the south coast with his genius: 'Now a more portly 36, George Best is anxious to once more regain acclaim of soccer's public after years in the wilderness wasted on gambling, drinking and fast cars. And Bournemouth's fresh-faced new manager Don Megson, who laments a dearth of star quality in the game today, was pleased to give him the opportunity.'

'We sat down and talked about the situation at Dean Court and I felt that bringing George in the team would not be weakened and it would provide a real star name for the fans,' explained Megson.

George also played an important role off the field as well, helping the new management team take the Cherries to their public. George said, 'The one thing I learned from playing in the United States was how important it is to get involved in the community… We are trying to do this here and the kids love it when we go out and coach them.'

For George it was good to hear the cheers once more and he said, 'The crowd have been tremendous towards me. We are in a position now where we are safe so we can concentrate on planning for next season which is the important thing.'

But it wasn't to be 'next season' for George Best. Not only was AFC Bournemouth v Wigan Athletic the last game he played for Bournemouth, it was also the last professional game he was ever to play. How would the referee for the day (although on the programme he was down as linesman), W. T. Phillips have known that he was reffing such a momentous, but somehow very sad match – of course he couldn't have known, but what he did do was to get the programme signed by George. Certainly something to keep to show the grandchildren!

The then manager of AFC Bournemouth commented, 'From my own point of view, and even more important the players, the short time George has spent with us he has been a great guy, trains hard, loves the game and joins in everything with enthusiasm without any superstar fuss. Whatever the future holds for George and he is not with us next year, I feel sure all at the club will join me in wishing him well.'

But life goes on. And on 20 May 2005 a website article was posted regarding another great find at AFC Bournemouth with a question in the title – 'The next best thing?' it makes interesting reading:

...Curtis Allen, apparently. A 17-year-old Bournemouth youth player: 'a young David Beckham' and 'the Irish Rooney'. He has scored 37 goals in 33 games this season.

'George Best, another phenomenal player from Northern Ireland, watched Curtis Allen play in a soccer match seven years ago. "This boy is one to watch out for. He's fantastic", Best said of the then 10-year-old Allen. The December 2004 edition of the "UEFA Champions League" magazine reported that Allen was one of five young players to watch out for in Europe.'

George commented, 'There are very few entertainers around now which is a shame for the game. It is still our national sport and the only way to bring back the crowds is to entertain them and that can only happen through individuals.'

George Best certainly lived up to that comment! Whatever situation he found himself in he definitely entertained, at times he was not under-stood and even more times he was used as cannon fodder for the press. No matter what, Saturday, 7 May 1983 was definitely a poignant day – it was the end of an era that spanned over 20 years and encap-sulated a life in football that started with the genius, the lad

off the streets of Belfast and ended in George Best still with that special something, and still 'being a nice guy' with the Cherries in Bournemouth.

Brisbane Lions
(Struggling Team)

3 July 1983 – 17 July 1983

3/7/83 Debut v Sydney Olympic
Won 2–1

8/7/83 v St George (H)
Lost 3–0

10/7/83 v Marconi (A)
Drew 1-1

17/7/83 Last game 0–4 home defeat
1,600 crowd

Appearances	Goals
4	0

Osborne Park Galeb

24 July 1983

24/7/83 v Melville Alemannia, won 2–1
Crowd approx 2,000

Appearances	Goals
1	0

EXTRA TIME

Tobermore
28 January 1984

Tobermore v Ballymena United
Irish Cup, lost 7–0

Appearances	Goals
1	0

TOBERMORE UNITED – WHO ARE THEY?

As the dawn of 1984 broke through the chimes of Big Ben and the reverberations of Auld Lang Syne, the more sceptical may have been considering that this turning point from 1983 to 1984 was in fact the beginning of Orwell's *Nineteen Eighty-Four* portrayal of the dangers of a perfect totalitarian society and the most extreme realisation of a modern-day government with absolute power. Others, in particular the 338 athletes from Great Britain and Northern Ireland, would certainly have been looking forward to the summer Olympics in Los Angeles, California.

For some in a small town in Northern Ireland, January 1984 meant a once-in-a-club's-lifetime footballing signing! Maurice Curry (Chairman), Councillor Ivan Linton and Billy Patterson (Manager), all from Tobermore – meaning 'The Great Well' – a small village in County Londonderry, Northern Ireland with a population of under 600, had dug deep into the well of footballing excellence and signed the 'greatest footballer in the world' to Fortwilliam Park, the home of Tobermore United.

Tobermore United was experiencing its first season in the

Irish League 'B' Division and had been drawn at home to Ballymena United in the first round of the Bass Irish Cup.

In the programme of the day, 28 January 1984, Maurice Curry said, 'I have great pleasure in extending a very special welcome to George [Best] and to thank him for coming here today. It is a marvellous opportunity for us all to see his great footballing talents.' It was hard for the South Derry fans to believe that they would have the chance to see this Irish International display his famous and much-talked-about footballing skills up close.

George Best was now 37 years of age, but, apart from playing international games at Windsor Park, the match between Tobermore United and Ballymena United was to be his first competitive game in the province. The game became an all-ticket affair and, as 28 January approached, those possessing a ticket clung on to it with anticipation.

Unfortunately, due to bad weather, the ground became unplayable and the match was called off but rescheduled for the following Wednesday. How much longer had the fans got to wait for George Best to play his first non-international game of football in his home country? The newly scheduled date of 1 February draw large crowds, but they were again disappointed as referee Jackie Poucher from Newry declared that the pitch conditions were yet again unplayable.

Was this a jinx to prevent Tobermore having the

experience, flair and sheer quality of George Best grace Fortwilliam Park?

Eventually, the following Wednesday (9 February) over 3,000 fans packed into Fortwilliam Park to witness this unique occasion in George Best's career. Unfortunately, the crowds went home disappointed and didn't see much of George's enchantment on the park.

Ballymena United with the Irish International goalkeeper Jim Platt went 2–0 up within the first 10 minutes. In the second half, the opposing team saw another five goals go over the line and hit the netting making the debut of George Best's non-international career in Northern Ireland part of a 7–0 defeat, with Ballymena eventually going on to win the cup.

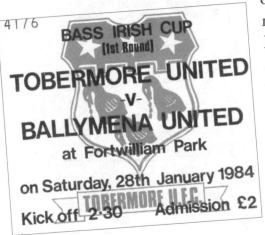

As some recompense, the crowds did see George come close to scoring in the closing minutes as a long-range shot went flying past the post.

Were the fans downhearted? Not likely!

Before and after the match they had the opportunity for George to sign autographs, and he did in their hundreds. And even in defeat actually being there in February 1984 when the great George Best played for their team and having his presence on the park made it such a historic occasion for everyone.

One young man, Steve Gilbert, was lucky enough to go to the Tobermore match. His family was best mates with the family that put up the money for George's fees on the night (he thinks the fee was around £2,000) and his flight to

George with young Steve, who skipped school to see the match.

Northern Ireland. The family owned a restaurant called Crawfords, which was closed for the evening so that George could dine in peace. But why was Steve there? Unfortunately, his Dad missed the match because he had to

George at Crawfords.

take Steve's sister to Durham and the Crawfords were looking after George for the day. What a day to choose! Steve not only got to watch the match, he was also invited to the meal at Crawfords where he was lucky enough to get photographs with the man himself. What a treat for a young Irish man.

Because of the match being cancelled and rescheduled for an evening, Steve was in a dilemma. He was at grammar school at the time, and no way was study more important to him than going to the match. He remembers being driven to the match in a Jaguar with the restauarant owner's son and getting out of the car when immediately the television cameras were on them. Imagine that – and, more importantly, Steve recalls thinking that he hoped his headmaster didn't see him on television when he should have been studying. Obviously not, as he lived to tell the tale.

Councillor Ivan Linton stated in his message within the programme, 'Despite the unrest that is with us all in this South Londonderry area, I believe that Tobermore United, whether win or lose, will give much credit and honour to the whole Magherafelt District by their courage and determination to keep playing football.'

Yes, there was still unrest in Northern Ireland and conflict between nations in 1984. In fact, later in the year, in October, the IRA detonated a bomb at the Grand Hotel, Brighton where Prime Minister Margaret Thatcher and her cabinet were staying during the Conservative Party conference. Five people were killed and several MPs seriously injured. But, amidst all that tragedy and turmoil, in a small town in County Londonderry many hearts were thrilled because of one man. George Best. Their memories of that day would stay etched within their hearts and minds.

A BRUSH WITH THE LAW

George Orwell's *Nineteen Eighty-Four* tells the story of Winston Smith and his degradation by the totalitarian state in which he lives. It also deals with his forbidden sexual relationship with Julia and shows his eagerness to rebel against the ruling party. The later part of the novel shows Winston being captured by the party and his imprisonment in the 'Ministry of Love'.

So what has all this got to do with George Best? Or perhaps the similarities are obvious...

George received a great deal of media attention when he was sent away for drink driving and assaulting a policeman.

In December 1984, Frank Keating wrote in the *Guardian*, 'Through the drizzly mock-gaiety of London's Christmas lights yesterday evening, the newspaper placards almost seemed pleased with themselves. Come-uppance at last. Christmas behind bars. In a way, it has taken an

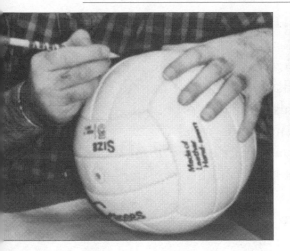

George doing porridge. *Clockwise from top left*: signing a football; being taken away by the police; with the other prisoners.

awesome and awful long time in coming to this.' George had been jailed.

In Keating's favour, however, he did admit that it was 'painful and horrible, dammit, yesterday's news still came as an awful blow, surely to any sports lover…'

George Best's personal life had become increasingly more difficult, with bouts of alcoholism, bankruptcy and the failure of his first marriage. A once great player, George was left to hawk his talents from pillar to post around the world before finally retiring from the game in 1983. Then, in 1984, he was convicted of drink driving and assaulting a policeman, and was jailed for 12 weeks. An appeal failed, and George spent Christmas in Pentonville Prison. During his prison term he did turn out for one more team – Ford Open Prison.

George claimed that the experience made him turn over a new leaf, but eight months later he was bound over for assaulting a man in a London pub. In 1998 he agreed, under pain of eviction, to leave the Chelsea flat he had lived in for the previous 13 years. He was £70,000 in mortgage arrears.

Some may say that it was an ignominious end to what should have been a glorious career for Britain's best ever footballer.

But, as the prison doors closed on George Best and he faced a Christmas behind bars, the judge called his three-month sentence 'neither excessive nor unduly deserved'.

The question should have been asked whether prison was the right place for George Best. No one can deny that he was found guilty of drink driving and assaulting a police officer, but other than Pentonville Jail XI what good would a prison sentence do for someone who was an alcoholic? George needed help with the disease that eventually killed him. Quite ironic that around the same time as George was imprisoned for an offence related to drinking the Labour Party issued a report, 'Cold Comfort', which suggested that the country needed a proactive not a reactive alcohol policy.

And so, when George's appeal was dismissed, he was driven off by car to Pentonville Jail where he spent the first few days of his prison term. By January 1985 George had been moved to Ford Open Prison where he joined other inmates in their daily shuffle around the compound. He admitted later that he found the whole experience degrading and made sure that he gained maximum remission for good behaviour.

But that wasn't the end of George's relationship with Ford Open Prison. In January 1986, just one year later, George returned to the prison – not because he had to, but by his own choosing. He organised a celebrity team to take on the inmates XI at Bognor – not something that was splashed across the headlines and blaring out from placards.

Consider the betrayed revolution, with which George Orwell had famously dealt in *Animal Farm*; the subordination of individuals to 'the Party' in *Nineteen Eighty-Four* and the rigorous distinction between inner party, outer party and everyone else. The judge's sentence, although perfectly proper, did not effect any rehabilitation of George who, on 2 February 2004, was convicted of another drink-driving offence and banned from driving for 20 months. So much for prison helping George to rehabilitate!

WEMBLEY STADIUM IS
ENHANCED BY THE BEST

'From a personal point of view, one of my favourite memories of Wembley was the 1987 FA Cup final between Spurs and Coventry City,' said John Motson of the match on Saturday 16 May. 'I was fortunate enough to commentate on that game and I felt, from a footballing perspective, that was one of the most memorable cup games of the late 20th century.' When you consider the memories Motto must hold of Wembley, that's quite an accolade.

What could have made this game so memorable to John Motson?

George playing in a
testimonial game
for Reading.

Probably the fact that the Sky Blues of Coventry City recovered from the shock of going behind to a Clive Allen goal in under two minutes to win the 106th FA Cup Final in exciting style. A classic match between Coventry City and Tottenham Hotspur of fluctuating fortunes, hard on the emotions of the two sets of supporters, was finally settled by a desperate own goal six minutes into muscle-cramping extra time.

John Motson was among the 98,000 people who watched that game in the stadium with the now long-gone, famous Wembley twin towers. Two other people were also among the crowd, one particular person there to support his team and the other an invited, distinguished guest whose past glories on the pitch would make him welcome to any footballing event – George Best. Both with lives worlds apart but brought together around the beautiful game.

As part of the absolute delight of seeing his team get to Wembley for the FA Cup, the football fan decided to take

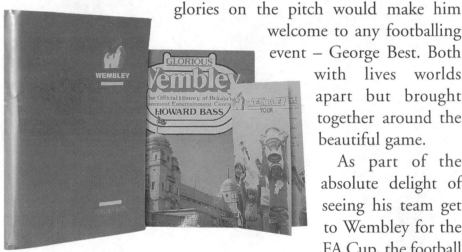

The Wembley folder signed by George.

a guided tour of the stadium. In doing so he was given a promotional folder full of books, postcards and posters, all relating to the history of Wembley Stadium. However, what made it even more special was that George Best took time out to sign the Wembley folder for him as he was walking through the backrooms of Wembley. Always time for people, George.

In 1983, George finally retired from the game, at the age of 37. His last games as a professional were with AFC Bournemouth, although he did go on to play four games for Brisbane Lions and one game for Tobermore United.

Just imagine how many fond memories George must have of playing at Wembley, even if he didn't actually receive an FA Cup winners medal! By 1987 he hadn't played competitive football for at least three years, but George was still held in high esteem by the footballing world – enough to be invited to the FA Cup that day, and enough to make the day even more memorable for one football fan in particular.

THE JOURNEY TOWARDS THAT SPECIAL MOMENT

In 1961, Manchester United's scout in Ireland, Bob Bishop, sent a telegram to United manager Matt Busby that read: 'I have found a genius'. No crystal ball could have predicted the journey that 15-year-old George Best – from the streets of the Cregaegh council estate on the outskirts of Belfast – would be starting, or the impact such a find would have on the life of the one 'found'.

The then six-and-a-half-stone George owned up in his book *Best of Both Worlds* that he 'wouldn't have known Bob Bishop if I had fallen over him...' and suggested 'take the usual image of the big club scout – big man, heavy overcoat, trilby and insight eyes – and Bob Bishop is just the opposite.' But clearly Bob Bishop had recognised a genius and had noted George Best!

It was a few days after a weekend of talking football and training exceptionally hard, with six other young hopefuls at Bob's seaside home of Helensbay. George arrived home from school, still very sore and stiff from the 6.30 am run-until-you-drop session, shocked to see Bob Bishop sitting in his dad's chair. He was even more shocked when the question from Bob to the schoolboy was, 'How would you like to join Manchester United?'

Shocked was an understatement! Surprised! Stunned! Amazed! In fact flabbergasted!

George was unable to take it in, unable to eat his tea, but still more than able to run out into the street to tell his mates that he was off to join the greatest team in the world, Manchester United, and recalled thinking at that particular moment that Matt Busby wanted him!

Just one week after that red-letter-day visit of Bob to the Bests' home in Belfast, George and Eric McCordie, another young lad spotted by the eagle eye of Bob Bishop, arrived in 'the big wide world of Manchester' and met United's chief coach, Joe Armstrong. After they'd had a kickabout with a football, the only bright lights they saw were those of the big city as daylight began to fade and they were introduced to their landlady Mrs Fullaway and her son Steve. Their night out was a stroll with Steve Fullaway

Sir Matt Busby proudly displays the European Cup.

along the banks of the River Mersey – not the coolest idea of nightlife from the broad, rich Northern Irish-accented young lads who had just left home.

Home!

As they walked along the riverbank they both missed home, and decided the next day they would tell Joe that they were homesick and wanted to go back.

Back home, as they were both happier among the familiar surroundings of council houses and their mates, George's dad decided to telephone Matt Busby. Matt said that if George could be persuaded to return to Manchester then he would forget the previous attempt to give him a trial because Matt felt that George could 'make the grade as a footballer'. George didn't need any more persuasion. He had not seen Mr Busby while in Manchester but the fact that the great man himself knew of him was enough. So back he went to the kindness of Mrs Fullaway, the home comforts of her semi in Chorlton and onto his road to a future no one could ever have forecast.

Six years later and George was an established Manchester United player. He responded best of all to the familiar words of Matt Busby before the team jogged out onto any pitch, 'Go out and enjoy yourselves. Play your game.' What an inspiration, how his players responded to the confidence he had in them all. However, one occasion when this familiar sound was not heard was an unforgettable Friday on 17 March 1967 (St Patrick's Day to any Guinness-loving Irishman). 'For one Irishman at least St Patrick's Day 1967 fell on a truly Black Friday.' That Irishman was George Best.

Mr Busby called a first-team meeting after the Friday training session. This in itself was a warning of things to come as it always meant that something important was about to be said. They all knew the format it would take, how he would go to each member of the team one by one, in front of everyone else and always give them a chance to respond if they wished.

True to form on the 'Black St Patrick's Day Friday' Matt Busby went through the same routine and eventually came face to face with George Best. George recalls with detail, 'He tore into me more hurtfully than any full-back had ever done. Oh yes, he had heard all about my late nights and free-for-all philandering. Everyone was telling him that was affecting my play. Then he dropped the bombshell. Without blackening my character completely, he seemed to side with the gossips for the first time when he added that, so far as he was concerned, there was no smoke without fire.'

George felt the barb of his comments so deeply. He didn't answer, as there was nothing he could say. He felt frightened and sick at heart. His blushes could be seen through his layered hair and he was deeply wounded and upset by the comments he had been given and everyone else in the dressing room had heard. That day George felt the 'boss' at work, something the public never saw or witnessed.

Years moved swiftly by with many accolades, successes, headlines and downfalls but still the somehow mystical fusion between the knighted Sir Matt Busby and the genius George Best remained intact. None more so than in September 1990, when, after 26 years of waiting, Sir Matt Busby watched his beloved Manchester United regain the league title. He was joined by United legend George Best. Together they shared the joy of the moment and Sir Matt was seen to wipe away a tear. Photographer Robert Aylott was right on the spot to capture the moment, and the photograph was called 'A Tear for George' which George himself claimed was his favourite photograph (see page 77).

From this shared moment in time something that will last

beyond both their now spent lifetimes was captured. Manchester artist Ralph Sweeney encapsulated this split-second special moment between the greatest football manager and the greatest football player, the two greats in a picture that spells out the combined affection each had for the other – aptly titled 'Almost Full-Time', a picture that George really loved, that has become much sought after in the collectors' world. Just a few months later Sir Matt died.

So what did George really think about Sir Matt Busby? Did the ill-fated 1967 Black St Patrick's Day roasting still have an impact on George's regard for the man?

It is commonly known that George Best gave Sir Matt Busby more headaches than probably the rest of his many players put together. But it is also commonly known that Sir Matt had a soft spot for Georgie because he was able to display a quality that made Matt go weak at the knees and not least because of Best's great creative play. There was an obvious mutual regard and respect.

George's love and respect for Sir Matt was explained to David Meek in the souvenir brochure for Sir Matt Busby's testimonial, Sunday, 11 August, 1991:

Sir Matt Busby became almost a father to me. I must have sorely tried his patience as a young man, but he never abandoned me and the older I got, the more I appreciated what he did for me.

Sir Matt became larger than life, but not to himself or those closest associated with him. Legendary figures are often disappointing when you come to meet them, especially in football.

But I have never heard anyone who has met Sir Matt disagree with the consensus that he is an outstanding man. It isn't just the big things he has done, but the little things that leave an imprint on another person's life.

When I first went to Old Trafford the young lads all knew their place. We were part of the family but there was a hierarchy to be respected. We were encouraged to mix but there was never any checking the elite players and there weren't any cliques, at least not until things went wrong at the end.

That was Sir Matt's influence and my other abiding memory of him is his capacity to remember people and things about them. For instance the first time my father went over to Old Trafford to see me play he brought a couple of pals with him. The next time he went to a game he had one of those friends with him again, and Sir Matt not only remembered his name but where he was from and what he drank. Little things perhaps, but the kind of interest that makes a person feel important in himself, and that can't be bad.

One thing he wasn't though was soft, despite what many people thought about him being easy on his players, especially me! I'd see players go in to see him, fully determined to demand this and that, and tell him exactly what they felt they were worth. Time after time they came out with a sheepish smile on their faces, but not feeling put down, for in that respect he was tremendous.

You might be called into his office for a dressing down – it happened to me numerous times – and he would really get stuck into me. Then, just as you were getting up to go, he'd wink at you. You knew you'd done wrong, but at the end of it all you knew you were still pals. That's how he managed to keep everyone happy… personality and understanding, and that's why I love the guy, someone very special.

'Almost Full-Time', classed as a stunning piece of artwork capturing a truly magical moment, is also a special possession for anyone who is fortunate enough to own one of the limited editions, signed by the artist with the brush, Ralph Sweeney, and the artist from the football pitch, George Best.

Sadly, within a few months of the final whistle blowing in 1993, after they had both watched Manchester United regain the title after 23 years, Sir Matt passed away. 'Almost Full-Time' captures the magic of this moment and freezes it in time. This poignant image of one who found another genius from among the raggy-trousered kids playing in the road on the council estate just outside Belfast speaks volumes to those who have the privilege to gaze upon that special moment, and in some way share it with them both.

A LAUGH-OUT-LOUD MOMENT

In his book *The Good, the Bad and the Bubbly*, George Best concludes that he 'can still look back on the old days and smile at the memories'. It is always interesting to discover what memories are really made of, but here is one 'laugh-out-loud moment' to savour.

It was in early 1992 that one of George's fans, Jason Farman, decided to go along to a book signing for George's latest autobiography, *The Good, the Bad and the Bubbly*. The book title summed up George's life from fame and fortune at the age of 19 to when, less than 10 years later, he walked out of Manchester United into a nightmare world. This nightmare world included lurid newspaper headlines, wild affairs, court appearances and battles with alcohol addiction.

Even so, Jason recalls that 'the place was heaving' with George's fans keen to get a look at the genius and to get an autographed copy. This was Jason's intention but, because of his fairly impatient nature, he thought he would give it half an hour and, if the queue hadn't diminished, he would just head off to the local for a pint.

Jason wasn't alone in his decision and after about 15–20 minutes someone else had the same idea. Yes, you may have guessed who!

George Best himself walked past Jason and gave him a signed copy of the book with the words, now written forever in Jason's memory, 'Here, you might as well f***ing have one as well!' How could that moment have been scripted? What brilliant material to make a memory of a laugh-out-loud moment.

George confessed in his book that 'If there's one thing lacking it's the buzz I used to get from appearing in front of

George's book signings always pulled big crowds.

Jason went to get his book signed by George – and got more than he bargained for!

a huge football crowd. Nothing has ever hit that height, and probably never will.' But he was still creating memories for so many and as the blurb on his book states: 'Still – even after all that has happened – the most famous footballer in the world.'

THE T-SHIRT FROM TENERIFE!

When Andy Corrie and a bunch of his mates booked an 18–30 holiday in Playa de Las Americas in Tenerife in the summer of 1993 they just couldn't wait to hit the bars.

One of their favourite watering holes was Lineker's Bar, and they certainly got to know the place really well that year. During one of their drinking sessions they noticed an advertisement to say that the footballer without equal, George Best, was due to visit the bar during one of the days of their holiday.

Sure enough, on the publicised day, the great man turned up and Andy and his mates queued up to get one of the famous Lineker's Bar T-shirts signed by the footballing genius. What a memorable moment it was for Andy as he shook George's hand and he signed the T-shirt 'Best wishes to Andy. George Best'. What a great memory Andy has of that moment as he recalls, 'What a real nice guy George was – a gentleman and very smiley.'

On returning home from sunny Tenerife, the beloved T-shirt was kept in a safe place and has moved from house to house with Andy. It has never been displayed (because his missus won't let him) and he has always been scared of washing it in case that famous signature gets washed out with the soap powder.

Finally, in 2006, Andy came to the decision that, although the signed t-shirt was truly a prized possession, a locked wardrobe was not really the place for it – and so decided to place it on eBay, the online auction site. After all, even if the T-shirt sold, no one could take away his memories of that hot sunny day in 1993 when he met George.

And so the bidding started! Not one, not two, nor even three or four people were bidding against each other to win the T-shirt. In fact, a total of 15 bids were eventually made. The winning bid was made by one of the authors of this book, Bernie Smith. But the story of the T-shirt doesn't end there.

One of the bidders was a young man, also named Andy,

who lived in the North East of England and who was gutted when he didn't have the winning bid. He was so disappointed that he kept emailing Andy (the previous owner) saying how upset he was. Andy then contacted the winner of the T-shirt and explained how upset the young man was and gave reasons why the winning bidder, Bernie, might want to think about letting him have the T-shirt.

Andy (the younger) was born in 1993, the year the T-shirt was signed by George, who incidentally is the boy's hero; he is a self-confessed 'mad George Best fan'. When he was five years old, Andy 'started loving George Best', and when he was 10 years old he joined a local club, Swalwell, where he tried to emulate his hero on the football pitch – and in fact still does. People may wonder why a 13-year-old boy holds George in such high regard – quite simply, George inspires him.

Bernie felt it was the right thing to do, to let the boy buy the T-shirt instead of him. The young man Andy is so delighted with it that he classes it as 'the most beloved possession I own', and that 'since I was a kid George Best is like my dad and hero'. He goes on, 'I know everyone might seem to care about him but I feel I love him the most out of the whole world. He simply inspires me. You might be thinking, he's just a kid, but I have the biggest space in my heart for George Best you'll ever know.' It is such a pity that George isn't still with us to hear such accolades and devotion from a true and dedicated young fan, who now proudly shows off his T-shirt signed 'Best wishes to Andy. George Best'.

So just where did this love of George Best come from?

The young Andy's dad, Martin, although from the North East and a Newcastle United fan, thinks that George Best was actually the best player in the world, and remembers seeing the skills of the man on form in 1971 when Man U played against Newcastle. He even recalls joining in with 'there's only one Georgie Best' – and there certainly was.

He also admits that his wife met George on a few occasions and she too said what a lovely man he was. So Andy is carrying on the family tradition with his admiration for George Best.

Life is full of surprises and it is interesting to note that, during the year young Andy was born, his idol was signing a t-shirt to another Andy in Lineker's Bar in Tenerife, and that the same T-shirt has been kept safe for the last 13 years just waiting for the young Andy to gain ownership.

You try telling Andy that George Best didn't sign it for him!

TOMORROW'S FISH AND CHIP PAPER

We must always remember that today's news – good, bad or indifferent – reported in any newspaper, either quality or 'gutter' press, will usually end up being tomorrow's fish and chip paper – or would have been before health and safety regulations stopped newsprint being used to keep your dinner warm on its journey home! But there are those special occasions when something of interest in a newspaper catches your eye, and in that instance the particular day's newspaper, or cutting might be kept. For what reason? Probably for no other reason than as a keepsake, or so you can have an 'I can remember that as if it were yesterday' moment when the cutting appears just when you are looking for something else.

We have all done it and will probably keep on doing it until our days are over. Then those that are left to sort out our earthly possessions will again come across the ageing piece of newsprint, read it with interest then either dispose of it or keep it themselves.

29 May, 1968: Man United 4–1 Benfica, European Cup Final, Wembley.

Perhaps no football match better encapsulates the career of George Best than Manchester United's European Cup 4–1 victory over Benfica. It was United's greatest triumph, and one of those momentous occasions for those fortunate in being one of the 100,000 watching and experiencing the unique performance that took place on the hallowed turf of Wembley, or even part of the millions who watched it from their armchairs around the world. All were able to witness, among others of the United team, George Best's wondrous skill, the savage way opponents often treated him and a need for individual expression that bordered on being vainglorious, or perhaps just a genius at work.

Newspapers the next day were full of the wonderful triumph grasped hold of by Manchester United. Sports writers all over the world displayed their journalistic skills in giving detailed paragraphs filled with kick-by-kick action for each history-making moment.

Among the many lines written about that remarkable and noteworthy game were those written in the *Daily Mail*. Alongside the columns of historic sporting news was the self-explanatory photograph where it looks as if Cruz

J.J.'s friend Peter was going to the hotel where this event was taking place.

is about to kick George after the ball has gone, with a caption 'Best in trouble – with Cruz'. George has his victorious arm in the air after scoring the famous goal at the start of extra time. It was a goal that spurred on the rest of the United team on the field to go on and win the European Cup.

This news report and picture from the *Daily Mail* became one of those cuttings that the father of Tim Flack took time to pull out from the newspaper and lay in a place for safe-keeping – namely the loft of his home. And there it was to stay, holding the history of that night in May 1968 in black and white until he came across it almost 30 years later in 1993.

Coincidentally, just after Tim's father, J.J. Flack, rediscovered the cutting and had lingered over the memories it brought back, one of his friends informed him of a weekend trip he was due to go on. J.J.'s friend, Peter, worked for Eagle Star (now known as Zurich). The Eagle Star staff were going away for a weekend to a hotel in Torquay. On the programme he had noted that one of the evening's events was an appearance by George Best and Rodney Marsh. (Also on the programme was a comedian who, as part of his act wore a horse's head and neck – à la Desert Orchid – but the less said about that the better!)

J.J. quickly dug out the newspaper cutting about George Best from 1968 and asked Peter if he would try to get it signed by the man himself. So the rediscovered sports page of 30 May 1968 was carefully prepared to go on its journey to Torquay to be endorsed by the player in the picture. Unfortunately, Peter didn't get the opportunity to corner George until the following morning when he spotted him in the lounge bar with two girls. So Peter gathered his courage and walked up to George clutching the 1968 cutting and asked him to sign it for his friend who had kept it all those years.

At first George was a little miffed about being interrupted (he was human after all), but, in his usual style of not wanting to disappoint people, George signed the picture of himself and then handed it back without another word. A very simple memory, but a poignant one.

The George Best in the photograph of 1968 literally had the world at his feet. He had the centre stage of football, the ability for a future that no other footballing hero had ever experienced before. The *Daily Mail* cutting of that day was for sure not the only one that was kept and preserved if for nothing else just for the memory of the triumphant match or the wonderful and thrilling goal – or even for the photograph of the teenage footballing whiz kid, George Best.

As a 'people person', George found the time to sign autographs for his fans.

The George Best that signed the photograph of George Best of 1968 now not only had to deal with the savage way defenders had treated him all those years ago, he also had to deal with savage attacks off the pitch as well. He could have quite easily told Peter to go away, but he didn't.

In the photograph of 1968 George was an up-and-coming people person and when he signed the photograph

229

The article, signed by the man himself.

in 1993 he was still a people person. Indeed, he was exactly that right up to when his last photograph was printed in the *News of the World* just prior to his losing his battle for life. George himself had asked for the photograph to be printed to show the terrible effects alcohol can have on someone. No autographs or signatures appeared on that particular picture, just a 'celebration' of the courage of George Best when he was in life's extra time. George is clearly suffering in the photograph as a result of his chosen way of life, but wanting others to see it as a warning. If that's not a people person, then what is?

1994 WORLD CUP FEVER IN MAGALUF

The 1994 Football World Cup held in the United States was won by Brazil who beat Italy 3–2 in a penalty shoot-out after the game and extra time ended 0–0. FIFA's decision in 1988 to hold the event in the United States over the bids of Morocco and Brazil surprised many considering the relative lack of soccer fans there (aside from a significant fanbase within the Latin American immigrant population). Despite these misgivings, in terms of attendance, the event was a rousing success. The average

attendance of nearly 69,000 shattered a record that had stood since 1950. The total attendance for the final tournament of nearly 3.6 million remains the greatest in World Cup history, despite the expansion of the competition to 32 teams in 1998.

Surprising as it may seem, the man who was considered 'the best', who won the UEFA Champions League in 1968 and the English Division One in 1965 and 1967, who was also British and European Footballer of the Year in 1968, George Best played for his country 37 times and scored nine goals but at no time were his abilities ever displayed on the World Cup stage.

So what was George Best doing while Brazil were winning the World Cup in the United States, apart from publishing his book *The Good, the Bad and the Bubbly*? For those who are not aware, the brother of former England striker Gary Lineker runs bars all over Spain and the one in Magaluf, Majorca, was one of his first. There are football videos playing all day and shirts on the walls from Gary's many international games. Not so good if you're not the sporty type, but an ideal place for George Best to relax in the sunshine, listen to regular updates from the world stage of football, read a few newspaper reports and sign the now much sought-after Lineker's Bar 94 T-shirts.

Quite poignant when you consider Michael Parkinson's summing up of the brilliance of George: 'He was quick, two-footed, beautifully balanced... He could hit long and short passes with equal precision, was swift and fearless in the tackle and he reintroduced the verb "to dribble". He was as imaginative and whimsical in midfield as he was economical and deadly given a chance at goal. He could also head brilliantly and he never shirked from defending when he had to. In short, he was the perfect footballer. But, while he was Roy of the Rovers on the field, sadly he was Roy of the Ravers off it.' All this talent and football magic, but George never adorned the World Cup stage.

It also seems ironic that at the same time the theatre of football was being cast in the United States, the film *The Madness of King George* was being released nationally and internationally – and only 12 months later was winning an Oscar, a Bafta and many other coveted awards.

Some may say that 'King' George Best was living in his own madness, that some of his actions were those of someone not completely in control. That George Best, the legend, one of the world's most brilliant soccer players, had to live with the fact that, as Tommy Docherty said, 'George was a fantastic player and he would have been even better if he'd been able to pass nightclubs the way he passed the ball.'

Best's explanations are interesting. Whatever he lacked in self-discipline, he was never less than honest with himself. 'I was born with a great gift,' he said, 'and sometimes with that comes a destructive streak. Just as I wanted to outdo everyone when I played, I had to outdo everyone when we were out on the town.' He once admitted that, when playing in the United States, he was living in a house by the sea, but as he had to pass a bar to get to the beach he never actually made it to the water.

The World Cup is sadly lacking any memories of George Best playing centre-stage in any of its performances – but we still have the T-shirt from Lineker's Bar signed by the great man himself so at least there are some memories of the World Cup relating to George.

GEORGE AND RODNEY

Rodney Marsh said it all when he was once asked if Beckham was as good as George Best. After pausing for a moment, he replied, 'He probably is. But George is 53 years old.'

Just to mention the names George Best and Rodney Marsh in the same sentence conjures up a series of images and memories in anyone's mind! First off would be the obvious, George Best – Manchester United, Rodney Marsh – Manchester City. After leaving the shores of the UK, both Bestie and Marsh ended up playing for the same team in the United States until they both returned to England to play for Fulham Football Club. Their lives took many different turns but George and Rodney remained the best of friends and reunited for a different kind of team talk.

There's no shock to any fan of either one of them that, after hanging up their boots, they decided to take on a new career and, just as they did with their football, they approached it and delivered it with flair, imagination and a desire to entertain. Their new career took them on the road again, not to away games but to various clubs and venues around the country for 'An Evening with…' or 'A Sporting Night to Remember'. Instead of a football pitch, their stage was in theatres, town halls, assembly rooms and civic halls up and down the land.

One such evening was at the Mere Golf Club in Cheshire where a steward and sometimes caddy, Peter, was in the right place at the right time to meet George and Rodney. They had just completed their evening of entertainment and were enjoying a relaxing drink before they were due to leave. Peter, a collector of Panini stickers, saw his opportunity and went up to ask George if he would sign his sticker of George Best that he just happened to have on him.

George and Rodney had a friendship that dated back to their playing days.

Rodney cheekily asked Peter if he had anything of him that he wanted signing, as he was a better player than George ever was. Although slightly worse for wear, but as quick as a flash and with that Irish glow still in his eyes, George replied, 'He was, you know, but only at f***ing darts!'

Peter had the privilege of meeting George on numerous occasions following that evening in Cheshire, and whenever they met he always asked George if he had beaten Marshie at darts yet. Just like George, he always remembered and gave that great, slightly to one side of his face, smile at the question.

On the road again, George and Rodney were making memories for their fans, and on one particular occasion in 1994 they were in Basingstoke. Basingstoke was about to experience the opening of a bar called Chicago Rock where Chris Wheatley was the DJ and part of the new set-up. To celebrate the opening of Chicago Rock, George and Rodney were invited to be guests – a certainty to pull in the punters.

They both arrived at around 10 pm and settled in to do a comical question and answer routine that went down like a ball (well, what else with two ex-football pros on stage?). They entertained the new 'Chicago Rockers' for about half an hour or so. As ever, following their performance, George and Rodney were pleased to sign autographs for customers and staff.

As DJ at Chicago Rock, Chris Wheatley was lucky enough to have a drink with George in the VIP area. What are his memories? Quite simply that George was a very down-to-earth guy with plenty of time to chat. They talked briefly and off Chris went back to his decks to play some music.

Another one of those everyday occurrences in the life of an ex-pro, or just more evidence that George Best was truly a people person who had time for anyone and indeed everyone. He created memories out of nothing – memories that are simple but meaningful, that those who encountered the man are more than happy to share.

Sadly there will never be any more evenings with George Best and Rodney Marsh as time was called on George in November 2005. But what about Rodney's memories of his team-mate, the other half of a performing duo and his friend?

Rodney has given his heart-felt memories and committed them in print on Yahoo Sports for us all to have an insight into what he really felt about his friend:

GEORGE BEST – A TRAGIC HERO

George Best is a 'tragic' hero. For a spell of around three years in the late '60s George Best was the best footballer in the world. That is my opinion and I don't care what anybody else says!

In that period Bestie was the quickest, the cleverest and

the most destructive player around. There was no one braver, he could head the ball, score and pass equally brilliantly with both feet and had an engine like Manchester City legend Colin Bell or Chelsea's Frank Lampard. He never stopped running.

The only reason Pelé is regarded as the best of all time is because he played in World Cup finals over a 20-year span, something George was never able to achieve. I've always said that the best judges of a footballer are the players themselves, and if you speak to anyone who trained

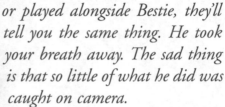

or played alongside Bestie, they'll tell you the same thing. He took your breath away. The sad thing is that so little of what he did was caught on camera.

Nowadays you see clip after clip of Zidane and Ronaldinho performing tricks and scoring goals. Bestie did that all the time and unfortunately the best stuff was only seen by the people that were in the crowd – there is no footage to prove his legacy. That's why youngsters today have no understanding of how

George Best

good George – and Pelé for that matter – really were. I'll give you an example. Long after Bestie retired from Manchester United and had done a stint in the USA, he returned with me and Bobby Moore to Fulham in 1976, for one last hurrah.

Now George had scored fantastic goals at all levels, all over the world but the greatest example of his inimitable ability came during a game for Fulham. He scored a goal against Peterborough away in the League Cup that typified his brilliance. At this stage of his career his body was paying the price for the years of damage he had suffered at the hands of the spoilers of the beautiful game – dopey defenders! Since he arrived at Old Trafford as a slight 16-year-old, he had been ravaged by crunching tackles from endless players trying to make a reputation for themselves by being the one who could stop 'the great one', by foul means or even more fouler means.

The game itself was terrible, 0–0 with an hour or so gone. The crowd, the majority of whom were just there to watch George in his twilight years so that they could say 'I was there', had started to fidget and boo at the lack of genuine quality and entertainment. Then, in a surrealistic instant in time, the stadium and both sets of players were to witness a stroke of genius that, if it were to happen today, would be shown over and over again on TV shows and thousands of times on the Soccer AMs of this world.

A loose ball out of Peterborough's defence bounced harmlessly to around the halfway line. It fell to Bestie who controlled it instantly. I was ten yards ahead of him and turned for a quick pass as their defence pushed out. As the ball stuck to his foot, he was already looking up. He did nothing. Time seemed to stand still. He was 45 yards from goal. Not one defender went to close him down. He just stood motionless as though he had called a 'time out'. And it appeared everyone on the pitch respected his space. I was amazed. Suddenly with no back-lift he put his left foot under the ball, flicked it up onto his right and struck a volley with such power that, as the ball flew into the net, the goalkeeper hadn't even had time to dive. The crowd was dumbstruck and for a moment nothing happened. Then they cheered in what seemed like slow motion, as though they had to do a double take to make sure that they could actually believe what they had seen.

I ran up to him, put my arms round his neck and said something to the effect of 'that was f***ing brilliant, pal' and as I did it, over his shoulder, out of the corner of my eye, I caught sight of the goalie on his penalty spot, openly clapping George's genius.

It was the ultimate respect!

Over the years people have criticised George, unmercifully in some cases. They don't know him. Yet they form opinions based on what they have read, about what he has (or hasn't) done OFF the football pitch. He's an easy target but these people don't know the real George. Personally I have witnessed countless acts of generosity, raising money for underprivileged children, appearing at hospitals to shake hands and take photos with terminally ill kids, signing autographs until everyone has his signature.

He is a quiet and gentle man, funny and generous.

But you shouldn't feel sorry for George Best. He is a deep thinker and extremely intelligent and he knows exactly the hand he has been dealt. He chooses to play it his way.

He is a genius, a flawed one maybe, but every true genius is.

From Rodney's tribute to his pal, it's clear that the glittery glamour world that the young boy from Belfast was thrown into at a very early age wasn't really able to take away from him what really made him tick. George has been criticised and, yes, at times he did things to encourage the criticism that was written about and spoken against him, but his values always remained the same. He was a gentle man, a caring person and a true genius, even if he was lacking, but still we're none of us perfect, are we?

Bestie and Marshie entertain off the pitch.

GEORGE'S OWN STORIES

Asked to comment on Bobby Charlton

When asked about his thoughts on Bobby Charlton, one of George's replies was: 'I have been asked about a comment on what has been said about Bobby Charlton, that he has said in the past that he tended to resent me slightly because of my so-called genius and by not giving my all to football, perhaps I had let people down – how do you feel about that? Quite simply, I do what I want to do, not what Bobby Charlton wants or anyone else. I have close friends who say I should have played for another 20 years, but funnily enough the rumours about Bobby and I continue. He used to get so frustrated with me and told this true story. He was playing a game, I think it was against Southampton, and he was getting so frustrated with me as he kept calling for the ball. He said that he had made this run, had beat the fullback and then again, then beat another fullback. "I was getting dizzy trying to catch Bestie and kept calling for it and shouted, 'Bestie, you greedy little… what a great f*****g goal, Bestie!'" And coming from Bobby that was a great compliment, from a great player. I could see his point. I wish I had played another 20 years for the club I loved.'

On playing football alongside Rodney Marsh

'We enjoyed playing together – we are great friends and have great ideas of how football should be played. It should be fun and when we went to Fulham they were getting crowds of 2,000 and it went up to 20,000, and if you watch the videos people are laughing and joking, taking their kids along. No violence, plenty of skill and atmosphere. It was a pleasure to play alongside him.'

Asked about Sir Matt Busby – what was he like?

'Sir Matt was a great, great man. He had a reputation for being a little bit soft but when he had to be hard he could – he was terrific. Down the years I have probably been the only person in the history of Manchester United that spent more time in his office than he did. Not many people know this but he was a great Scotsman, and behind his desk he had the stag at bay as his wallpaper. Not many people will know this but there are 3,674 stags on the wallpaper, because when he was giving me a b******ing I was nodding my head and counting the stags.'

On Denis Law

'It was suggested that I was once elected by the lads to go in for a pay rise. I reflected that Sir Matt had a great way of doing things, and in those days we had so many great lads, great players. We decided because of the increase in crowds to go in for a pay rise. It wasn't me that went in – I wouldn't have gone in. It was Denis Law that drew the short straw, and to this day he doesn't realise we set him up. And we were encouraging him – "go on, Denis, you sort it out"– he was such a great player and such a great character. So he went in and was gone about 30 seconds and came out saying, "I sorted it out boys we're taking £10 a week less for the rest of the season."'

... and Kenny Lynch on George

'A Kenny Lynch story! True story! Me and Bestie, you know, used to share a flat together in Manchester. I was his best friend for 25 years – well, somebody had to carry the crates! The second game after England had won the World Cup in 1966 they played Northern Ireland and went over there with them. He thought it was going to be sunny but I had a jumper on and I went over with Mike Summerbee and watched the game, and they got beat 2–1. After the game we went back into the dressing room to pick Bestie up. Went to get a cab and couldn't get one anywhere – so we walked all the way back into Belfast. Anyway on the way we went past some kids playing football up against the wall. We got to a corner and I began calling out for a cab and these kids came shouting, "Eh! that's Georgie Best, so it is," and a little kid next to him said, "And he's got Cassius Clay with him."

THE 'BEST OF TIMES' FOR A
LIFELONG SUPPORTER

In 1996 George Best celebrated his 50th birthday, so many years since his 15th birthday in 1961 when he joined Manchester United, and so many events in his life throughout those years. (Incidentally, 1961 was the same year Jimmy Hill and Cliff Lloyd of the PFA were putting the flags out with delight at the eradication of the maximum wage for footballers.)

When George walked away from Manchester United Football Club at the age of 27, some people didn't think he would see past 30, but he did. The time between his departure from the 'Theatre of Dreams' and his enjoying his half-century (and beyond) was indeed filled with other forms of excitement, but also included his drinking addiction, gambling habits, beautiful women and being in and out of the papers for what editors thought newsworthy happenings in his life. He also got married and became a father to a fine-looking and adored son, Calum.

It was during the mid-1990s that George joined up with Rodney Marsh, not on the football pitch this time but as part of their famous 'An Evening with…' around the country when fans could enjoy an evening of questioning their idols while socialising with their friends and families.

One person who enjoyed an evening with 'Best and Marsh' was Steve Brown. The following is his memory of meeting George Best: 'Although I am a loyal Chelsea fan I have always been amazed by George Best, not only because of his skills on the football pitch, but also by his very colourful and quite often sad life. However, my mother-in-law has been a lifelong fan of his, so when in the mid-1990s we saw that there was an evening with

George and Rodney Marsh on at Bedworth Civic Hall, we decided to go.

'The evening was not quite as we had expected. Although obviously fans of the two, we found the audience to be very disrespectful and did wonder why two legends of the game had put themselves in this position that obviously made them feel awkward. The questions being asked were not of his football achievements, but more about his personal exploits, ladies and drinking mainly.

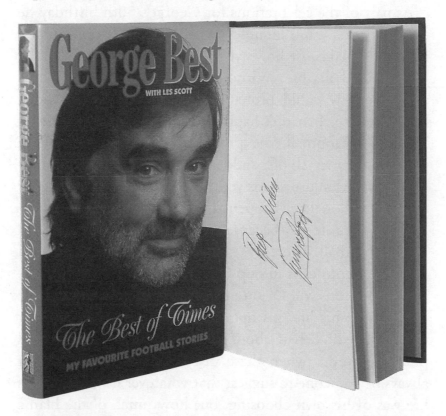

'At the end of the evening George made himself available for signing books that were purchased on the night. I took my mother-in-law up to meet George and get his signature in his book *The Best of Times* written by George with Les Scott, in 1994.

'We both found George to be charming, but also a little nervous and unsure of himself. To my mother-in-law's absolute delight George kissed her, he then shook my hand whilst thanking us for our support over the years. It is a moment I will always remember!'

It was just another evening for George and Rodney, even with the abuse they had to endure, but what a fantastic memory George gave to two people who at this once-in-a-lifetime meeting felt the warmth of him as a person.

As part of the celebrations for George's 50th birthday he took part in a frank interview with Michael Parkinson and tried to explain just how everything around football really had affected his life. Without laying any blame, George said, 'Nobody could protect me, advise me. They didn't know how to. It hadn't happened to a footballer before... Now every footballer is protected. Of course it was a problem for me. All of a sudden I had to employ three full-time secretaries just to answer the 10,000 letters a week. At the time I thought it happened to every footballer.

'I wasn't protected because it hadn't happened before in English football. There was no precedent. I was being asked for more photo-calls in pop magazines than sports ones.'

Deliberations will for sure continue as to whether George Best wasted his life, his opportunities and his talents, but there can be no debate about his pure genius on the football pitch. However, when these discussions arise there must always be someone to suggest that whatever he did with his life was of his own choosing, but how much of the blame should rest with others who perhaps didn't see the need to protect the shy but very talented lad from Belfast? George would never have suggested this but we have the liberty to say it with hindsight.

Clearly, even at the age of 50, George was still a charmer

as he wowed Steve's mother-in-law with a kiss at Bedworth Civic Hall, and by signing her book with his best wishes. He was also a genuine guy, still a little nervous and perhaps underneath it all still that shy 15-year-old that joined Old Trafford in 1961.

IT'S A GIFT

The millennium! It was predicted that so many things would happen at the stroke of midnight as we moved from one millennium to another. But as the seconds ticked past that magical hour of 12 o'clock on 31 December 1999, nothing happened, except perhaps a few more fireworks being set off! But it was something special – not only a brand new year stretching out before each one of us, but also the start of another 1,000 years. Just for a moment

Old Trafford – an unusual choice for a wedding venue!

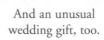

And an unusual
wedding gift, too.

consider what has taken place over the last 1,000 years, then ponder on what the world will be like at the turn of the next millennium. Hard to imagine, isn't it?

But looking forward to the year 2000 meant more than just a few more fireworks lighting up the sky for one particular couple, Gill and her husband-to-be, who were busy planning for their marriage in July that year.

Planning for a wedding can be stressful, but it can also be quite fun, particularly when deciding where the knot is going to be tied. Forget a Norman church, a quaint little chapel or even a majestic cathedral for the happy event – focus on the Theatre of Dreams at Old Trafford, Manchester, as that's where this eagerly antincipated marriage was to take place – whatever the cost. How fantastic, particularly as the husband-to-be was a big Manchester United fan.

The plans were in place, the wedding-gift list distributed to those who wanted to celebrate along with the happy couple. But what wasn't on this list was one specific gift. Particularly for Reds fans, quite an unusual gift was given to the bride and groom – and this is what the label stated:

PRODUCT FROM ITALY BY COLLINA SERRAGILLI 1996... BARBERA D'ALBA DENOMINAZIONE DI ORIGINE CONTROLLATA 75cl 12% vol

A 'cheeky' bottle of quite appropriate red wine was the delightful gift – in fact, it was a characteristic red nectar: ruby, dry and generous, a very versatile wine which holds up well with ageing.

If that wasn't symbolic enough to celebrate a wedding conducted at Old Trafford, the label of the bottle read 'PRESENTED BY GEORGE BEST', with a picture of

Manchester's greatest, George Best, alongside his famous and desired autographed name.

How about that to raise your glass to?

That prized bottle, its contents and the label have been kept safely for the memory, and because it just didn't seem right to open it – after all, it is quite special, just like the one that presented it!

THONGS FOR THE MEMORIES, GEORGE – AND RYAN GIGGS'S FOOTBALL SHORTS!

Tony Dorigo and George Best never played with or against each other because their footballing talents missed each other by about ten years. However, the defender (Tony) born in

Australia, and the winger (George) born in Belfast were brought together one unsuspecting evening at a charity do sometime in the late 1990s. This episode has given us a lasting and quite typical memory of the great man himself concerning something as simple as a thong!

The 'bit of a do' was in aid of BEN (a charity set up to help families linked in any way to the motor industry. This includes big car manufacturers right down to local garages and bodyshops). Tony Dorigo (ex Aston Villa and Chelsea, to name a few), was invited as he was a customer to a local BMW dealer, and George Best was a guest speaker at the same event held at Elland Road football ground.

Tony Dorigo

While the BMW dealer (Tony Robinson) and Tony were having a drink the auction got under way, with one of the lots being a gold-coloured thong made from satin and lace. George Best signed the thong in bold, black ink, right across the crotch! With the drink still flowing and all the guests getting into the swing of the auction, Tony Robinson won the bids for the thong, causing quite a bout of laughter – particularly from Tony Dorigo.

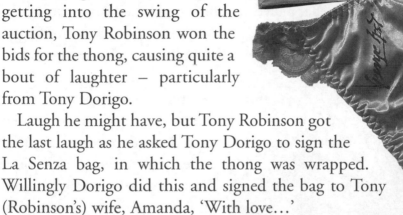

Laugh he might have, but Tony Robinson got the last laugh as he asked Tony Dorigo to sign the La Senza bag, in which the thong was wrapped. Willingly Dorigo did this and signed the bag to Tony (Robinson's) wife, Amanda, 'With love…'

The Elland Road event was at a time when George was 'on the wagon', and perhaps he was comparatively so by drinking several bottles of wine and a few whiskeys – but that was George, although as Parkinson remembers '…drinking didn't make him [George] happy.'

The gold-coloured thong conjures up many different thoughts to do with George Best. It could be that he has left his 'mark' on many thongs throughout a life where as Parky remembers 'Women offered themselves and he took them. Simple as that.'

Parkinson may have commented that 'George Best was sometimes a difficult man to defend in the aftermath of a drunken episode.' However, many people say that the golden boy of Belfast, who abused his liver with alcohol, was a naturally gifted footballer with a huge heart. He was the guest speaker at the auction where the golden thong was sold to help others, and this typifies the man.

Around this time in George's life he was often called upon to be the guest speaker at numerous auctions and dinners in aid of charity. And of course George could never say 'No' – not that he would have wanted to.

On one particular Saturday afternoon, George was making his way out of Old Trafford after watching Man U play, and he happened to call into United's dressing room

where he spotted Ryan Giggs' football shorts. Knowing that he was due at an auction the same evening, George sneaked the shorts out and duly signed them before putting them in pride of place at the auction. Just imagine winning the bid on Ryan Giggs's shorts that would probably still have had the grass stains from the Old Trafford pitch and possibly the smell of his sweat too!

What of the gold thong? Bought for around £100 at the auction held at Elland Road, it was signed by George; the bag was signed by Tony Dorigo with his love and they had been left in a drawer since that day in the late 1990s; and what of the Ryan Giggs shorts? Now the pretty gold thong and the shorts have come out of the dark to remind us of a man of whom, as Michael Parkinson said, 'What was never a problem was to talk of his genius as a player and to love him as a friend.'

BLESSED IN MILTON KEYNES

For any local newspaper reporter there are days that are routine, and there are also red-letter days that live with you forever. On very few occasions you get to interview the great! There was one of those days for a *Milton Keynes News* reporter in December 2002.

The assignment was to visit Ottakers for a book-signing session by George Best for his latest autobiography *Blessed*, a fully revised and updated paperback version of the life and times of the greatest Manchester United player ever.

Still a crowd puller, George's fans massed around their hero whose previously scheduled appearance at the shop in the August of that year had been cancelled when he was rushed to hospital for a liver transplant. George was so pleased to have finally made it to Milton Keynes, just one of the three book signings he conducted throughout the country promoting *Blessed*, and said, 'It's great because I nearly wasn't here at all.'

'Blessed' could also describe how the reporter felt when he met the great man himself, as he recalls George being generous with his time, particularly as his people wanted to restrict the interview to three or four quick questions and answers. But, true to form, George was happy to sit and chat and expand on all the questions asked, and would have been happy to talk all day. Craig, the reporter, recalls how George needed little introduction. That, although he had never personally seen him play, the footage he had seen of George playing proved he certainly was one of the best ever.

For Craig, this was the first and only meeting with George Best. On this special occasion he did get a signed copied of *Blessed* and he also got to speak with the man himself and felt his sense of delightful generosity in a relaxed and unhurried interview resulting in a couple of newspaper columns.

A book can be lost, stolen or even sold. A newspaper: read and archived. But the memory of that day will live forever for Craig. At this meeting he was able to formulate his own media opinion of this generous, delightful and genuine man who, when seeing his fans flock to the Milton Keynes book signing, commented 'The turn-up is phenomenal.' What a champion!

MEDAL OF HONOUR

In 2002, the borough of Castlereagh, situated on the outskirts of East Belfast, decided to honour their famous son and former Manchester United star George Best by giving him the freedom of the borough. The decision was made and the motion, which was proposed by the SDLP and seconded by the DUP, was passed unanimously by the borough council.

Just prior to the decision, George, his wife Alex and their pet dog Red had moved to live in the County Down fishing village of Portavogie, and George had been fighting a very public battle against alcoholism in recent months. DUP Deputy Leader Peter Robinson said that it was an ideal way to honour the area's most famous son, who grew up on the local Cregagh Estate.

The freedom of the borough of Castlereagh has been bestowed on 10 occasions to organisations; significantly it has only been bestowed on two individual citizens, George Best and Alderman PD Robinson MP.

In recognition of this notable event, 300 commemorative medals were made, giving people a unique opportunity to have a limited-edition medal. The medal combined the borough with the man. On one side, the design shows a raised head and shoulder of George Best and on the reverse is the borough's coat of arms.

At the time of the special event, the father of one Irish girl, Jackie, acquired around 25 of these medals with the intention of giving one to each boy in his junior football team a medal. But for some reason the medals were never given out.

Four years later, Jackie noticed that an identical medal had been sold on eBay for over £300! As her father is a collector of junk, they delved into his many collections to find the abandoned medals. Fifteen were found, while the others were definitely stashed away somewhere. Both Jackie and her father were amazed at what the medals were worth – obviously a further tribute to George and what people will pay to have something to remember him by.

The mayor of Castlereagh decided who was invited to the luncheon on the day and all guests were given one of the commemorative medals. They also received a booklet produced for the occasion. The honour of receiving the freedom of the borough occurred in April 2002 when the soccer legend George Best returned in triumph to his home city and got an unexpected treat. Not only had the Manchester United hero been given the freedom of Castlereagh, but the local council had secretly flown in one of Best's old friends and colleagues, Denis Law, and the two legends hugged each other like long-lost brothers.

Lloyd, who had the honour of officiating at the luncheon as Master of Ceremonies, knew that, like all corporate functions, people had to be treated as VIPs. Knowing that George Best was in attendance made it all the more important and enhanced the event.

Lloyd recalled that George was extremely forthcoming to him and in fact to all the staff involved with the event. It was a pleasure to be in George's company. Lloyd said that there were not many occasions in his line of work when he had the chance to meet such heroes as Best and Law, but the event of George receiving the freedom of the borough surpassed all events hands down.

At the ceremony it was reported that George looked healthier than he had done for some time, was accompanied by his wife Alex and said, 'No matter where I have been this has always been my home. I had no clue Denis might be coming and it was a wonderful surprise.'

Later in the day George was asked to unveil a plaque at the family home where his father, Dickie, still lives. At Dickie Best's small terraced house on Burren Way, a tiny plaque on the wall told visitors this was the family home of soccer legend George Best, and that he was awarded the freedom of the borough of Castlereagh in April 2002. It is evidence that a sporting superstar was raised in this working-class neighbourhood.

The conferment of the freedom of the borough of Castlereagh on George Best was given in recognition of his exceptional sporting talent and his outstanding contribution to the game of soccer which made him an international celebrity and put Castlereagh and Cregagh forever on the world map.

In recognition Peter Robinson spoke on behalf of the borough, 'People in Castlereagh for a very long period of time have recognised that they have had someone in George Best who was recognised throughout the world as probably the greatest soccer star, indeed the first superstar in soccer terms that the world has seen.'

And what of the commemorative medals that had been stashed away? They have been released back into the marketplace where those who want to can purchase that little bit of George Best history; a piece of history, and also perhaps a special memory of a great person who was openly honoured by the people in his home town.

A BRIEF ENCOUNTER

When anyone has a brief encounter with someone whose name is known to thousands, it has to be memorable. But when anyone has a brief encounter with someone they have idolised for a long time, who has at one time had the world at his feet, and that person is George Best, then that has to go down in history.

That 'anyone' is Chris Abbott, a lifelong Manchester United and George Best fan, who holds many memories of seeing and watching George in his heyday as he shaped his magic on the football pitch; but this particular memory was of a one-time meeting with the man himself – although quite a sad and thought-provoking encounter.

Chris had just returned from a 2002 trip to Barcelona and, as you do after a trip abroad, he met up with some friends in a pub on the Kings Road just for a catch-up, a drink and a chat.

As the friends were enjoying one another's company, they noticed George come into the pub and order what looked like a pint of white wine spritzer. Obviously aware of who he was, Chris and his friends also noticed that George looked the worse for drink – but he was on his own and kept looking over to the group, the way someone does when they would really like to be part of what is happening. Others in the pub took no notice of George as they were probably regulars and used to him being there.

It was Chris's round so as he went to the bar he just said hello to George and told him that he was a Manchester United fan and that he was one of his heroes. George acknowledged what Chris had to say when another one of the group joined them and bought George a drink.

Nothing unusual! But, for Chris, his memory of George is how lonely he looked, how he seemed to want to join in the chat and how, when they invited him over, George seemed to go all shy.

There was no doubt that George was really drunk and couldn't really get his words out. It was so sad for Chris to see George like this because, as much as George wanted to talk, when he did it was very incoherent and Chris felt almost embarrassed for his hero.

After a short time George got up and left the pub on his own.

The wretched effect that the craving for drink had on George's life created grief and desolation, and attracted a lack of understanding from his critics, who seemed content to walk by on the other side and perhaps even point the finger. But for Chris it was a brief encounter with his hero; it was a sad encounter too, but as for all that knew or met George, albeit briefly, still a memorable occasion.

Some three years later, Chris, a real United fan who attends home and away games, was present in Old Trafford at the WBA George Best tribute match, just after George had died.

As the whole of Old Trafford remembered George, Chris recalls that those present could almost touch the atmosphere, it was so moving, with a silence that was only disturbed by the intruding noise of the electric fans. The eerie silence surrounded everyone as Old Trafford stood for its adopted son who had once been described as 'a gift from God to say sorry for the loss of the Busby Babes'.

During this golden silence tears naturally rolled down Chris's face, and those who were around him experienced the same selfless show of sadness as they all remembered George Best.

GEORGE'S LAST REQUEST

George Best and Jimmy Greaves are two of the greatest footballers ever to come out of Britain. After exiting the football pitch, they transferred their talent for entertaining onto the stage, and wowed audiences around the country with their wit, football stories and memories.

George Best and Jimmy Greaves... what a combination! Put them in the same side, and what a team you would have.

Unfortunately, it was a treat football fans never had, as Bestie and Greavsie never played in the same side. But decades after they hung up their boots – prematurely – they teamed up for a series of 'An Evening with George Best and Jimmy Greaves'.

George Best was football's first superstar, he was probably the most naturally gifted footballer ever to come out of the British Isles, but he quit top-class football at an early age.

Greavsie was also a flawed genius. He was probably the best finisher England has ever had, but was famously kept out of the 1966 World Cup Final team by Geoff Hurst. In just 57 starts for England, he scored 44 goals. Most of his career was spent at London clubs – Chelsea, Spurs and West Ham. Like Best, he retired from top-class football early, and he also fought alcohol addiction. So, all in all, they've had a lot in common. They were both born enter-tainers – geniuses on the football pitch and witty raconteurs on television and stage. Jimmy Greaves is now a contented man, but it was not always so, which is why he sympathises with his friend George Best who unfortunately is no longer with us.

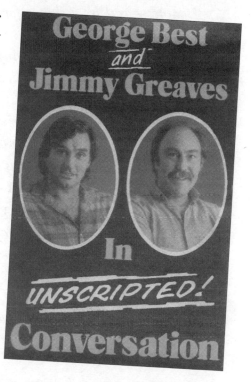

In 2005, Jimmy Greaves was interviewed by the *Observer*'s Kevin Mitchell, here reflecting on his friend George Best:

Jimmy Greaves looks out of the window of the hotel room in Docklands and a smile breaks out on his well-worn but boyish face. We're talking about George Best, about Paul Gascoigne and a little bit about Wayne Rooney. If you had the four of them in the same room, you would be sitting with the royalty of footballing rascals.

'Up until a year ago,' he says, 'we were doing our theatre shows with George. They were phenomenal successes. We did the Birmingham Symphony Hall, which holds 1,500 – packed solid. And Chopper came along, good old Chopper Harris.

'We did four really big theatres all over the country

and they all sold out. It was George who pulled them in, though. He was great... but unfortunately, things have got the better of him... and that's sad. It's a crying shame – and it's a shame for us, because we had a good show going.

That is the upside of having gone through hell yourself: snatching back your life allows you to laugh at even the grimmest of circumstances.'

Jimmy Greaves stopped drinking in 1978 and he knows that if he hadn't then he would be dead by now. That's the plain and simple fact. He has got his life together and he is contented with life as it is now. He says, 'When I'm allowed to, I play a bit of golf, do a bit of gardening, walk the dogs. I try very hard to make as much space for myself as possible. I live in a beautiful village, Little Baddow. Got 200 acres of woodland at the bottom of the road, golf course beyond. If you were parachuted into there, you wouldn't know you were in Essex. Because everyone has a weird idea about Essex. I love it. Been there since 1981.'

Of his friend George he said, 'He's a great bloke, George. I'm not going to moralise one way or another except to say he's a man who's made up his mind what he's going to do and no one's going to change it. He's a very warm and kind man. He's decided that whatever time he's got left, he's going to live it the way he wants to. Fair enough. Really, he's a sensible, intelligent guy, George. He knows exactly what he's doing.'

Kevin Mitchell aptly suggests that 'The moralists were never far away when Best slipped into one of his physical collapses. Few people of fame can have inspired more premature obituaries. In recent weeks, the opinion formers pored over the final moments of his turbulent life. He drank too much. He loved too much. He spent too much. He wasted his genius. He was every good thing gone wrong, a relic from the defining age of excess. And, with his beautiful face and his four-letter name, he was a gift to Fleet Street. Once, some of the chroniclers had been his friends. Now they found it hard to balance sermonising with compassion. They were careful not to damage his legacy because they knew that, for all his failings, he was universally cherished.'

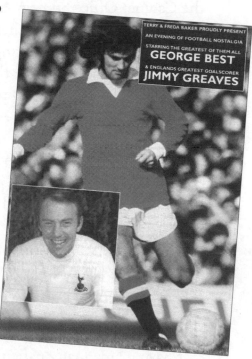

Towards the very end of his life George Best released a photograph showing the shocking extent of his suffering and was at the time of the photo release described as being in a 'dangerous' condition and struggling to survive on a life- support machine. His long-time friend and agent Phil Hughes said George had insisted he take the picture minutes before the former star was transferred to an intensive care unit, as a warning to others against the dangers of heavy drinking.

George's liver specialist, Professor Williams explained: 'Cirrhosis is an irreversible liver condition, which can lead to the complete failure of the organ. Without a transplant, as George Best had in 2002, the result is death.

'In the last 10 years, deaths from cirrhosis have doubled. The rate has increased eight times in men, the increase mainly affecting the 45–55 age group – that is, those still in active working life; indeed, often those at the height of their working or professional lives. It now causes more deaths in men than Parkinson's disease. Alcohol consumption is on the increase: one in three men drink above the recommended safe levels, according to a 2003 report from the Cabinet Office Strategy Unit.

'Dying unnecessarily is the ultimate disaster. But, before then, there is much suffering, with illness and disability. People were shocked to see the pictures of the late George Best released, but he wanted to stop people going down that same path. A quarter of all A&E admissions are related to excessive drinking; injuries and accidents are common.

'Alcohol misuse can lead to loss of brain function, terribly painful inflammation of the pancreas – the worst pain that people can experience – awful head and neck cancers, indeed cancers affecting many other organs of the body. And, although alcohol may increase sexual desire, performance is decreased – embarrassing for the couple concerned. And then there are all the social consequences – breakdown of marriage, loss of that better job, disqualification from driving, bankruptcy in health, wealth and outcome.

'I have many, many patients who have successfully dealt with their problem, are remaining in good health and living a happy life. Tackle the problem now – it won't go away.'

Millions of people suffer from alcohol problems ranging from heavy drinking to dependency. It is estimated that just one in 10 have treatment for their drinking – despite one million people in the UK being dependent on alcohol and five times as many drinking more than is good for them. For the heavy drinkers, common treatment may involve a consultation with their GP or brief counselling from an alcohol specialist. But if the condition is more serious –

dependency – a whole range of options are available from counselling to drug therapy.

On Alcoholics Anonymous' website you can read: 'Once a pin-up boy for his generation, the last, harrowing photographs of George Best graphically show the extent to which decades of alcohol abuse ravaged his body.

'Best's drinking problem was affecting his health by the time he was 25, when he admitted he was drinking a bottle of spirits a day. As his footballing career began to decline, his drinking increased and so did his girth. By the 1980s, he was living in the United States and already in a cycle of drinking and treatment that characterised his life.'

Taken at the end of his last week on this earth, just hours before he was admitted to intensive care, George Best's skin was yellowing and his body covered in tubes. He authorised the pictures himself, telling his agent: 'I hope my plight can act as a warning to others.'

PARKINSON'S BEST MATE!

When George Best made his debut appearance for Manchester United against West Bromwich Albion at Old Trafford in 1963, Michael Parkinson was there and, it would seem, was with him throughout the rest of his life until George's departure in November 2005. It was at this red-letter-day football match where Michael became an instant fan of George and they became and remained friends for more than 40 years.

It is almost impossible to think of Michael Parkinson without also thinking about George Best – such was the closeness portrayed by them both either when speaking to each other – on Parky's show – or about each other in interviews and news articles. Many will recall one such television interview when Michael asked George, 'What was the nearest to kick-off that you made love to a woman?' to which George replied with his naturally, quick-witted humour (or truth, maybe), 'Er – I think it was half-time actually.' Certainly many interviewers may have wanted to ask the question, but for sure it was the friendship between them both that allowed such comments to be made on national television.

Another much-remembered appearance of George was when Michael's wife, Mary, joined Michael on the chat-show sofa during the 1980s. A video clip shown on one of the shows was that of George Best dressed as Father Christmas which showed his delightful and caring interaction with children as they asked Santa for their Christmas toys. One of the children on Santa's knee was George's own son Calum. Such a touching moment was revealed when Calum realised, as George removed his long white beard, that the Father Christmas whose knee he was sitting on was actually his daddy, George Best.

Michael Parkinson is a much-loved celebrity who even though the majority of his fans may never have met him still feel they know him. Throughout his television career from *Where in the World* (1960), *Give Us A Clue* (1984–92), *Going For a Song* (1995/99), to *Auntie's All Time Greats*, and of course his ever popular *Parkinson* show, his friendship with George Best was as consistent as his broadcasting career. A friendship that survived through celebrating George's successes to Michael supporting him in his sadness; a friendship that experienced the magnificence of his talent and genius while weeping with him through his times of desolation.

But did Michael ever discover why George needed to drink so much? Unfortunately, this was one question

George could never answer. Through the many hours they spent together George always avoided any such questions and treated them more as a joke. One thing Michael did know is that drinking didn't make George happy. So why? 'I used to think it was because he was bored,' said Parky. 'He was the supremely gifted athlete who found playing football a simple matter.'

Michael has often been quoted as saying, 'Of all the great players I have seen, George gave me the most pleasure. I

suppose it is because he was lucky enough to embrace all the talents they possessed and more. I don't know if he was as good as Pat Jennings in goal, because I never saw him play in goal but I wouldn't want to bet against it.'

Perhaps it was after hearing such comments from his old mate Parky that George gave him a team photo entirely made up of George Bests. George said that it was his favourite team and, judging by Parky's comments, it must have been his too!

In 1975, Michael Parkinson wrote *Best: An Intimate Biography*, published by Hutchinson Publishing Group. With thanks to Michael Parkinson for his approval and endorsement, the following are selected extracts from his honest and 'intimate' thoughts on his friend George Best. The selected extracts briefly touch on: George Best, pre-United; George Best, genius, talents and skills; and understanding George Best.

George Best, pre-United
(Chapter 1, pages 14 & 15)

I joined a boys' club, The Cregagh, and we had a manager called Bud MacFarlane. He used to tell me that I was one of the best players he had seen and that I ought to think about making it a career. He used to write to Irish clubs about me and they'd send their scouts down but all of them said I was too small. Mind you they had a point. I looked like a stick of rhubarb. I weighed about seven stones and I was as thin as a matchstick.

I was very unattractive and I remember the birds teasing me. They used to shout 'Look out the skinny, ugly sod' when I walked past them. I used to want to grab them and thump them because it was true. Instead I put birds to the back of my mind. I didn't bother with them. You could say I made up for it later. When I wasn't playing I used to watch. My dad used to take me to a local soccer tournament called the Chicken Run held in the local dust bowl. Twenty-seven games in a day and the local St. John's Ambulance Brigade were the busiest people on the field. They had some players who made Norman Hunter look normal... It used to make me upset when I saw scouts on the touchline and I'd play brilliantly and they'd just shake their heads and Bud would tell me later they'd say, 'Which refugee camp did you find him in?' There used to be a director of Glentoran football club who lived on our estate. He had a house right next to our soccer field and I used to pray before every game that one day he'd spot me and whisk me away to play for his team. He never showed.

MY FAVOURITE TEAM

I was fifteen and feeling rejected. I'd just about given up any thoughts of being a soccer player. Dad suggested that I get a job as an apprentice printer when I left school. I agreed. I'd have said yes to anything because if I couldn't play soccer it didn't really matter what I did and I'd be bored stiff in any case. My talent gave me that, my physique fitted me for apprentice dwarf in a circus.

One day I was playing and I saw a guy on the touchline. An ordinary guy wearing an open-necked shirt and a cloth cap. I asked Bud who he was. He said he was called Bob Bishop and he was a scout. I met him later at our house. He told me Manchester United wanted me to go for two weeks' trial. That night I ran down our street to the soccer pitch. The girls shouted, 'Where you going to, long streak of piss?'

'I'm off to play for Manchester United,' I shouted back.

'He's gone bloody mad,' they said.

I nearly did – but it took a while.

George Best, genius, talent and skills
(Chapter 4, pages 35 & 36)

He had more confidence in his ability than I had ever seen in any other sportsman [said Matt Busby] *He was always able to use either foot (sometimes he seemed to have six!) His heading was devastating. If he had a fault in those younger days it was that he wanted to beat too many opponents when he could have passed the ball to better advantage. You could see him beat two or three or even four and then lose the ball and you would be having apoplectic fits and saying to yourself, 'Why the hell don't you pass the ball more?' Then he would beat four men and score the winner. What do you do about that?*

The same question was often asked by opponents who found themselves spending a fruitless afternoon chasing after this extraordinary player. He posed them problems they had never even considered before. More often than not they countered skill with brute force but Best's unique balance enabled him to evade the most savage tackle and his remarkable speed of acceleration from standing start took him clear of the scything tackle designed to bring him down to his opponents' speed and playing level.

Understanding George Best
(Chapter 14, page 135)

I first saw him when he was seventeen and frail as a stick of undernourished rhubarb, and I watched him ripen into the finest soccer player I have ever seen and decline into a confused, unhappy young man who ultimately turned his back on his own great gifts.

The tragedy of George Best – and I believe it to be nothing short of tragic that he should seek a living in nightclubs rather than on the soccer field – is twofold. Firstly soccer needs players of Best's ability and appeal as an example of how soccer should be played.

The game is consistently in danger of being taken over by dreary theorists who reduce soccer to trench warfare when what spectators want is a cavalry charge... Any lover of the game can only feel a bitter disappointment that he is forever denied the sight of a great athlete on the field of play. But the real tragedy of George Best is that he himself will never know how good he might have been. He will never have the satisfaction of knowing the full extent of his great gifts, will never understand where his extraordinary imagination and remarkable athleticism in perfect accord could have taken him.

Michael last saw George about two months before he died when he joined him at a reunion of players who were at Old Trafford with him. (source *Daily Telegraph*, 25 November 2005)

He sat all evening without a drink and reminisced. He said to me later that it was one of the most enjoyable occasions he could remember. I said: 'That's because you were sober.' He said: 'Whatever, I was certainly very happy.' Michael thought, not for the first time, maybe, just maybe, we'd got him back. However, sadly a week later he was drinking again and the final spiral of his life had begun.

George Best was sometimes a difficult man to defend in the aftermath of a drunken episode. What was never a problem was to talk of his genius as a player and to love him as a friend. That was easy.

On the other hand, I suspect that his friends – or most of them I know – had a better time than George did. There was within him a profound melancholy, not altogether attributable to Celtic gloom.

If Best had no regrets then it would be presumptuous of those lucky enough to have watched him and known him to have felt cheated. Yet the fact remains he left the game aged 27, before he reached his prime. We don't know what might have been. The ultimate affliction of George Best was neither did he.

Michael Parkinson speaks for us all when he suggests that George Best was the finest of them all, that if we live to see one better, not only would we be remarkably blessed, but also we would all be twice blessed.

ANGELO THANKS GEORGE FOR THE MEMORIES

Look at any of the photographic coverage of George Best's funeral and you will see among the many thousands of tributes, flowers, scarves, shirts and messages, the now very famous red Manchester United Best number 7 shirt hung alongside a green Northern Ireland Best number 7 shirt, with a poignant message that could speak for the hundreds of thousands of fans: 'Thanks for the memories, Georgie'.

These particular football shirts, with such moving messages, were placed on the garden fence of George's dad's Belfast home by a lifelong Manchester United and George

Best fan, Angelo Agathaggelos. Known to everyone as Angelo, he is the proud proprietor of the Red Star Sports shop, the first Man U supporters' shop (www.redlegends.co.uk), situated in the shadow of Old Trafford.

You will see a close-up of these shirts on the back cover of this book, selected to represent the thousands of tributes to George Best.

It is interesting to note that the Greek meaning of the name 'Angelo' is 'heavenly messenger', and so it seems only fitting to have a more detailed tribute from Angelo as he shares his own memories of George:

The first time I met George Best was in the 1980s in a hotel in Manchester. Because he was such a superstar, George had the usual crowd around him. When the chance came to meet him, I was surprised more than anything to meet a man who was so genuinely friendly and down to earth, not like the person I thought I was going to meet.

Please don't forget that this was the greatest player in the world and, by rights, George knew it but didn't need anyone to tell him so. As I got to know George Best, let me say that he was a humble man with a heart to go with it, but with a hint of naivety, not to mention a bit gullible – which was one of the things that people loved about Georgie.

As I got to meet George a few times I got to know him as the real person that he was. This was completely the opposite to what the newspapers always wrote about him and portrayed him – which was upsetting to the people that knew him best, especially in his bad times which was never far from the headlines.

To be completely honest with you I want to take this

opportunity to say it as it was, and not what people want to hear. I will tell you, the person, George Best, was, and how I'll will remember him, the Best – he was one of the old guard. By that I mean he was a gentleman who never refused anyone a signature or a minute of his time. I would describe George as an innocent and gullible man, who was good-hearted, but was always taken advantage of because of his good nature. The problem he had was that he couldn't say no to anyone or anything, and always had time for anyone who wanted his attention – and there were quite a few. The word "no" just wasn't in George's vocabulary.

George Best was the greatest football player the world has ever known, and if anyone knows anything about football then they would know that even to this day there has never been anyone who has come near to what George Best was. He was a one-off, there was no duplicates; he was the original, the special one, the superstar, the greatest player in footballing history.

George had a last wish and that was to be remembered as the Best. Well, George, you have got your wish, you were simply as your name says. THE BEST!

The last thing I can say is, "Thanks for the memories Georgie, God Bless!" Angelo.

Sadly, the last meeting Angelo had with the legend was at the Marriott Hotel in Worsley just six months before George had his liver-transplant operation.

The so recognisable Manchester United Best number 7 shirt signed by Angelo is now part of the tribute to George Best at Old Trafford Museum. Angelo can still be found at his Red Star Sports shop, which George himself used to call into when he first joined United and continued to visit throughout all those colourful years of his life. This shop is the world's original Manchester United souvenir shop that has traded since the 1950s, and is where George Best used to go when he was a 17-year-old – for what reason? Because he fancied one of the shop assistants!

For sure George's memory will always be held within the walls of the Red Star Sports shop – as long as Angelo has any say of course.

MIKE'S STORY...

There are in our existence spots of time,
Which with distinct pre-eminence retain
A renovating Virtue, whence,
... our minds
Are nourished and invisibly repaired

William Wordsworth

'Spots in time' for William Wordsworth are past experiences through which he can trace his own development, as a man and as a poet, and which continue to echo with new meanings many years after the events themselves. Many of Wordsworth's 'spots of time' arise out of moments of activity. Others come in response to a particular feeling, or a time of emotional intensity, such as the death of his father.

For Wordsworth, spots in time were key moments in his life; they formed amazingly clear memories. He talks about the compression of time, the heightened senses, the feeling of being inside something important. He experienced spots in time again and again in nature, and, although many call his experiences 'mystical', Wordsworth denied any supernatural element to these moments. Rather, they are about as grounded in this earth as you can get.

Some of us acknowledge that there are certain moments that we experience in our lives which are retained in our memories. Although seemingly insignificant, when revived, these memories are brought to the forefront of reality again. We can also have spots in time that come flooding back just when we're not expecting them.

Lifelong fan and later friend of George Best Mike Graham has such a story to tell that includes a series of spots in time that focus on various episodes from the life of George.

Mike's dad was born in Northern Ireland and he absolutely loved Manchester United. Of course, he encouraged his son to follow the team with the same passion. Mike recalls his first day at secondary school when other students were taking their bright, shiny briefcases into the new world of secondary education. Not Mike; he proudly carried his Manchester United haversack, brandishing the name 'George Best'.

Some years later, Mike recalls meeting George for the first time in 1993 at the Becks Theatre in Hayes, Middlesex, on one of the infamous Best/Marsh tours. It was here where Mike first shook the hand of George. However, it was in 1998 when Mike's fascination with George Best really kicked in, particularly after watching the video *Best Intentions*. This caught Mike's imagination and he decided to read one of the many books written about George, *The*

Good, the Bad and the Bubbly. Once he started to read it he just could not put it down. This was about the time that George had grown a full beard and was drinking for his country – but, to Mike, he was still the kid off the streets of Belfast with that natural talent about which his dad had often spoken so passionately: the man who was a true gift to football – even though he was now making more headlines for womanising, drinking, gambling and nightclubbing than he was for his footballing talent. Mike also recalls the headlines announcing George's liver damage which really put into perspective George's philosophy that life is full of risks.

At this particular time, Mike was a national manager for Royal Doulton. He recalls watching George Best appear on the *Wogan* chat show and decided to put pen to paper to write him a letter in which he included an unwritten Christmas card, asking him to sign and send it back to him.

It was sometime in the following January that Mike received the card back from George duly signed with a short note, 'Sorry it's late – Happy 1993'. What a certain spot in time that must have been for Mike, and what a real touch of humanity for George to bother to sign and return the card.

Time moved on for both Mike and George, and Mike recalled another spot in time that showed him the intuitive and sensitive sides to George's nature. Mike was having an association with a female who wasn't his partner and was more than just a friend. They were in an area where Mike knew that George frequented one of the pubs and, although Mike hadn't met George since shaking his hand in 1993, decided to call in for a drink. A short time after they had settled with a drink, in walked George. Mike took the opportunity to speak with George, to introduce himself and to invite him to have a drink with them – which George did. In fact he spent most of the evening with them chatting away and putting the world to rights. Mike and his companion left the pub after thanking George for his time and company.

Just after they had left George noticed Mike's wallet on the seat beside him and picked it up. As he ran outside he saw Mike's car pulling out of the car park. George took the time to take the wallet back inside to the pub landlord and suggested contacting Mike. Of course, the landlord was pleased to and said that he would phone the home number in the wallet. Quite intuitively, George sensed that the person Mike was with wasn't the person who would be answering the phone at home, and suggested that the landlord phone the work number he had found in the wallet too. This was done the next day and Mike was very grateful that he and his wallet were reunited.

It was such spots in time that went some way to Mike deciding to embark on the journey of producing the bronze figurine 'Moment in Time' which captured George Best scoring the winning goal in the 1968 European Cup. He recalls sitting with a friend and colleague in the British Legion one day, having been made redundant from Royal Doulton. They were both remembering the 1968 Cup Final and how Mike went into school the following day knowing that his club were the European champions.

Mike was genuinely looking for something to do; after all

he had spent the majority of his redundancy money on drink and women! Some kind of mirror image of his hero seemed to have materialised.

Mike had been thinking about getting a figurine produced for some time; he had even approached his contacts at Royal Doulton to do something; and so Mike, being quite artistic, and his friend, who had a career in advertising, decided to do something about it themselves.

Although Mike recalls that George had long become public property, he found that working on getting the 'Moment in Time' cast in bronze was a coming together of his love for George with his passion for fine art. The cold-cast porcelain statue of that well-known one-arm-in-the-air, goal-scoring celebration was created; the journey had taken a massive leap forward towards the finished bronze product, but Mike wanted it to be more than just another tribute to George – he wanted George to have a part in this creation.

Through George's agent, Phil Hughes, Mike managed to meet with the man himself to show him the porcelain statue and to get his approval before it was to be cast in bronze. Imagine being asked to go to the home of your hero for him to look at a tribute made of him. But that's exactly what happened.

George was so thrilled to see himself in porcelain, to see the fine detail right down to the odd-sized football boots, one 8½ the other size 9, and the scar on his temple. He was delighted to endorse the figurine with his signature on the base, and to provide another signature to be used in the casting. But even seeing himself portrayed in such a work of art George didn't believe he was worthy of the accolades.

Only three of these fine porcelain figurines were even made – one is now in Manchester United's collection, another is the one signed by George and still in the possession of Mike and the third one was given to George as a gift from Mike on his 55th birthday.

How fantastic, the only figurine in the world endorsed by George Best himself was ready for the next step to become immortalised in bronze. That step has been taken and the finished product is now in existence but only 1968 have been cast – to replicate the year this legendary moment in time happened. George's son, Calum, has said that it is the most lifelike portrayal of his father he has ever seen. In fact all who have the pleasure of either seeing or owning one of these fantastic tributes can almost sense the occasion and atmosphere of that spot in time in 1968.

George Best gave hope to so many people and there is so much people can learn from him even today. He was the first to make the profession of football attractive but unfortunately the support and protection wasn't around when he needed it.

What of Mike's lasting thoughts of George?

Mike recalls himself as a lad sitting on his father's knee watching the funeral of Winston Churchill, not really understanding what was going on but knowing that this man must have been of some importance because his funeral was being shown on television. Coincidentally, in December 2005 the same picture transpired but this time it was Mike's son sitting on his father's knee watching the televised funeral of George Best, and his son perhaps wondering why, but knowing that the man must be of some importance because of the throngs of people wanting to be a part of the day – another spot in time for Mike, right to the end of George's time on this earth.

And what of a last thought or comment from Mike on his spots in time with George Best? Quite simply, 'I miss my hero!'

THE DAY I FIRST MET GEORGE

Jane's story

Jane Godwin was George Best's hairdresser and, George being George, he took a keen interest in her son's footballing exploits, Jane explains:

When I first cut his hair my hands did shake a bit. I told him that this was the first time I had cut the hair of a superstar.

He was almost embarrassed, very quiet and withdrawn, very shy. But he became open and warm as I got to know him. He took a real interest in my son Alex and his football. He always asked me how he got on. There was one particular week that my son got a yellow card and I was horrified.

He just laughed and said, 'Oh, that's nothing. You don't want to know anything about what I've done over the years.'

One Christmas Alex sent him a present. It was a chocolate football with a No. 7 and it said, 'You're the best.' He opened it and he didn't smile, his eyes almost filled with tears. I felt very sad for him then.

One day, I told him about a breast cancer fundraising event I was hosting with a friend. He took the details and said he'd see what he was up to. I never expected to see him there. But on the day, Alex was looking out of the window and suddenly shouted out, 'Mum, George Best is on the drive!'

He stayed for an hour, drinking only a glass of sparkling water. He joined in the quiz and even got one of the football questions wrong.

My son is so sad right now, George Best touched our lives and he was a lovely person.

Meg's Story

Meg Williams worked in a bar on the Thames that George used to frequent:

I met George while I was working at a pub on the Thames. He used to come in on Saturday afternoons for about a year.

The thing that sticks in my mind is that he always made time for anyone who came up to him – and that was a steady stream from the moment he got there. He would often help us out collecting glasses and clearing ashtrays if we got a rush.

He asked for our names the first time he came in and he never forgot them, much to the surprise of one of the barmen who thought it would be funny to sneak off and leave me on my own in the middle of a busy summer afternoon – the look on his face was priceless and he never snuck off again.

He would always treat us with respect and involve us in conversations, which made an otherwise boring shift highly enjoyable.

I feel proud to have known him even if it was only for a short time. He was always genuine and fun to be around.

Taken from BBC News Website – Have Your Say

GEORGE BEST BY MARTIN KNIGHT

British-born author Martin Knight is mainly associated with working-class culture and football literature. Born in 1957, Martin has co-written a book on Jimmy Stockin, a gypsy prize fighter. He is also the author of biographies on the Chelsea great Peter Osgood as well as Spurs, Derby and

Scotland football hard-man Dave McKay, among other fiction and non-fiction books. In 2003 he collaborated with George Best on his final memoirs, *Scoring at Half Time*.

Martin wrote the following article just after George had died and he is pleased to have it reproduced again in this celebration of the life of George Best. In the article Martin gives an insight into the life and times of a genius, as well as showing the real heart of a man, who was caring, considerate, kind and well aware of his faults and failings. Our thanks go to Martin Knight for sharing his thoughts, and his insight into such a great and talented footballer, a multifaceted person that had some uncomplicated qualities:

I wouldn't mind betting that George Best holds the distinction of being the person that people have wanted to be at some time in their lives more than any other. There was a time when millions of schoolboys the world over wished they were Georgie – Georgie – Georgie – Best. This was a simpler time when climate change was known as spring, summer, autumn and winter and the world marched to the tunes of The Beatles. The Fab Four were another phenomenon to behold and although millions idolised them and wanted to be near them they didn't necessarily want to be them. Here, perhaps, is the key to the public's passionate and turbulent relationship with this extraordinarily gifted but seemingly self-destructive man. I would also wager that there were times George himself was one of the people that had no desire to be George Best.

George was born in working-class Belfast in 1946. His father worked at the Harland & Wolff shipyard and his mother in the Gallaher tobacco factory. From a very early age he displayed dazzling skills with a football at his feet and in 1961 a scout for Manchester United whisked the 'boy genius' over to England. Over the next few years Matt Busby, the Manchester United manager, the Northern Ireland international selectors and the Old Trafford faithful were blissfully aware that this shy slip of a kid was something special but it was not until a live televised European Cup quarter-final tie against Benfica did George enter the public consciousness at large. United won 5–1 against a pre-eminent Benfica who boasted in

their team Eusébio – the European Player of the Year. But it was George Best that staged the virtuoso performance by running, dribbling, nutmegging, scoring twice and generally making the Benfica defenders look like bewildered cart-horses.

The television-watching millions had never seen an individual performance like it and on his return from Lisbon George received a pop-star airport welcome, the press dubbed him El Beatle and the ride had begun.

Two years on in 1968 George figured prominently in helping United become the first English club to win the European Cup beating Benfica again at Wembley Stadium. For the club this was the fairytale ending to the long journey led by Matt Busby from the dark days of the Munich air disaster where the cream of the Busby Babes team had perished ten years earlier. Few living rooms across Britain remained dry-eyed when manager and protégé embraced like father and son at the end of the game. George was awarded English and European Footballer of the Year and was arguably now the most famous man on the planet. His playing performances continually delighted and amazed and the exquisite triumvirate of Best, Law and Charlton in attack was an Englishman, Scotsman and Irishman story that for opposing teams was far from a joke.

His on-field impudence and flamboyance was contrasted by his shyness off it and one can only imagine the impact that extreme fame and adulation had on a far from worldly-wise kid from Belfast. Few people have been in the position of being feted by the great and good, worshipped by millions of boys and men, lusted over by most young women he came into contact with (and plenty he didn't) whilst simultaneously arousing the maternal instincts of the nation's housewives. None of us can really say how we would have coped. George made light of it all often by trotting out his well-worn 'Where Did It All Go Wrong?' hotel porter story but many of those close to him are convinced that it was this pressure-cooker existence that led him into becoming a heavy drinker.

Over indulgence in alcohol is far from rare among young men and if the opportunity to live the champagne lifestyle is presented few would reject it. Many will embrace the clubs, the birds and the booze with gusto and only drop out only when relationships, careers and a quieter life start to appear more enticing. Tragically, this was not the case for George, as his own group of close and

loyal friends gradually threw in their partying towels he seemed to accelerate his drinking habit. Medical science has yet to be able to prove this theory either way but it may be that George, like thousands of others, possessed some sort of alcoholic gene and that he had little choice in the matter. Possibly, it is no coincidence that George's mother who did not have a long history of drinking died from alcoholism in her fifties.

By 1970 George's footballing star was waning. Over-enthusiastic hard-men defenders were determined to take him out, this often led to trouble with referees, which in turn caused problems with the FA's disciplinary commission. In the middle of all this though was the glorious, now legendary, spectacle of him scoring six goals against a shell-shocked Northampton Town in the FA Cup. As the decade progressed George was making the headlines more for his missing training and even matches than for his brilliance and skill and his relationship with Manchester United inevitably deteriorated. In 1974 aged only 27 George played his last game for the team.

His subsequent career was a series of cameo roles for such diverse clubs as Dunstable Town, Stockport County, Cork Celtic, LA Aztecs, Hibernian, San Jose Earthquakes, Bournemouth, Brisbane Lyons and most notably Fulham. Here he teamed up with Bobby Moore and Rodney Marsh and although out of condition managed to fleetingly enthrall and entertain English crowds once again with his genius.

George's first marriage to Angie Macdonald ended in divorce although the union did produce a son, Calum, in 1981. The following year George was made bankrupt and then in 1984 he hit his personal nadir when he also hit a policeman who was attempting to arrest him in connection with a drink-drive charge and he subsequently served eight weeks in prison. Although George's drinking exploits were by now legendary and the subject of much urban myth an appearance on Terry Wogan's early evening chat show in 1990 where he was paraded live and very drunk possibly marked a turning point in the public's robust affection for him, cancelling out the goodwill generated by several sober and charismatic appearances on the Michael Parkinson show.

However, as his public profile dimmed, his personal life began to recover. He was discharged from bankruptcy and under the strong but sensitive management of his closest friend Phil Hughes he kept busy with personal appearances and punditry. For the first time in many years his finances were in order and there was a structure to his day-to-day life. In 1995 he married Alex Pursey and relative domesticity ensued. His searingly honest autobiography Blessed *was enthusiastically received by the British public and if sales are anything to go by it was proof that the people had forgiven their wayward son. It seemed that the George Best story could have a happy ending after all. In 2000 though his liver failed and due to the efforts of Professor Williams and the staff at the Cromwell Hospital he was stabilised but his name was urgently added to the waiting list for a liver transplant. A condition of being allowed on the list was that George gives up drinking and this he did. Two years later a transplant was successfully performed.*

I met George at this time when he was recuperating at his and Alex's lovely barn conversion in the Surrey countryside. I had been invited to work with him on a follow-up to Blessed. *Although shocked by his frailty I felt that he was truly happy with his two red setters and Alex tenderly and lovingly caring for him. I was saddened when their marriage collapsed later because they seemed so well matched, always affectionately calling each other Bestie. Over the following weeks as we met regularly and worked on the book I watched him grow in strength and relished his company. He was reserved, humble, self-deprecating and natural, also intelligent with a quick wit. It was impossible not to like him. He was a nice man.*

On a couple of occasions he was very reflective. He told me how Sir Matt Busby was a lovely man, and how Denis Law was a lovely man and dear Shay Brennan was a lovely man and how much he missed him. These were not empty compliments. There were no cameras – just me, him and a red setter – and his eyes were moist. I asked him if he had any regrets and he looked at me sternly –

'Of course,' he said. He joked about his drinking and remarked that he went from El Beatle to El Vino in six years but felt that he would never drink again. That evening he really believed it and so did I.

It could be frustrating doing the book with him. His attention could wander. Heaven knows he had told these stories a thousand times and it was the devil's job to fish out something new. It didn't help when he said, 'Do you mind if I just watch Fifteen to One?' and when that finished, him having answered nearly every question correctly, he zapped over to Countdown or The Weakest Link and then when I finally got down to switching the tape recorder on I'd look up and he was sucking his pen bent over the Telegraph crossword. As he returned to health he began using the local gym where he would tell me which horses he would be backing that afternoon. Then he started to visit the betting office where he was gambling modest sums and I wondered how he could stand for hours in there amid the smoke and the banter. It was like being in a pub. Then I realised that was why he was spending the hours in there.

George Best's final tumble off the wagon has been painfully and painstakingly documented over recent months. His last battle with death has been reminiscent of the man at his peak. Dipping, swerving and pulling back a ball and suddenly, somehow, he is up, regaining possession and charging goalward with his hair streaming in the wind, socks rolled down and shirt hanging out. The staff at the Cromwell Hospital have said they had never seen a patient fight against the odds like he did. Even as far back as a week ago, at one point his doctors were measuring his life expectancy in hours. On Friday, the final, final whistle was blown and George Best left the arena for the last time. History will record him as the greatest British footballer of all time.

Debate will rage over whether George wasted his talent, he will be condemned for destroying his liver and someone else's; he will be accused of throwing away his own life. I believe that George would not see it that way. He wanted to live a full life and he did. Although he has died prematurely he notched up several lifetimes awarding himself a small percentage of the pleasure he had given others in his heyday. His heroic fight to stay alive is proof enough that he loved life and adored those close to him; his dear, tough old dad, his brothers and sisters and their families, Calum, Phil and the others. He did not want to leave them and cause them pain. His alcoholism was a disease that had blighted him since he was in his twenties. He did not want to drink himself to death. George Best called his definitive autobiography Blessed *but he could have just as aptly named it* Cursed.

Article first appeared in the *Sunday Herald*

Our thanks go to Martin Knight for this tremendous eulogy to George Best: the son; the husband; the father; the brother; the footballer; the friend; the genius; the talent; the courage and the one that touched so many lives and still lives on within the memories of so many.

BELFAST BOY IN A LIFE LESS ORDINARY

As concern grew over George Best's fading health, Bill Elliott remembered a fun-loving man who was nobody's fool:

Mac, the village newsagent, had the Sun *open on the page led by the medical bulletin on George Best. He pointed at the story. 'He's an idiot, isn't he?' he asked. It was, of course, a rhetorical question but it still deserved an answer. And the answer is 'no'.*

Like, I suspect, millions of others, Mac only knew – or thought he knew – one George Best. The one who was weak, unable to say no to almost anything, a man lost in a shambolic world, an alcoholic who never managed to beat properly the old foe. Now, a week on from that first bulletin, comes more of the same, confirmation again of his weakness. But an idiot? No, never an idiot.

And so I tried to tell Mac about the Best I knew in the late 1960s and the 1970s when I was a Daily Express *soccer reporter in Manchester, covering United and City and travelling with the Northern Ireland team for its matches. And trying to keep up with Georgie Boy and a fast life that captured the times. It was fun but, Christ, it could be difficult as well.*

Those were the days when reporters still had real contact with the stars. First priority was to have a contact number. I had one for Bobby Charlton, one for Denis Law. For George, at his peak, I had 19 telephone numbers in my book. These included his old digs in Chorlton-cum-Hardy and his 'second mum' Mrs Fullaway, who fussed over him and to whose modest home he retreated when he needed a break from the bollocks, and where the local kids guarded his E-Type Jaguar from the scratchings of envy.

There was the number for the home he had built, an ultra-modern place with a huge television set that disappeared up a fake chimney. It had more glass than brick in its construction, so the fans could see straight in and George was forced to sit with the blinds down. He loved looking at his house, but he hated living there. So, soon after he moved in, he moved out.

The other telephone numbers were for a bunch of his best pals, a few were for women and the rest were for the various clubs and pubs that George frequented, places such as The Brown Cow or Slack Alice's or Blinkers. It was in these places that he would be protected as he drank his then alcohol of choice – vodka and lemonade – and held court quietly and shyly. He was, almost always anyway, friendly with everyone except the fools and, of course, he was especially friendly if the interloper wore a micro-mini and sported long, blonde hair. There were a lot of these about at the time and George made friends with all of them.

The rest of us young men could only watch all this with a mixture of fascination and envy, but if we were gobsmacked by his pulling power, we were even more impressed when we watched him play. London back then had Michael Caine and Twiggy and The Rolling Stones as it swung, Liverpool had The Beatles and the rest of the Mersey sound but Manchester – grey, old Manchester – had The Hollies and Bestie. Mancs, to a man, felt they had the better of the deal.

The old TV pictures of George playing do him some justice but not enough. England legend Tom Finney once told me George was by far the best, most complete player he had ever seen, a view echoed by former Liverpool manager Bill Shankly. What was he like? You had to be there to appreciate the brilliance, the imagination, the balance, the commitment, the goals. Most of all, he had the belief.

In 1976, Northern Ireland was drawn against Holland in Rotterdam as one of its World Cup group-qualifying matches. Back then, the reporters stayed at the same hotel as the team and travelled with it on the coach to the game. As it happened, I sat beside George on the way to the stadium that evening.

Holland – midway between successive World Cup Final appearances – and Johan Cruyff were at their peak at the time. George wasn't. I asked him what he thought of the acknowledged world No. 1 and he said he thought the Dutchman was outstanding. 'Better than you?' I asked. George looked at me and laughed. 'You're kidding, aren't you? I tell you what I'll do tonight… I'll nutmeg Cruyff first chance I get.' And we both laughed at the thought.

A couple of hours later, the Irish players were announced one by one on to the pitch. Pat Jennings, as goalkeeper, was first out of the tunnel to appreciative applause. Best, as No. 11, was last. 'And now,' revved up the PA guy, 'No. 11, Georgie [long pause] Best.' And out trotted George. Above him, a beautiful blonde reached over with a single long-stemmed red rose.

Five minutes into the game, he received the ball wide on the left. Instead of heading towards goal, he turned directly infield, weaved his way past at least three

Dutchmen and found his way to Cruyff who was wide right. He took the ball to his opponent, dipped a shoulder twice and slipped it between Cruyff's feet. As he ran round to collect it and run on, he raised his right fist into the air.

Only a few of us in the press box knew what this bravado act really meant. Johan Cruyff the best in the world? Are you kidding? Only an idiot would have thought that on this evening.

The age.com.au (online newspaper in Australia)

GEORGE BEST (1946–2005)

The footballer and 'genius of popular culture' George Best is remembered by Eamonn McCann:

It was Van Morrison who put George Best into proper context, which was apt. 'Too long in exile,' sang the Man on the title track of his hugely underrated 1993 album. 'Just like George Best, baby... just like Alex Higgins.'

Three of maybe half a dozen authentic geniuses of popular culture to have emerged from Ireland in the last half century, and they had this in common, that they were tight wee working-class Protestants from Belfast, and never at ease with celebrity. Had they been Catholics, Nationalists, they might have slid into riches and fame as if this were their natural environment and begun talking celeb like native speakers. But there's an awkwardness about Prods, particularly Prods from a proletarian background, as they make their way, if they can, in the upper reaches of the wider world.

This is sometimes expressed in drunkenness, grumpiness or uncool outbursts of atavism, perhaps resenting the way their identity isn't esteemed, perhaps resenting their identity. Or maybe just confused. Northern Protestants have never been any good at guff.

George Best left for Manchester in 1961, made the break definitive when he signed at 17 as a pro for United in May 1963, the month after the release of The Beatles' first LP. He was soon to be dubbed 'the fifth Beatle' and it's plain he seized on the sobriquet with alacrity. Pictures from the period show him modelled on the Fab Four – collarless jacket, mop-top hairstyle and all.

Back in Belfast in 1963, the Unionist leader Lord

Brookeborough departed for retirement to the fastness of Fermanagh and was replaced by Terence O'Neill, from the drawing room school of Unionism. The first stirrings of change were everywhere, but as yet there was no pervasive sense of threat. The youth-quake epicentred on Liverpool had sent its shudders of anticipation rippling

across to the North, seeming to suggest, as the old order rapidly faded – or so it seemed – that the young and the urgent of Ulster might find a new sense of themselves in rock and roll and freedom.

George was the exquisitely timed, perfect epitome. No one who saw him live in the flowering of his genius can ever forget, because it's on permanent play on a loop in the mind, his feint and dribble, his slalom and surge, the way he'd pause and sway and then spasm in an instant through a cluster of defenders to arrive as an apparition in the area, his nonchalance and daring, his beauty.

He had such balance as, it was observed, might have made Isaac Newton think again about gravity. Plus, he was a great header of the ball, a great reader of the game, a great tackler back when he had to be. He was everything a footballer could or should be. He was brilliant. Millions draped their dreams around him.

In Blessed *– published in 2001, sharply intelligent and much the most thoughtful of his unsatisfactory drafts for an autobiography – he recalled with wonder the pride of his neighbours on the Cregagh Estate on the occasions he went home after making it big-time.*

He scored his first goal for United in a Christmas 1963 fixture against Burnley and was home next day when the Belfast Telegraph *shouted it out from an exultant back page. '[It] just seemed so unreal to me and to all my mates. Kicking a ball around in the streets, we had all pretended to be playing for some big club. Now I had scored for Manchester United, and there was the picture in the* Belfast Telegraph *to prove it! There was a sense of disbelief among Tommy, Robin and the others… My goal was a big talking point on the estate. It was as if I'd scored for them, too, which made me a bit weepy.' You have to wonder if he was weepy because he sensed, too, this was sort of goodbye.*

The age when footballers came home from the top flight for the off-season and bought pints for their mates and shared glory around the neighbourhood were gone, or at least going. After that first senior goal, there is no indication that he ever celebrated another footballing feat as a sort of communal achievement. Tommy, Robin, and the others aren't mentioned again in Blessed.

His visits home became fewer and fewer. 'Off the field in 1964,' he wrote, 'something odd was happening. All the old values in life were changing as the Sixties began to take hold, led by pop groups like the Beatles and the Rolling Stones... I didn't mix with the other first-team players socially, partly because they were older and many of them were married. I was part of this new generation...'

Part of the price of being the first pop celebrity footballer was that he was detached from players around him even as he was tugged out of contact with the people he'd come from. It was commonly remarked that there was vulnerability about him, a sense of him always standing alone, even, or especially, as applause cascaded upon him. He was always out on his own. No guru, no method, no teacher is all very well, except if, really, you're lost.

In Blessed, *George strove to describe his roots in the Protestant community but managed only to make clear his uncertainties. He'd spent a mere three of his teenage years on the Cregagh Estate, during the least rowdy interlude in Northern Ireland's existence. The material realities of Belfast life impacted upon him lightly. The intersections between politics and popular culture eluded him. 'In those days, even football support was divided on sectarian grounds,' he wrote. 'If you were a Protestant, you automatically supported Linfield, and if you were a Catholic you supported Glentoran.'*

George just didn't get it about the Belfast Big Two, that while the Glens, unlike Linfield, weren't characterised by strident Loyalism and had some Catholic support, their fans, too, were overwhelmingly Protestant. He tells that his family were 'Protestant, Free Presbyterians to be exact'. But they were not. If they had been, they'd have had no time for secular fripperies like football.

There is a startling naivety about his suggestion that, 'We used to get a few taunts from the Catholics, calling us Proddy bastards and we would call them Fenians… It was a bit like being a member of the Rotary Club or the Freemasons.' These are the observations of a man, not recalling at leisure the culture, which had shaped him, but trying and failing to imagine what its content must have been. He'd been exiled too long, too far; too soon, to feel secured by a real rootedness.

We have to hope that he knew in the end how much he was loved and that he found in this the solace and validation, which was surely his entitlement for the delirium of joy, which his genius gave to us all.

© Copyright Socialist Worker (unless otherwise stated)

MORE THAN A MERE GENIUS?

When Tony Dunne signed for Manchester United in 1960 from Shelbourne as cover for Noel Cantwell or Shay Brennan, his big chance came when he replaced Brennan in the line-up for the 1963 FA Cup Final victory against Leicester City. Tony was always thought of as a brave, speedy defender and he went on to cement a place in the first team and missed only six league games over the next four seasons.

That FA Cup winner's medal was only the start. The Irish fullback also helped United to win the title in 1965 and 1967 and the European Cup in 1968. He played in every round en route to the final and deserved his medal as much as any of the stars that scored the goals.

Dubliner Tony Dunne played 33 times for Ireland and made a remarkable 530 first-team appearances for Manchester United in a team that included George Best, Denis Law and Bobby Charlton – the side that Matt Busby led to European Cup glory with that 4–1 victory over Benfica at Wembley in the 1968 final.

The pinnacle of Tony Dunne's international career came in 1969 when he was appointed captain of his country for the first time – an honour he had on a further four occasions. He will always be remembered as a player of tigerish tackling ability, great skill and total commitment.

Back to 1968 when Tony was a part of the European Cup winners' side alongside George Best. David Meek recalls the two Irishmen linking up with each other on the pitch – which made all the difference. Writing about George, David said, 'There was one, though, with ice in his veins. Nerves never troubled George Best and within six minutes of the start, unaffected by the rockets and shrieking 80,000 crowd, he leapt to head home Tony Dunne's free-kick and gives his team an ideal start. Then after another six minutes David Herd headed Harry Gregg's goalkick down and into the path of Best who streaked away on a solo run to score and put United further ahead.'

Among the myriad of tributes written about and for George Best following his death, Tony Dunne added his thoughts and memories:

George was the Beatle of the football world. He had everything, the looks, the talent and the high profile. When we started playing together in the early '60s the Beatles were just becoming big and girls were screaming at them. They'd never screamed at us before but they were soon screaming at George; they recognised that there was something special about him.

He was just a boy when he came over to Manchester United, about 14 or 15, and at the time it was a very hard thing to get into. The story is that he went back home after a while because he was so homesick but the club chased after him and convinced him to come back. He got a job because that was a club rule at the time – so he worked in an outside job by day and played football in the evenings.

He looked very slight and not that strong, and at the start he just seemed like any other player. He certainly had talent but there were one or two other boys who were also very good so his skill wasn't a noticeable thing at first. But then he developed into a genius, one of a kind. He just had this God-given talent that is so rare.

I think his problems were because he was an introvert off the pitch and an extrovert on it. When he got the ball he just changed into somebody else. But he was a shy lad away from home in a foreign country, and he had no one to guide him. He needed someone like a schoolteacher, to say 'don't do this' and 'don't do that' and keep an eye on him.

Of course as a group of young men we would all go out to the bars and have a few drinks. And in the bars George found it very easy to talk to women because he was as good looking as you could get.

He got in with a certain crowd and from there his problems seemed to begin but no one really noticed at first. We had a strong manager at the time that seemed to be in control, but even he didn't realise what a major problem it was. His drinking began to escalate but it didn't affect his game so the problem just slipped by unnoticed. It didn't affect his performance on the field so nobody did anything about it. But once drink gets hold it's a terrible disease and he couldn't seem to fight it. It's a very sad thing.

George and Tony Dunne shake hands.

We were both part of the '68 team that won the European Cup and we got together regularly over the years since. The last time I saw him was last year and he seemed to be struggling a bit. But he was off the drink at the time.

I don't think his talent was wasted but maybe someone could have helped or guided him when he was younger. Maybe if he'd had some mentoring he could have chosen a different path. But, regardless, during his football career he was just electric. When he was playing, the crowd would be waiting for him to get the ball, even the supporters for the other side would want him to get it.

I've played with and against some of the best players in the world and there's no doubt that he's up there with the best of them. He was one of the chosen few who had a talent above everyone else. Anyone who ever watched him play would know that he was one of the most gifted footballers to ever play. There's no question that he's up there with Pelé and Maradona and anyone who says otherwise is mad.

People call him a legend now but he's not, he's more than that. The word 'legend' is attached to so many people who show average talent but George truly was one of a kind and is deserving of a much bigger compliment than that.

Any tribute made to someone who has died is always pleasing and supportive for those close to the lost loved one. But when the tribute is made from a fellow countryman and a fellow player from the same era, and the content of the tribute includes such heartfelt comments and memories, then that must be extra special, and that's just what Tony has done for George.

Tony Dunne has been described on the Manchester United webpage as: 'An unsung hero of Sir Matt Busby's trailblazing side of the 1960s, Tony Dunne is one of the greatest full-backs in the club's history.' He was Irish Footballer of the Year in 1969, a rare personal award for such a team player. He left Manchester United for Bolton Wanderers in August 1973. He helped Bolton win the Football League Second Division in 1977/78. He joined Detroit Express in the NASL in 1979. So Tony Dunne was certainly a seasoned player and must be quite knowledgeable about the beautiful game.

Yes, Tony Dunne is probably 'an unsung hero' but he certainly knew George Best, and was proud to play alongside the genius and acknowledged his outstanding abilities. A genius and an unsung hero both on the same side – what more could you ask for?

NIGEL'S FOOTBALL CARDS

George Best was among many footballing icons to whom tribute was paid through the production of cards from around the 1960s onwards. In the late 1980s the trend was to sell stickers to young fans who could collect them, swap them and complete books on their favourite teams, just as fans had done with football cards.

Below is Nigel's, from Tasmania, Australia, tribute to George through a collection of George Best cards with a chronological sequence of information and notable comments on the great man himself.

George made his debut for Manchester United against West Bromwich on 14 September 1963, aged 17 years and 4 months. Six months later he made his debut for Northern Ireland, being still under 18 years of age. His entry into football cards during the period occurred in 1965 when he was selected as one of 25 world players to be featured in an excellent set produced by Reddish Maid.

In the period from 1963 to 1968 George Best was considered to have been at his peak as a football player. Sadly his 'decline' is dated by some to begin when he was aged only 22.

In 1967/68 A&BC Gum issued their Star Players set of 55, now better known as 'black backs'. While George had appeared in the black and white photographs of the 1966/67 A&BC collection of Footballers (set size of 220) the black backs showed George in full colour.

In the same year his Typhoo Tea card states: 'Signed a professional for his present club on his 17th birthday in 1963, George Best played an important role in his team's 5–1 win over Benfica (Lisbon) in February 1966 and the press christened him "El Beatle". Voted third in the Footballer of the Year Award in May 1966, he already has 13 full Northern Ireland caps to his credit and is hailed as one of the outstanding world-class footballers of the future.'

Two years later his Typhoo Tea card states: 'George Best joined Manchester United in May 1963 and is now one of the world's most famous footballers. With 13 full caps to his credit he has often played a decisive role in many important matches. After his third place in the 1966 Footballer of the Year Award he won the award in 1968. His versatile and individual style of play has now put him in the front rank of "all-time greats" in the game.'

In the 1967/68 season George Best actually won both the Footballer of the Year and the European Player of the Year trophies. In 1969/70 his picture graced the front cover of the FKS Wonderful World of Soccer Stars in Action album. He was a staunch supporter of the Manchester United side.

He is quoted in Shoot's London Football No. 1 Special as saying 'All I know is that London hasn't had a League title look-in for quite a few years. The game isn't, well... so dedicated down there.' Did he actually say these words?

He is also quoted as saying: 'I get a fair deal from London crowds, I must admit. That's why I love playing in London. But your teams don't seem to get real encouragement from the fans. Seems the crowds get despondent if their side is a goal down, especially to us – yet that's when the cheering and urging should get even louder.'

The 1970/71 Lyons Maid card sings his praises: 'George is one of the greatest all-round players in the world. A genius of dribble, his shooting also matches the best. United signed him when he was 15, giving him his senior chance in 1963/64. In six seasons he has 100 goals, his 28 in 1967/68 making him top-level League scorer. Now he's a fixture in the Northern Ireland team.'

In the early 1970s Best was reportedly disinterested in the game. His 1971/72 IPC Magazine card states: 'A brilliant and exciting entertainer with a football and scorer of fantastic goals for United and Ireland. Born in Belfast, the wee lad joined United as an apprentice in 1960 and won his first Irish cap before his 18th birthday. He's now a No. 1 personality.'

The 1971/72 Top Sellers card states: 'Perhaps the most brilliant ball player in Britain, with "Pelé-type" following. Can weave his way past the tightest defences, but is inclined to be temperamental... First made name in Belfast schoolboy football.'

The 1972/73 Barratt card states that George is: 'Perhaps the greatest footballer in the game. Has magic in both feet, and is the biggest draw in Britain today. Has allied his skill to getting goals now. Temperamental gets into trouble often, but is often the victim of vicious tackling. Voted the No. 1 player in the world by most sports journalists.'

In January 1974 George Best left Manchester United, aged only 27 years. His final League match for United was against Queens Park Rangers on New Year's Day 1974. In total, he made 361 League appearances for United scoring 136 goals.

After leaving Manchester United he played a small number of games for a number of clubs for many years, including in the United States in the late 1970s.

The 1977/78 Topps card of Best in Fulham strip states: 'George proved that, unlike boxers, you can make a comeback as a footballer. The biggest box-office draw in soccer looked as if his career in the League was finished until Fulham gave him a contract in 1976. A world-class player.' George ended up making 42 appearances for Fulham in the 1976/77 and 1977/78 seasons.

In a set of cards issued in 1977/78, promoted as Bobby Charlton's selections of World Cup Aces, Best is described as having: 'The best ball control of any British player with an eye for goals. Premature departure from big-time football didn't hide the fact he had a period when he was uncatchable in the box.'

Soccerstamps were another collectable in the early 1970s. Following on from the undoubted success of the Swap cards the *Sun* followed up in 1971/72 with the ambitious Soccerstamps collection. The Soccerstamps were stamps, rather than cards, and came in a wide variety of sizes, shapes and colours.

The tokens for Soccerstamps appeared in the *Sun* each day. The *Sun* only accepted tokens in lots of six, plus 5p, to get you 12 Soccerstamps by return post. The stamps were to be mounted in the spaces for them in the 164-page Football

Encyclopaedia and Soccerstamp Album (available from newsagents for 10p). The album suggests that you stick them in with stamp hinges. Collectors of these stamps therefore distinguish between those, which were (a) never stuck into an album, (b) stuck in with stamp hinges or (c) stuck in as stamps.

The *Sun* claimed at the time that over 60 million Soccerstamps were to be printed, which means that they often turn up today. The size of the set was 500 stamps.

It perhaps goes without saying that the stamps for George Best were enthusiastically looked for, collected and saved by so many of his fans.

Nigel goes on to comment that George Best was one of those rare sporting talents who only come along once or twice in every football fan's lifetime. The only current equivalent is Wayne Rooney, and it is interesting to compare the two. George Best played at a time when the game was less well refereed. He was therefore always subject to 'attention' from some of the tough backs of the time. In spite of this he managed to stay relatively injury-free. His speed and strength (for a little guy) were enough to keep him away from too much trouble. He seemed to love the game of football, and knew he was a phenomenal talent. He appeared to care about the game as entertainment, and about winning games, more than he necessarily cared about winning the big trophies. He therefore embodied what most fans see in football – the beautiful game. Rooney is the same – an incredible talent who seems to know that there is a level of football higher than most of his peers can ever play. The other attraction with George Best was the human side of him. A vulnerable man who loved the attention, power and benefits that came from being a celebrity, but who ultimately couldn't keep all of the facets of his life together. It would be wrong to dismiss him as a 'flash-in-the-pan'. He appeared a total of 470 times for Manchester United, right up there in 11th position in all-time appearances for the club. He then went on to play for at least another 12 or so clubs, so he was no quitter. The attraction of the George Bests and Wayne Rooneys is that they can connect with those who know the joy of playing and watching football of the highest possible quality.

Unfortunately, as Nigel lives in Tasmania he never met George Best or indeed watched a League football match but clearly he has a notable respect for his absolute genius. As he walks us through the social history of football cards, he shows a series of comments from that of 'outstanding world-class footballer of the future' to that of 'a number-one personality'. The journey through the cards highlights the interesting contrast of observations made by a variety of people as the focus on George changed throughout the years.

When George Best died on 25 November 2005, Nigel, along with hundreds of thousands of other people, declared, 'He will be sadly missed by all those who remember him and those who have become aware of the contribution he made to the great game of football.' And with a final tribute Nigel stated a phrase echoed by so many: 'Thanks George, and farewell!'

LAUREN'S DEBUT AND GEORGE'S FAREWELL

The atmosphere around Old Trafford on Wednesday, 30 November 2005 was a mixture of sadness and celebration. George Best had died just a few days before the fixture between Manchester United and West Bromwich Albion – irony in its truest sense as George's debut first-team appearance in 1963 was against West Brom.

Everyone knew that this would be an emotional affair. The whole of Old Trafford, whether wearing red and white or blue and white stripes, all honoured the late, but great, footballing legend with a minute of silence and a moving ceremony.

Sir Bobby Charlton, who was representing the club and the fans, and in fact the world of football, said, 'I would just like to say on their behalf, a big thank you to George Best. And to just say, you will never be forgotten.' Several of George's former team-mates reunited at Old Trafford to honour him and to show their respect to him. Members of the 1963 West Brom team also gathered on the pitch together with George's son Calum. Both United manager Alex Ferguson and West Brom manager Bryan Robson (who once played for United) held floral arrangements as their players followed them onto the pitch.

The Manchester Utd vs West Bromwich Albion tribute match.

Hundreds of banners and signs adorned the stadium 'R.I.P. You are the Best, George' and 'George Best – Genius in Red' were just a couple of the flag-waving admirations displayed for George, arguably the most talented soccer player the UK has ever produced, a player with exceptional speed and consummate skill.

Thousands of fans from both teams received posters of George Best showing his youthful, fresh, good-looking face wearing the Mighty Reds colours. These simple but moving posters were held aloft in unison and admiration for 'The Best'.

Every person that witnessed this tribute will have their story and their own memories. None more so than eight-year-old Lauren who was getting really excited as she was being taken to her first football match at Old Trafford with her dad, a Manchester United fan. Lauren's debut appearance at Old Trafford had been planned well before

A sea of floral tributes outside the Best family home in Belfast.

the sad news of the death of George Best – but what a day for her to experience.

She witnessed tears in the eyes of many fans as the song 'There's only one George Best' echoed all around the stadium for what seemed like the whole of the match, and the black armbands with red-lettered R.I.P. worn by so many within the crowd.

The thousands of banners and posters held up in

remembrance of George was a sight that Lauren will hold in her memory for many years to come, as well as witnessing Calum Best accept something, although Lauren doesn't know what, from Sir Alex before he made a touching speech about how George will be remembered for his talent and skills on the pitch.

So much of that tribute day is still held by Lauren as she often talks about how magical the whole experience was.

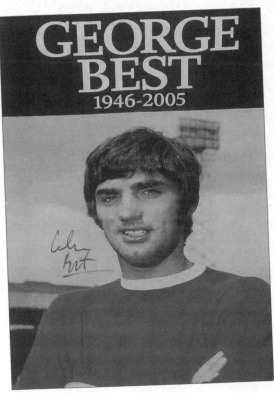

The programme from the day signed by Calum Best.

What a day to choose as your first visit to Old Trafford! How could Lauren have known that when her dad, Gary, arranged her treat it would be a tribute match to someone who has been called the greatest foot-baller ever? Such a young child in such a vast crowd – maybe not really understanding everything that was going on but content to experience the magic and the emotion of the moment.

When one considers George Best's love of children and how he always had time for them, it seems quite plausible that he wouldn't have seen Lauren being there as insignificant, quite the opposite, he would have welcomed her presence in the crowd. Let's hope you have found peace, George – then be sure to rest in it.

'SHINE THROUGH THE GLOOM…
AND EARTH'S VAIN SHADOWS FLEE'

The driving rain on Saturday, 3 December 2005 couldn't dampen the warmth poured out for George Best by those invited to his funeral at Stormont together with those who invited themselves to line the four-mile route of the cortege, or those who watched and listened to the events of the day on television or radio. 'The warmth of humanity. Warmth which flowed along the crowded four-mile route from the symbolically modest Best home – a listed council house now – and flooded the Stormont grounds with a public act of mass homage not observed since Princess Diana took her final journey.' (Jeff Powell – *Daily Mail*, 5 December 2005)

The carefully planned order of service included many who were invited to pay tribute to George Best and who put on hold any threat to peace in Belfast – at least for a short time – as the masses remembered. Local singer Brian Kennedy was invited to sing for George 'You Raise Me Up', with his individual evocative voice.

Viola player Ashley Mason, one of the two who played in the string section that performed in Stormont Sinfonia and accompanied Brian Kennedy and Peter Corry, has his own memories of the day. Memories from a perspective of not actually knowing the man George Best but having the privilege of being involved at a very memorable occasion:

Having rehearsed the previous day we were asked to assemble in a car park about half a mile from the Stormont estate at 7.30 on the morning. We were to be driven into the estate in a coach flanked by police motorcycles. As we drove past the main entrance at the foot of the hill there were already thousands of people queuing to gain entrance to the grounds. We entered the estate through the Dundonald House entrance and drove to the rear of the main building. There were many television and news crews setting up their camera positions in front of the building.

Viola player Ashley Mason.

The orchestra was already set up and at around 8.30 we took our places for a run-through of all musical items. My own seat was right up against the staircase in the centre of the room, it was clear that I would not get a very clear view of the proceedings.

Once we had finished our rehearsal all the musicians and the choirs were given a cooked breakfast in the large canteen in the basement of the building. Prior to the service starting we were free to mingle with the assembling guests. Of particular note was Alex Best, George's ex-wife, who sat alone and somewhat apart from many others of the guests. I went outside the front of the building to take some photos from the steps looking down towards the gates. By now they had been opened and there were many thousands of people lining the road.

It was soon clear that there would be many well-known faces from the worlds of not only sport but also politics. Sven Goran Eriksson, Sir Alex Ferguson, Ole Gunnar Solskjaer, Barry McGuigan, Denis Law, the list was quite extraordinary.

As the service drew nearer we finally took our places and waited for the arrival of the coffin. The first signal we got to indicate its imminent arrival was the playing of the bagpipes by a single piper, firstly from a distance but slowly drawing nearer. I think the tune was 'Jesus Wants Me For A Moonbeam', but I am not certain.

A hush fell upon the 300 or so members of the congregation as George's casket was carried into the hall. Unfortunately, from my position, seated next to the stairs, I could see nothing of its arrival or indeed any of the service.

We were given a cue and began to play the first song, 'Bring Him Home'. We all had our fingers crossed that Peter Corry, a personal friend of mine, would be able to sing as

George Best
1946 – 2005

Pages from the programme from the memorial service.

well as we know he can given the emotion of the occasion. He did a fabulous job! None of us knew at this stage that the music would be released as a CD but I doubt that Peter or Brian Kennedy could have done better in a recording studio. The words of one of the songs, 'Vincent', *had been changed, references to 'Vincent' were changed to 'George' with permission of the music publishers, which gave the rendition a very personal touch. This was a solo*

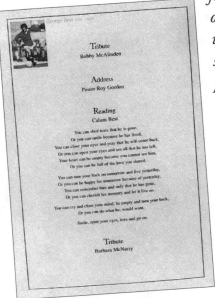

for Brian Kennedy accompanied only by a solo guitarist, Jonny Scott, who again did a fantastic job. It sounded to me as if they had performed this song together many times but in fact this was the first time they had worked together.

The service started and there were a number of speakers who gave some of their memories of George. For me three will remain with me for many years. Firstly Denis Law, who spoke of his friendship with George when they were both players at Manchester United. Secondly Calum, George's son, who gave a moving reading. Finally Professor Roger Williams who had been treating George and had gotten to know him well.

The service eventually ended and Eamonn Holmes summed up the feeling of all present. Brian stood and we performed 'You Raise Me Up' as the casket was removed.

Once the family had departed many of the guests mingled and I'm sure shared memories of George. One of my colleagues, a fanatical football supporter, took some photos of the guests and even had his photo taken with Sven and Sir Alex.

The choirs and orchestras were invited to a lunch to be held in the 'Long Room' upstairs overlooking the mile-long approach road, but I had to leave immediately as I was departing for Edinburgh later that afternoon.

It was an extraordinary event and I felt honoured and privileged to have taken part. The logistical side was phenomenal, it seemed that no expense had been spared to get it right on the day. The rumour was that the Secretary of State, Peter Hain, who had given permission for the building to be used, had given instructions that, if it was going to happen in the way it did, then everything should be perfect for the family. I think it was.

The commemorative edition front page from the *Manchester Evening News*.

Jeff Powell suggests, 'He [George] must have been chuckling all the way up those 66 steps [of Stormont]. Not only that but smiling as, with a last shiver down our spines, he demonstrated the extra-ordinary power over the people which can be exerted by the game he made divine.'

LIMITED EDITION IMMORTALISES THE BEST

When it was decided to commemorate the life of a legend, George Best, by issuing a limited-edition £5 note, fans couldn't wait to get their hands on something that was a fitting tribute to his contribution to football.

On 26 October 2006, it was announced that George Best was to be honoured on a limited-edition £5 banknote to coincide with the first anniversary of his death. Ulster Bank's decision to have George featured on the note showing both his Manchester United and international football strips was an accolade to his footballing genius and enabled his fans to have a lasting keepsake of him.

The notes were limited to one million issues and made available through all branches of the Ulster Bank throughout Northern Ireland or by mail order from further afield, so waiting fans were desperate to 'buy' one on the release date of 27 November 2006 – although application forms were made available online from 13 November. Incidentally, this was the first time the bank had ever commissioned a commemorative banknote.

Online application was phenomenal! Those not acting quickly enough received the following information: 'Due to the overwhelming demand in Ulster Bank's limited-edition George Best Commemorative Bank Note we have now closed the postal application process. Any applications received via the postal service after Close of Business on 21

November will not be processed and will be returned along with payment to unsuccessful applicants.'

The *Belfast Telegraph* reported on 24 November: 'Some half a million of the eagerly awaited limited-edition £5 notes commemorating Ulster soccer legend George Best are believed to have been snapped up in just over one week since their official launch. The Ulster Bank printed one million of the unique notes, which were officially launched on November 13.

'It confirmed the postal applications finished on November 21 when the allocated number of notes had been reached.

George's father, Dickie, with the commemorative notes.

'From November 27, the remaining bank notes will be available over the counter from the 90 Ulster Bank branches across the province.'

A spokesman for the Ulster Bank said: 'We are surprised and delighted by the response to this unique bank note. We believed it would be a popular commemorative note and it has certainly proved to be the case.'

The Ulster Bank issued this special publication on the day the banknotes were released.

One particular person, Nicola, queued at the Donegal Square branch of the Ulster Bank in Belfast and was able to purchase the limit of 10 notes per person. As far as she knew they were the last branch to have any of the much-sought-after bank notes left. The day after Nicola bought her notes the queues were worse, as for most people this was their payday – and so the branch very quickly sold out just a few days after the release date.

Nicola felt very proud that Northern Ireland was the only country to have commissioned the banknote. Although she saw it as a way of making some money out of selling some of her purchased treasure, she also felt that she was doing others who didn't live in Northern Ireland a favour in obtaining some treasure for them too.

The Chief Executive Officer of the Ulster Bank, Cormac McCarty, said, 'We wanted to make it possible for fans throughout Northern Ireland and further afield to own their very own piece of unique George Best memorabilia. By selecting the most affordable note denomination, five pounds, we have tried to make the notes as widely accessible as possible.'

What George would have thought about his well-known

face and footballing action captured on a £5 note, no one can really say. He would probably have wondered 'Why me?' and have smiled with his unique almost Mona Lisa-style smile: the kid off the streets in Belfast, who loved to kick a ball about, was adorning the money of the realm, and indeed people were actually queuing to buy that money! One thing is for certain, there was absolutely no doubt that George Best was special and the commemorative fiver says it all!

JOHN REMEMBERS GEORDIE

Below are the recollections of just one of Ireland's senior citizens who queued to buy some of the five-pound notes issued by the Ulster Bank to commemorate George Best. He also tells of one memory he has of George when the drink got the better of him, but certainly not the better of his skills on the football pitch:

Dear Bernie,
We were outside the bank about 45 minutes before it opened and then about another hour. Most people were, like my wife and I, pensioners and were getting the notes as Christmas presents for children and grandchildren. Mostly for grandchildren. Later on some mothers who had dropped their kids off at school joined us. So most of the talk was about Christmas and grandchildren.

My wife and I had also applied by post for the fivers but there was no way of knowing if we would get any that way so we went to the bank. We were restricted to ten each and five wallets each. That was at our local branch. Later that day we were in the centre of Lisburn where the main branch is, there wasn't very many in the line so we queued up again for half an hour and got 20 more.

On the way home there was no queue at all at the other branch so we went in and got 20 more. The next week we got another 20 and about three weeks later we got all we applied for by post. So we have quite a few to sell.

There was very little talk about Geordie, just a few people saying that somebody had to die to give him a second chance and it was a pity he couldn't take it.

Most people here view George as the greatest footballer that ever lived. I used to live in Manchester and saw him play many, many times and I have to agree with them.

Many times I had a drink with him both in Manchester and Lisburn. The Woodland Hotel in Lisburn (which has been demolished for housing) was where the Northern Ireland team used to stay. My brother-in-law and sister-in-law both worked there, and one Friday night before the international match the next day – I think we were playing Wales – we were having a drink about 3 o'clock in the morning. Somebody noticed George was missing. We searched the hotel top to bottom with no sign of George. We did not know what to do – some suggested getting the police.

The brother-in-law and I and a couple more decided to search the outside. We found George passed out lying in the middle of a bush. We carried him into the hotel and put him to bed.

The next day – or to be precise that day – George played a blinder and was man of the match.

Best Wishes
John Moore

John and his wife were among many that queued to buy the commemorative five-pound notes. He is also among the many that wish that George was still around to take that second chance.

BEST, BECKHAM AND THE AMERICAN DREAM

Best or Beckham? Beckham or Best? Which one would you vote for? Does it really matter – it is after all just a matter of opinion, but the debate will go on. What is perhaps more interesting are the comparisons between the two talents both on and off the pitch, and more importantly the differences the time-gap between them entering the green-grass stage of top-flight football and the effects that has had.

Let's go back to their individual roots. George Best was the boy who grew up on the outskirts of Belfast and lived football; David Beckham grew up on the outskirts of London in East End Leytonstone and lived football.

Both George and David were spotted at an early age by the great Manchester United, they were 'blooded' in the youth team, brought into the first team at a comparatively early age and are both in the sport's archives for particular and spectacular goals. For example, George scoring a record-breaking six goals against Northampton and David for the corker struck from the halfway line against Wimbledon.

Their individual and varied hairstyles have been copied, commented on and indeed criticised. Their love of clothes and fashion – albeit from differing decades – have been the centre of gossip pages, re-created in fashion shops. Some designers have cherished their clothes which have been worn by George or David as, after the stars appeared in them, the designers became overnight successes. They have been front-page, back-page and centre-page pin-ups in newspapers and magazines throughout the world and on the wish list for many a teenage (and not so teenage) female.

Both have been used to promote the most unlikely of commodities, but between them their individual names have helped sell a whole list of stuff: sausages, oranges, sunglasses, Pepsi and, of course, football boots.

As teenagers, both George and David enjoyed the sweet smell of success. Everyone wanted a piece of them – but all they really wanted to do was to play football. Books and magazine articles have been written about them, by them and with them.

By 1998, David Beckham said that he didn't get the twisted values of the celebrity world: 'It's difficult and hard to understand. Once I was on the front page of a newspaper for wearing a sarong and then I turned to page five and read about a train crash. That amazed me.'

By 1999, David Beckham and Victoria Adams (Posh Spice) were married. Alex Ferguson once accompanied Becks and Posh to Elton John's pad on the Riviera and wrote about how frightening it was to see how they were hounded by the press – 'When he first started being exposed to all that stuff, David naturally enough found it all pretty exciting. But I get the impression that he has come to hate it.'

But Ferguson seemed to think that Beckham had other priorities and, ultimately, it led to the breakdown of his relationship with the Manchester United manager, the man he had called a father figure.

Sounds familiar, doesn't it? Wasn't Matt Busby equally George Best's 'father figure'? And Busby once said of him: 'He was unique in the number of his gifts. He remained deceptively skinny looking but he was strong and courageous to a degree that compensated amply. Every aspect of ball control was natural to him from the start. He had more confidence in his ability than I have seen in any sportsman.' But former Wales manager Bobby Gould said, 'Best's rare talent was allowed to fade before its time. When George looked at how Alex Ferguson handled the likes of Eric Cantona, I wonder whether he regrets that someone did not handle him in the same way.' It was Sir Matt Busby who came closest to playing that role for Best.

Ultimately it was the bright lights of success off the pitch that came between the father and son relationship both Matt and George had at one time treasured. Didn't that breakdown also lead to the parting of ways for George and Manchester United?

Best and Beckham's separate journeys took different routes but both at one time in their careers have ended up in the United States. For George it was to try to get away from it all and to make some kind of living while dealing with his addiction to alcohol. That was way back in the 1970s and '80s when he graced such clubs as Fort Lauderdale, LA Aztecs and San Jose Earthquakes all in the NASL. And now Beckham's journey has also landed him in the United States. To the US public, Beckham is better known as a familiar face from glossy magazines who just happens to play football than as a sports star in his own right. But will his signing for LA Galaxy have changed all that?

Lots of numbers were involved in David Beckham's deal with LA Galaxy: US$200,000,000 in endorsements and US$50,000,000 over the five years of his contract. But the most important number wasn't necessarily headlined, 2,000 season tickets to LA Galaxy games were sold once the news of David Beckham's signing was announced, that the former Manchester United and Real Madrid midfielder had joined the US gravy train.

Of course that wasn't the league that George Best played in – in fact, that league, the NASL (National American Soccer League), is no longer around. But where did it all start and how did MSL (Major Soccer League) replace it?

The 1966 World Cup Final was televised live by NBC in North America and generated so much interest that sports promoters decided to start a pro league. However, two rival groups couldn't agree on a number of matters and, therefore, two rival leagues started in 1967, the FIFA-sponsored United Soccer Association and the renegade National Professional Soccer League.

After one disastrous year, they merged to form the North American Soccer League. The new NASL continued to lose a tremendous amount of money during the 1968 season. After all but five teams folded, the 1969 NASL season almost didn't happen.

In 1970 the league lost another team but gained two former American Soccer League teams. Throughout the rest of the early 1970s, the league was slowly increasing overall attendance. US-born players were now becoming stars and the likes of Dallas Tornado star Kyle Rote, Jr. and Philadelphia's Bob Rigby became nationally prominent. The NASL continued to expand and increased to 20 teams for 1975.

The signing of Pelé by the New York Cosmos forever changed the league in 1975. More clubs signed international stars to keep up. The quality of play and attendance increased but player salaries increased at an even higher rate. The rapid increase in attendance prompted the league to expand to 24 teams for 1978.

This marked the beginning of the end for the league. As teams in weaker markets had problems with profitability, this moved on an almost yearly basis, or folded altogether.

The rival indoor league, the MISL, competed with the NASL for players and popularity. Teams continued to fold and, by 1984, the league was down to nine teams. The league tried increasing the Championship from a single game to a three-game series to draw attention, but it was too little, too late. The Chicago Sting defeated the Toronto Blizzard on 3 October 1984 to take the Championship 2–0 in the last NASL game ever played.

In contrast to most other established professional sports leagues in the United States and abroad, but like most recently founded leagues, MLS (Major Soccer League) is organised as a 'single-entity' organisation, in which the league (rather than individual clubs) contracts directly with the players, in an effort to control spending and labour costs, share revenue, promote parity and maximise exposure. This also differs from most other soccer leagues around the world. Still, clubs may do their own scouting, and, if they identify a potential signing, and MLS can negotiate a salary with the player, the discovering club will typically get that player. Each club has an owner/investor and the league allows an owner to have more than one club, although this may be more because of the lack of willing investors than the single-entity structure itself.

The league assigns a home region to each of its 13 clubs for player-development purposes. The clubs have the right to develop a limited number of players they select in their home region and retain the rights to these players. Further, the league also requires each club to operate youth academies and to field youth-academy teams in 2007.

Players developed by the club in their home region may be signed by the club and placed on the club's first team directly without that player being entered into the annual player draft.

Consequently, not all high-school and college players will go through the MLS SuperDraft. Instead, each club's youth-development programme will retain the rights to players, ensuring clubs a steady stream of talented teenagers beyond those cultivated by colleges and US Soccer's residency programme in Bradenton, Florida (run in conjunction with IMG). Thus, as Deputy Commissioner Ivan Gazidis told media, MLS today consists of clubs not merely teams. With vertical player development in 2007 based closer on the European model, MLS organisation is different from other US sports.

George Best's American dream was part of US professional soccer that had already been down the path of signing bright stars in North America, only to watch them flicker and disappear. Some of the game's most luminous names, such as Pelé and Franz Beckenbauer, were recruited and paid significant money to play in the North American Soccer League, which fizzled under the weight of its own ambition in 1984.

David Beckham and indeed George Best are far from being the only British footballers to ply their trade in the United States. MSN have kindly put together their pick of players – in alphabetical order – who had a go on the other side of the Pond (the Canadian teams mentioned played in the same North American leagues as the US teams).

1. Alan Ball – Philadelphia Fury, Vancouver Whitecaps
2. Gordon Banks – Fort Lauderdale Strikers
3. Peter Beardsley – Vancouver Whitecaps

4. George Best – Los Angeles Aztecs, Fort Lauderdale Strikers, San Jose Earthquakes
5. Mike England – Seattle Sounders
6. Trevor Francis – Detroit Express
7. Archie Gemmill – Jacksonville Tea Men
8. George Graham – California Surf
9. Geoff Hurst – Seattle Sounders
10. Mo Johnston – Kansas City Wizards
11. Willie Johnston – Vancouver Whitecaps
12. Brian Kidd – Atlanta Chefs, Fort Lauderdale Strikers
13. Peter Lorimer – Toronto Blizzard, Vancouver Whitecaps
14. Rodney Marsh – Tampa Bay Rowdies
15. Booby Moore – San Antonio Thunder, Seattle Sounders
16. Jimmy Nicholl – Toronto Blizzard
17. Harry Redknapp – Seattle Sounders
18. Bruce Rioch – Seattle Sounders
19. Graeme Souness – Montreal Olympique
20. Nobby Stiles – Vancouver Whitecaps

They could have also included Phil Parkes, Peter Osgood, Steve Morrow, Peter Withe, Steve Howey, Justin Fashanu and many, many more. Former West Ham midfielder Ian Bishop even played for a team called the New Orleans Shell Shockers.

Now David Beckham can be added to the list. The phenomenon of his intended arrival swept in like a winter swell on a Malibu beach. US soccer fans salivated, women swooned and corporate marketers planned sexy sales pitches. Hollywood giggled in anticipation. Bubbling up somewhere between Beatlemania and Fernandomania on the lunacy scale is Beckhamania.

Months before David Beckham played a game on US turf 'Beckham Comes to America' ads blared out his impending arrival in Los Angeles. David Beckham's appeal lies beyond sport, which is perhaps why he made the voyage. David commented, 'The decision to join the Galaxy wasn't hard because I've been to LA… I think there's a huge opportunity out there… with me, it's about football – that's what I'm all about. I'm coming there to make a difference. I'm coming there to play football.'

George Best was as talented and charismatic a footballer as the British Isles ever produced. The late and the great soccer star later played for the Los Angeles Aztecs and other NASL teams in the 1970s. George had his best years with Manchester United, as did Beckham, but his soccer talents truly were supernatural, if ultimately dulled by too many pub crawls.

Now comes Beckham, a one-word wonder in a city where vapidity long ago was raised to an art form.

The poet William Blake once wrote, 'the road of excess leads to the palace of wisdom'. And strangely perhaps David Beckham will personify that comment. The cynical would say that Beckham is just lining his pockets for one final payday in the sun. Surely the lad from Leytonstone, who won almost everything at Manchester United, just wants to add a fistful of dollars to his sizeable bank account. By now everybody knows about his background, lifestyle and celebrity wife. Millions of magazine column inches have been swallowed up by the phenomenon that is Beckham. But nobody can condemn a man who gave heart and soul to the game he loves.

So what if the Beckhams will now live out the fantasy existence that most of us can only dream about? Beckham may never have been the most articulate member of the football profession, but he does not play football to show off his public-speaking prowess. Unfortunately George Best did not make the 'palace of wisdom' for many reasons.

Let's for one moment consider the laddish bell boy who was delivering the room- service champagne, who witnessed the tens of thousands of pounds confettied on the Birmingham hotel bed of George Best, alongside his Miss World girlfriend scantily dressed in a see-through negligee.

Then contemplate yet again those well-worn words 'Mr, Best, where did it all go wrong?' that have been used to death to question George's lifestyle, but somewhere on the printed pages have lost the irony and sarcasm that was surely meant by the young man. Perhaps there was that chance that he wasn't questioning George's wrong-doing, but in that moment in time in a first-class hotel bedroom, seeing the handsome, talented play-

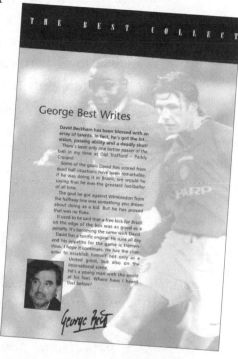

boy-lifestyle footballer with a very beautiful woman, the most expensive champagne and money strewn about, he was actually questioning the very people who were suggesting it had all gone wrong for George.

Two questions that will not really have answers, but merely induce opinions:

1. What if David Beckham had been exposed to the celebrity limelight without the much-needed protection and security that surrounds him? How would he have managed without such protection with agents, PR and security at every hand?

2. How different would things have been if George Best had been in David Beckham's position, having the now well-oiled systems of protection and security in place and playing in the greatest league in the world, the Premiership?

Prior to the new season in 2007, LA Galaxy's manager, Frank Yallop, said that he was planning to play Beckham in his favoured central midfield position. He said, 'The one conversation I had with him was all about football… he was not interested in the weather, the lifestyle or the beaches. That was encouraging.' In the United States David Beckham enjoys a stress-free life, £70,000 a day and a beach house. If George Best's bellboy were still around, would he be asking of David too, 'where it all went wrong'?

TIME FOR REFLECTION

In the May 2006 edition of *CRUX*, Manchester Cathedral's monthly news, the following was written:

Family, friends and fans of football legend George Best converged on Manchester Cathedral in March to celebrate and give thanks for his life. The service, televised live on BBC News 24, was devised by George's family and friends, and featured personal tributes from friends and players including David Sadler, Eddie Gray, Wilf McGuinness and Malcolm Wagner. The Dean of Manchester the Very Revd Rogers Govender said, "George had God's gifts to play, to win, to entertain and to bring joy. We are richer for having known him, and he will always belong to us.' George's family, who travelled from Belfast for the service, said 'Manchester always had been a special place in George's heart. We are proud to be here, and proud of our boy.'

GEORGE BEST - GENIUS
1946 - 2005

THE LEGEND LIVES ON
THE GEORGE BEST FOUNDATION
www.georgebest.com

For More information on the George Best Foundation visit
www.georgebest.com

Take a little time to reflect, even just for a moment, on a couple of the items from George's funeral. Songs from the day included 'The Long and Winding Road', perhaps a reflection of the latter part of George's life, but certainly not about his former life, full of excitement and creativity on and off the pitch. More poignant was possibly 'Vincent – Starry, Starry Night' as it had been George Best's favourite song. Perhaps the world was never meant for one as beautiful as you, George.

WHY *GEORGE BEST – A CELEBRATION?*

George Best – A Celebration has been written for a number of reasons. In 2005, Bernie Smith made an invited, professional visit to the State of Victoria, Australia, to share the community aspects of the work developed over a number of years in his school Four Dwellings High School and the adjoining Quinzone Vocational Learning and Teaching Centre with schools and multi-agency services over there.

During his time in Australia, Bernie was introduced to 'Chances for Children', a charity that gives chances to children in a community where finance could be a barrier to their aspirations. It also gives opportunity for people, businesses and services to give and support the charity while demonstrating their social responsibility. Bernie knew straight away that 'Chances' was needed for the young people, children and families of the Quinzone schools where he and Maureen work. He decided to look for collectables that had a story linked to them, but couldn't decide on a focus. He felt that writing such a book was a way of using enterprise to create the 'Chances' charity and to give people a chance in life.

On the day of George Best's funeral Bernie was listening

to the commentary of the funeral on his car radio and began to think that he had at last found his focus. As a lifelong Manchester United and George Best fan, and knowing he already had one or two pieces of George Best memorabilia, Bernie soon became an avid collector of everything to do with the late, great man, including collecting from people their stories of their objects linked to moments in George's life.

Very soon Maureen Hunt became part of the idea and together Bernie and Maureen began to write and bring alive the stories and memories people held of George Best, and saw the book as a tribute and a celebration of his life. The book has given the opportunity for many people to celebrate George Best. It has also given Bernie and Maureen the opportunity to create 'Best Chances' charity; to which they will donate a tenth of any profits made from the sale of the book. Maureen and Bernie hope that by contributing in this way others may wish to give to those less fortunate in their own community (see www.chancesforchildren.com in Victoria Australia).

'Best Chances' will be a part of the Edgbaston Foundation in Birmingham and will be administered through the Birmingham Foundation, based in the Jewellery Quarter of Birmingham. Bernie and Maureen thank David Bucknall (Chairman of Bucknall Austin, and Chairman of the Birmingham Foundation) and Tim Watts (Chairman of Pertemps and President of the Birmingham Foundation) for inspiring, leading and developing the Birmingham Foundation to be what it is today. Details of which can be found on www.bhamfoundation.co.uk.

'Best Chances' is an opportunity to help ensure that the absence of money does not stand in the way of a person's ability to achieve their maximum potential, be it in educational, social or cultural pursuits which contribute to the realisation of their goals – and the enhancement of their contribution to the community where they live.

It seems appropriate, in the same way George Best was given a chance in life by Manchester United, that the sale of a book celebrating his life will give chances in life to many other people.

For more of the Best, visit www.georgebestacelebration.com

PICTURE CREDITS